CLEP

College Level Examination Program

Analyzing + Interpreting

Literature

D0814684

Jessica Egan
Heather M. Hilliard
XAMonline

Copyright © 2016

All rights reserved. No part of the material protected by this copyright notice may be reproduced or utilized in any form or by any means, electronic or mechanical, including photocopying or recording or by any information storage and retrievable system, without written permission from the copyright holder.

To obtain permission(s) to use the material from this work for any purpose including workshops or seminars, please submit a written request to:

XAMonline, Inc.
21 Orient Avenue
Melrose, MA 02176
Toll Free: 1-800-509-4128
Email: info@xamonline.com
Web: www.xamonline.com
Fax: 1-617-583-5552

Library of Congress Cataloging-in-Publication Data
Wynne, Sharon A.
CLEP Analyzing and Interpreting Literature / Sharon Wynne.
ISBN: 978-1-60787-508-6
1. CLEP   2. Study Guides   3. Analyzing and Interpreting Literature

Disclaimer:
The opinions expressed in this publication are the sole works of XAMonline and were created independently from the College Board, or other testing affiliates. Between the time of publication and printing, specific test standards as well as testing formats and website information may change that are not included in part or in whole within this product. XAMonline develops sample test questions, and they reflect similar content as on real tests; however, they are not former tests. XAMonline assembles content that aligns with test standards but makes no claims nor guarantees candidates a passing score.

Printed in the United States of America
CLEP Analyzing and Interpreting Literature
ISBN: 978-1-60787-508-6

Table of Contents

Meet the Authors

Jessica Egan

With a Master's Degree in English Education from Florida State University, Jessica Egan has expertise in the areas of literature, linguistics, and educational psychology. Jessica has worked as an instructional technologist and has experience in teaching secondary English, English as a Second Language (ESL), college-level composition and Adult Basic Education (ABE). She has authored lesson plans, teacher certification materials, and test preparation texts.

Heather M. Hilliard

Earning her bachelor's degree in New Orleans and her two masters degrees from the University of Pittsburgh, Heather M. Hilliard serves as an Adjunct Professor for her undergraduate alma mater, Tulane University. From teaching - both at the collegiate level as well as special courses at a leading independent high school - to her corporate endeavors, she has consciously focused aspects of her career and volunteerism on education. She has received several commendations for her achievements, has been inducted into the national honor society for public health and is one of fewer than 1,000 internationally Certified Emergency Managers in the world. She has published on a variety of topics and edited textbooks as well as other fiction and non-fiction work and focuses on strategic communications and improvements for clients - including writing and editing for XAMonline preparation content and tests including Advanced Placement exams, CLEP materials, and the SAT.

About XAMonline

XAMonline – A specialty CLEP publisher

XAMonline – A publisher specializing in CLEP

The College Board CLEP series offers thirty three tests. If your goal is to survey the field and see which of the tests fit into your college curriculum schedule then a good first step resource is XAMonline's

- CLEP 33 ISBN 978-1-60787-575-8

CLEP has clusters of subjects: English; languages, sociology, history, math, science, and business. Each one of these clusters has numerous tests. XAMonline specializes by subject with full length sample tests and explanations.

- CLEP Literature Sampler ISBN 978-1-60787-583-3
- CLEP Foreign Language Sampler ISBN 978-1-60787-577-2
- CLEP Sociology Sampler ISBN 978-1-60787-579-6
- CLEP History Sampler ISBN 978-1-60787-578-9
- CLEP Math Sampler ISBN 978-1-60787-581-9
- CLEP Science Sampler ISBN 978-1-60787-580-2
- CLEP Business Sampler ISBN 978-1-60787-582-6

Another way XAMonline specializes is to focus your attention to what historically has been the most popular tests according to Nielson rankings. CLEP 5 is most popular among civilians, CLEP Military favorites are most popular according to military statistics. Each book comes with numerous tests and full explanations.

- CLEP 5 Favorites ISBN 978-1-60787-576-5
- CLEP Military Favorites ISBN 978-1-60787-551-2

Once you know what specific test you feel most comfortable with you can get a complete picture of your understanding with XAMonline products. True to format content and full length sample tests give you the opportunity to practice under test day conditions. Specialized content is available in the following study guides that will align with all the CLEP standards and you can be assured that you are studying in the most focused way possible.

- CLEP Algebra ISBN 978-1-60787-530-7
- CLEP College Mathematics ISBN 978-1-60787-532-1
- CLEP College Composition/Modular ISBN 978-1-60787-527-7

- CLEP Analyzing and Interpreting Literature ISBN 978-1-60787-526-0
- CLEP Spanish ISBN 978-1-60787-528-4
- CLEP Biology ISBN 978-1-60787-531-4
- CLEP Introductory Psychology ISBN 978-1-60787-529-1

Our competitive advantage

As of 2016, the College Board are administrators of the CLEP Spanish test and do not make full guides for this test or any other test. For Spanish, they offer "official" material that has 100 of the 120 questions. It provided answers but failed to include explanations or content. The material is not a former test. It has no audios to go along with the listening sections. You must decide for yourself if you think a sample test is a study guide or is it a study resource? Is it "Official" if it is not a real test? Is it 2016 if it is essentially the same product as it has been in many past years.

Over the last 20 years, XAMonline has helped nearly 600,000 test takers. Our commitment to preparation exceeds simply providing the proper material for study - it extends to helping you gain mastery of the subject matter, ushering today's students toward a successful future.

Overview of the Test

I. The College-Level Examination Program _____

How the Program Works

CLEP exams are administered at over 1,800 institutions nationwide, and 2,900 colleges and universities award college credit to those who perform well on them. This rigorous program allows many self-directed students of a wide range of ages and backgrounds to demonstrate their mastery of introductory college-level material and pursue greater academic success. Students can earn credit for what they already know by getting qualifying scores on any of the 33 examinations.

The CLEP exams cover material that is taught in introductory-level courses at many colleges and universities. Faculty at individual colleges review the exams to ensure that they cover the important material currently taught in their courses.

Although CLEP is sponsored by the College Board, only colleges may grant credit toward a degree. To learn about a particular college's CLEP policy, contact the college directly. When you take a CLEP exam, you can request that a copy of your score report be sent to the college you are attending or planning to attend. After evaluating your score, the college will decide whether or not to award you credit for a certain course or courses, or to exempt you from them.

If the college decides to give you credit, it will record the number of credits on your permanent record, thereby indicating that you have completed work equivalent to a course in that subject. If the college decides to grant exemption without giving you credit for a course, you will be permitted to omit a course that would normally be required of you and to take a course of your choice instead.

The CLEP program has a long-standing policy that an exam may not be taken within the specified wait period. This waiting period provides you with an opportunity to spend additional time preparing for the exam or the option of taking a classroom course. If you violate the CLEP retest policy, the administration will be considered invalid, the score canceled, and any test fees will be forfeited. If you are a military service member, please note that DANTES will not fund retesting on a previously funded CLEP exam. However, you may personally fund a retest after the specified wait period.

The CLEP Examinations

CLEP exams cover material directly related to specific undergraduate courses taught during a student's first two years in college. The courses may be offered for three, four, six or eight semester hours in general areas such as mathematics, history, social sciences, English composition, natural sciences and humanities. Institutions will either grant credit for a specific course based on a satisfactory score on the related exam, or in the general area in which a satisfactory is earned. The credit is equal to the credit awarded to students who successfully complete the courses. Please see page 345 for the complete list of the titles we offer for CLEP exams.

What the Examinations Are Like

CLEP exams are administered on computer and are approximately 90 minutes long, with the exception of College Composition, which is approximately 120 minutes long. Most questions are multiple-choice; other types of questions require you to fill in a numeric answer, to shade areas of an object, or to put items in the correct order. Questions using these kinds of skills are called zone, shade, grid, scale, fraction, numeric entry, histogram and order match questions.

Some of the examinations have optional essays. You should check with the individual college or university where you are sending your score to see whether an optional essay is required for those exams. These essays are administered on paper and are scored by faculty at the institution that receives your score.

Where to Take the Examinations and How to Register

CLEP exams are administered throughout the year at over 1,800 test centers in the United States and select international sites. Once you have decided to take a CLEP examination, you can log into My Account at https://clepportal.collegeboard.org/myaccount to create and manage your own personal accounts, pay for CLEP exams and purchase study materials. You can self-register at any time by completing the online registration form.

Through My Account you can also access a list of institutions that administer CLEP and locate a test center in your area. After paying for your exam through My Account, you must still contact the test center to schedule your CLEP exam.

If you are unable to locate a test center near you, call 800-257-9558 for more information.

ACE's College Credit Recommendation Service

The College Credit Recommendation Service (CREDIT) of the American Council on Education (ACE) enables you to put all of your educational achievements on a secure and universally accepted ACE transcript. All of your ACE-evaluated courses and examinations, including CLEP, appear in an easy-to-read format that includes ACE credit recommendations, descriptions and suggested transfer areas. The service is perfect for candidates who have acquired college credit at multiple ACE-evaluated organizations or credit-by-examination programs. You may have your transcript released at any time to the college of your choice. There is a one-time setup fee of $40 (includes the cost of your first transcript) and a fee of $15 for each transcript requested after release of the first. ACE has an additional transcript service for organizations offering continuing education units.

The College Credit Recommendation Service is offered through ACE's Center for Lifelong Learning. For more than 50 years, ACE has been at the forefront of the evaluation of education and training attained outside the classroom. For more information about ACE CREDIT, contact:

ACE CREDIT
One Dupont Circle, NW
Suite 250
Washington, DC 20036

ACE's Call Center is open Monday to Friday, 8:45 a.m. to 4:45 p.m., and can be reached at 866-205-6267 or CREDIT@ace.nche.edu. Staff are able to assist you with courses and certifications that carry ACE recommendations for both civilian organizations and training obtained through the military.

If you are already registered for an ACE transcript, you can access your records and order transcripts using the ACE Online Transcript System: https://www.acenet.edu/transcripts/.

ACE's Center for Lifelong Learning can be found on the Internet at: http://www.acenet.edu/higher-education.

How Your Score Is Reported

You have the option of seeing your CLEP score immediately after you complete the exam, except in the case of College Composition, for which scores are available four to six weeks after the exam date. Once you choose to see your score, it will be sent automatically to the institution you have designated as a score recipient; it cannot be canceled. You will receive a candidate copy of your score before you leave the test center. If you have tested at the institution that you have designated as a score recipient, it will have immediate access to your test results.

If you do not want your score reported, you may select that as an option at the end of the examination *before the exam is scored*. Once you have selected the option to not view your score, the score is canceled.

The score will not be reported to the institution you have designated, and you will not receive a candidate copy of your score report. You will have to wait the specified wait period before you can take the exam again.

CLEP scores are kept on file for 20 years. During this period, for a small fee, you may have your transcript sent to another college or to anyone else you specify. Your score(s) will never be sent to anyone without your approval.

II. Approaching a College about CLEP _____

The following sections provide a step-by-step guide to learning about the CLEP policy at a particular college or university. The person or office that can best assist you may have a different title at each institution, but the following guidelines will lead you to information about CLEP at any institution.

Adults and other nontraditional students returning to college often benefit from special assistance when they approach a college. Opportunities for adults to return to formal learning in the classroom are now widespread, and colleges and universities have worked hard to make this a smooth process for older students. Many colleges have established special offices that are staffed with trained professionals who understand the kinds of problems facing adults returning to college. If you think you might benefit from such assistance, be sure to find out whether these services are available at your college.

How to Apply for College Credit

Step 1. *Obtain, or access online, the general information catalog and a copy of the CLEP policy from each college you are considering.*

Information about admission and CLEP policies can be obtained on the college's website at clep.collegeboard.org/search/colleges, or by contacting or visiting the admissions office. Ask for a copy of the publication in which the college's complete CLEP policy is explained. Also, get the name and the telephone number of the person to contact in case you have further questions about CLEP.

Step 2. *If you have not already been admitted to a college that you are considering, look at its admission requirements for undergraduate students to see whether you qualify.*

Whether you're applying for college admission as a high school student, transfer student or as an adult resuming a college career or going to college for the first time, you should be familiar with the requirements for admission at the schools you are considering. If you are a nontraditional student, be sure to check whether the school has separate admissions requirements that might apply to you. Some schools are very selective, while others are "open admission."

It might be helpful for you to contact the admissions office for an interview with a counselor. State why you want the interview and ask what documents you should bring with you or send in advance. (These materials may include a high school transcript, transcript of previous college work or completed application for admission.) Make an extra effort to have all the information requested in time for the interview.

During the interview, relax and be yourself. Be prepared to state honestly why you think you are ready and able to do college work. If you have already taken CLEP exams and scored high enough to earn credit, you have shown that you are able to do college work. Mention this achievement to the admissions counselor because it may increase your chances of being accepted. If you have not taken a CLEP exam, you can still improve your chances of being accepted by describing how your job training or independent study has helped prepare you for college-level work. Discuss with the counselor what you have learned from your work and personal experiences.

Step 3. *Evaluate the college's CLEP policy.*

Typically, a college lists all its academic policies, including CLEP policies, in its general catalog or on its website. You will probably find the CLEP policy statement under a heading such as Credit-by-Examination, Advanced Standing, Advanced Placement or External Degree Program. These sections can usually be found in the front of the catalog. You can also check out the institution's CLEP Policy by visiting clep.collegeboard. org/search/colleges.

Many colleges publish their credit-by-examination policies in separate brochures, which are distributed through the campus testing office, counseling center, admissions office or registrar's office. If you find a very general policy statement in the college catalog, seek clarification from one of these offices.

Review the material in the section of this chapter entitled "Questions to Ask about a College's CLEP Policy." Use these guidelines to evaluate the college's CLEP policy. If you have not yet taken a CLEP exam, this evaluation will help you decide which exams to take. Because individual colleges have different CLEP policies, a review of several policies may help you decide which college to attend.

Step 4. *If you have not yet applied for admission, do so as early as possible.*

Most colleges expect you to apply for admission several months before you enroll, and it is essential that you meet the published application deadlines. It takes time to process your application for admission. If you have yet to take a CLEP exam, you may want to take one or more CLEP exams while you are waiting for your application to be processed. Be sure to check the college's CLEP policy beforehand so that you are taking exams your college will accept for credit. You should also find out from the college when to submit your CLEP score(s).

Complete all forms and include all documents requested with your application(s) for admission.

Normally, an admission decision cannot be reached until all documents have been submitted and evaluated. Unless told to do so, do not send your CLEP score(s) until you have been officially admitted.

Step 5. *Arrange to take CLEP exam(s) or to submit your CLEP score(s).*

CLEP exams can be taken at any of the 1,800 test centers world-wide. To locate a test center near you. clep.collegeboard.org/search/test-centers. If you have already taken a CLEP exam, but did not have your score sent to your college, you can have an official transcript sent at any time for a small fee. Fill out the Transcript Request Form included on the same page as your exam score. If you do not have the form, visit clep.collegeboard.org/about/score to download a copy, or call 800-257-9558 to order a transcript using a major credit card. Completed forms should be faxed to 610-628-3726 or sent to the following address, along with a check or money order made payable to CLEP for $20 (this fee is subject to change).

CLEP Transcript Service
P.O. Box 6600
Princeton, NJ 08541-6600

Transcripts will only include CLEP scores for the past 20 years; scores more than 20 years old are not kept on file.

Your CLEP scores will be evaluated, probably by someone in the admissions office, and sent to the registrar's office to be posted on your permanent record once you are enrolled. Procedures vary from college to college, but the process usually begins in the admissions office.

Step 6. *Ask to receive a written notice of the credit you receive for your CLEP score(s).*
A written notice may save you problems later, when you submit your degree plan or file for graduation. In the event that there is a question about whether or not you earned CLEP credit, you will have an official record of what credit was awarded. You may also need this verification of course credit if you meet with an academic adviser before the credit is posted on your permanent record.

Step 7. *Before you register for courses, seek academic advising.*
A discussion with your academic adviser can help you to avoid taking unnecessary courses and can tell you specifically what your CLEP credit will mean to you. This step may be accomplished at the time you enroll. Most colleges have orientation sessions for new students prior to each enrollment period. During orientation, students are usually assigned academic advisers who then give them individual help in developing long-range

plans and course schedules for the next semester. In conjunction with this counseling, you may be asked to take some additional tests so that you can be placed at the proper course level.

Questions to Ask about a College's CLEP Policy

Before taking CLEP exams for the purpose of earning college credit, try to find the answers to these questions:

1. *Which CLEP exams are accepted by the college?*
   A college may accept some CLEP exams for credit and not others — possibly not the exams you are considering. For this reason, it is important that you know the specific CLEP exams for which you can receive credit.

2. *Does the college require the optional free-response (essay) section for exams in composition and literature as well as the multiple-choice portion of the CLEP exam you are considering? Will you be required to pass a departmental test such as an essay, laboratory or oral exam in addition to the CLEP multiple-choice exam?*
   Knowing the answers to these questions ahead of time will permit you to schedule the optional free-response or departmental exam when you register to take your CLEP exam.

3. *Is CLEP credit granted for specific courses at the college? If so, which ones?*
   You are likely to find that credit is granted for specific courses and that the course titles are designated in the college's CLEP policy. It is not necessary, however, that credit be granted for a specific course for you to benefit from your CLEP credit. For instance, at many liberal arts colleges, all students must take certain types of courses; these courses may be labeled the core curriculum, general education requirements, distribution requirements or liberal arts requirements. The requirements are often expressed in terms of credit hours. For example, all students may be required to take at least six hours of humanities, six hours of English, three hours of mathematics, six hours of natural science and six hours of social science, with no particular courses in these disciplines specified. In these instances, CLEP credit may be given as "6 hrs. English Credit" or "3 hrs. Math Credit" without specifying for which English or mathematics courses credit has been awarded. To avoid possible disappointment, you should know before taking a CLEP exam what type of credit you can receive or whether you will be exempted from a required course but receive no credit.

4. *How much credit is granted for each exam you are considering, and does the college place a limit On the total amount of CLEP credit you can earn toward your degree?*

   Not all colleges that grant CLEP credit award the same amount for individual exams. Furthermore, some colleges place a limit on the total amount of credit you can earn through CLEP or other exams. Other colleges may grant you exemption but no credit toward your degree. Knowing several colleges' policies concerning these issues may help you decide which college to attend. If you think you are capable of passing a number of CLEP exams, you may want to attend a college that will allow you to earn credit for all or most of them. Check out if your institution grants CLEP policy by visiting clep.collegeboard.org/search/colleges.

5. *What is the required score for earning CLEP credit for each exam you are considering?*

   Most colleges publish the required scores for earning CLEP credit in their general catalogs or in brochures. The required score may vary from exam to exam, so find out the required score for each exam you are considering.

6. *What is the college's policy regarding prior course work in the subject in which you are considering taking a CLEP exam?*

   Some colleges will not grant credit for a CLEP exam if the candidate has already attempted a college-level course closely aligned with that exam. For example, if you successfully completed English 101 or a comparable course on another campus, you will probably not be permitted to also receive CLEP credit in that subject. Some colleges will not permit you to earn CLEP credit for a course that you failed.

7. *Does the college make additional stipulations before credit will be granted?*

   It is common practice for colleges to award CLEP credit only to their enrolled students. There are other stipulations, however, that vary from college to college. For example, does the college require you to formally apply for or to accept CLEP credit by completing and signing a form? Or does the college require you to "validate" your CLEP score by successfully completing a more advanced course in the subject? Getting answers to these and other questions will help to smooth the process of earning college credit through CLEP.

III. Preparing to Take CLEP Examinations _____

Test Preparation Tips

1. Familiarize yourself as much as possible with the test and the test situation before the day of the exam. It will be helpful for you to know ahead of time:

   a. how much time will be allowed for the test and whether there are timed subsections. (This information is included in the examination guides and in the CLEP Tutorial video.)

   b. what types of questions and directions appear on the exam. (See the examination guides.)

   c. how your test score will be computed.

   d. in which building and room the exam will be administered.

   e. the time of the test administration.

   f. direction, transit and parking information to the test center.

2. Register and pay your exam fee through My Account at https://clepportal.collegeboard.org/myaccount and print your registration ticket. Contact your preferred test center to schedule your appointment to test. Your test center may require an additional administration fee. Check with your test center and confirm the amount required and acceptable method of payment.

3. On the day of the exam, remember to do the following.

   a. Arrive early enough so that you can find a parking place, locate the test center, and get settled comfortably before testing begins.

   b. Bring the following with you:

      • completed registration ticket

      • any registration forms or printouts required by the test center. Make sure you have filled out all necessary paperwork in advance of your testing date.

      • a form of valid and acceptable identification. Acceptable identification must:

         ○ Be government-issued

         ○ Be an original document — photocopied documents are not acceptable

- Be valid and current — expired documents (bearing expiration dates that have passed) are not acceptable, no matter how recently they may have expired
- Bear the test-taker's full name, in English language characters, exactly as it appears on the
- Registration Ticket, including the order of the names.
- Middle initials are optional and only need to match the first letter of the middle name when present on both the ticket and the identification.
- Bear a recent recognizable photograph that clearly matches the test-taker
- Include the test-taker's signature
- Be in good condition, with clearly legible text and a clearly visible photograph

  Refer to the Exam Day Info page on the CLEP website (http://clep.collegeboard.org/exam-day-info) for more details on acceptable and unacceptable forms of identification.

- military test-takers, bring your Geneva Convention Identification Card. Refer to clep.collegeboard.org/military for additional information on IDs for active duty members, spouses, and civil service civilian employees.
- two number 2 pencils with good erasers. Mechanical pencils are prohibited in the testing room.

c. Leave all books, papers and notes outside the test center. You will not be permitted to use your own scratch paper; it will be provided by the test center.

d. Do not take a calculator to the exam. If a calculator is required, it will be built into the testing software and available to you on the computer. The CLEP Tutorial video will have a demonstration on how to use online calculators.

e. Do not bring a cell phone or other electronic devices into the testing room.

4. When you enter the test room:

a. You will be assigned to a computer testing station. If you have special needs, be sure to communicate them to the test center administrator *before* the day you test.

b. Be relaxed while you are taking the exam. Read directions carefully and listen to all instructions given by the test administrator. If you don't understand the directions, ask for help before the test begins. If you must ask a question that is not related to the exam after testing has begun, raise your hand and a proctor will assist you. The proctor cannot answer questions related to the exam.

c. Know your rights as a test-taker. You can expect to be given the full working time allowed for taking the exam and a reasonably quiet and comfortable place in which to work. If a poor testing situation is preventing you from doing your best, ask whether the situation can be remedied. If it can't, ask the test administrator to report the problem on a Center Problem Report that will be submitted with your test results. You may also wish to immediately write a letter to CLEP, P.O. Box 6656, Princeton, NJ 08541- 6656. Describe the exact circumstances as completely as you can. Be sure to include the name of the test center, the test date and the name(s) of the exam(s) you took.

Accommodations for Students with Disabilities

If you have a disability, such as a learning or physical disability, that would prevent you from taking a CLEP exam under standard conditions, you may request accommodations at your preferred test center. Contact your preferred test center well in advance of the test date to make the necessary arrangements and to find out its deadline for submission of documentation and approval of accommodations. Each test center sets its own guidelines in terms of deadlines for submission of documentation and approval of accommodations.

Accommodations that can be arranged directly with test centers include:
- ZoomText (screen magnification)
- Modifiable screen colors
- Use of a reader, amanuensis, or sign language interpreter
- Extended time
- Untimed rest breaks

If the above accommodations do not meet your needs, contact CLEP Services at clep@info.collegeboard.org for information about other accommodations.

IV. Interpreting Your Scores _____

CLEP score requirements for awarding credit vary from institution to institution. The College Board, however, recommends that colleges refer to the standards set by the American Council on Education (ACE). All ACE recommendations are the result of careful and periodic review by evaluation teams made up of faculty who are subject-matter experts and technical experts in testing and measurement. To determine whether you are eligible for credit for your CLEP scores, you should refer to the policy of the college you will be attending. The policy will state the score that is required to earn credit at that institution. Many colleges award credit at the score levels recommended by ACE. However, some require scores that are higher or lower than these.

Your exam score will be printed for you at the test center immediately upon completion of the examination, unless you took College Composition. For this exam, you will receive your score four to six weeks after the exam date. Your CLEP exam scores are reported only to you, unless you ask to have them sent elsewhere. If you want your scores sent to a college, employer or certifying agency, you must select this option through My Account. This service is free only if you select your score recipient at the time you register to take your exam. A fee will be charged for each score recipient you select at a later date. Your scores are kept on file for 20 years. For a fee, you can request a transcript at a later date.

The pamphlet *What Your CLEP Score Means*, which you will receive with your exam score, gives detailed information about interpreting your scores. A copy of the pamphlet is in the appendix of this Guide. A brief explanation appears below.

How CLEP Scores Are Computed

In order to reach a total score on your exam, two calculations are performed.

First, your "raw score" is calculated. This is the number of questions you answer correctly. Your raw score is increased by one point for each question you answer correctly, and no points are gained or lost when you do not answer a question or answer it incorrectly.

Second, your raw score is converted into a "scaled score" by a statistical process called *equating*. Equating maintains the consistency of standards for test scores over time by adjusting for slight differences in difficulty between test forms. This ensures that your score does not depend on the specific test form you took or how well others did on the same form. Your raw score is converted to a scaled score that ranges from 20, the lowest, to 80, the highest. The final scaled score is the score that appears on your score report.

How Essays Are Scored

The College Board arranges for college English professors to score the essays written for the College Composition exam. These carefully selected college faculty members teach at two- and four-year institutions nationwide. The faculty members receive extensive training and thoroughly review the College Board scoring policies and procedures before grading the essays. Each essay is read and scored by two professors, the sum of the two scores for each essay is combined with the multiple-choice score, and the result is reported as a scaled score between 20 and 80. Although the format of the two sections is very different, both measure skills required for expository writing. Knowledge of formal grammar, sentence structure and organizational skills are necessary for the multiple-choice section, but the emphasis in the free-response section is on writing skills rather than grammar.

Optional essays for CLEP Composition Modular and the literature examinations are evaluated and scored by the colleges that require them, rather than by the College Board. If you take an optional essay, it will be sent to the institution you designate when you take the test. If you did not designate a score recipient institution when you took an optional essay, you may still select one as long as you notify CLEP within 18 months of taking the exam. Copies of essays are not held beyond 18 months or after they have been sent to an institution

Description of the Examination

The CLEP Analyzing and Interpreting Literature examination covers material usually taught in a general semester undergraduate course in literature. Although the examination does not require familiarity with specific works, it does assume that candidates have read widely and perceptively in poetry, drama, fiction, and nonfiction. The questions are based on passages supplied in the test. These passages have been selected so that no previous experience with them is required to answer the questions. The passages are taken primarily from American and British literature.

The examination contains approximately 80 multiple-choice questions to be answered in 90 minutes. A recommended passing score is calculated at "50".

Knowledge and Skills Required

The exam measures candidates' knowledge of the fundamental principles of rhetoric and composition and their ability to apply the principles of standard written English. In addition, the exam requires familiarity with research and reference skills. In one of the essays, candidates must develop a position by building an argument in which they synthesize information from two provided sources, which they must cite. The requirement that candidates cite the sources they use reflects the recognition of source attribution as an essential skill in college writing courses.

Questions on the Analyzing and Interpreting Literature examination require candidates to demonstrate the following abilities.

- Ability to read prose, poetry, and drama with understanding
- Ability to analyze the elements of a literary passage and to respond to nuances of meaning, tone, imagery, and style
- Ability to interpret metaphors, to recognize rhetorical and stylistic devices, to perceive relationships between parts and wholes, and to grasp a speaker's or author's attitudes
- Knowledge of the means by which literary effects are achieved
- Familiarity with the basic terminology used to discuss literary texts

The examination emphasizes comprehension, interpretation, and analysis of literary works. A specific knowledge of historical context (authors and movements) is not required, but a broad knowledge of literature gained through reading widely and a familiarity with basic literary terminology is assumed. The following outline indicates the relative emphasis given to the various types of literature and the periods from which the passages are taken. The approximate percentage of exam questions per classification is noted within each main category.

Within the questions of the CLEP, the mixture of genre types falls typically almost 80-90% between poetry and prose (both fiction and non-fiction within the prose selections) and the remaining on drama. The entire test is balanced between three main eras - Renaissance/17th Century, 18th/19th Century, as well as 10th/21st Century; in the past, there is a slightly heavier emphasis on 18th/19th work, and usually there is one passage from the Classical/pre-Renaissance period.

Optional Essay for This Test

Because writing about literary texts is central to the study of literature, some colleges may require candidates to take an optional essay section in addition to the multiple-choice section. The essay section is 90 minutes long and is made up of two 45-minute questions. One question asks candidates to analyze a short poem, the other asks them to apply a given generalization about literature (such as the function of a theme or a technique) to a novel, short story, or play that they have read. The essay section is still administered in a paper-and-pencil format; the essay responses are graded by the institution, not by the College Board.

Section I: Reading Comprehension – Skills You Need To Succeed

Chapter 1: Techniques Used in the Reading Comprehension Passages and Questions

The CLEP Analyzing and Interpreting Literature focuses its multiple choice section on examples of rhetoric in different styles and eras of literature. Many people throw general language around, and you have probably even said yourself, "Is that a rhetorical question?" However, most people don't understand rhetoric – and if you make the assumption that you do, your test score on this exam will likely suffer.

So, let's review some of the essential foundations of rhetoric and the techniques used in the multiple choice portion of the Evidence Based section of the exam.

What is rhetoric?

When someone refers to rhetoric, it is a way to describe a manner of speaking or writing that is meant to generate a substantial effect on its audience. Some people say a person uses rhetoric well when they claim "she has a way with words" or perhaps state "he makes a good argument." It may also refer to the study of the way someone speaks or presents words – but for this exam, it is the way an image is created through word choice, emphasis, and the intent to influence beliefs. This counts when you are reading passages in the multiple choice section as well as the passages for your essay prompts (if you choose to take the optional essay portion).

Be cautious, as rhetoric is not just a philosophy being presented, a means of persuasion, or merely speaking well. Rather, it is the intention behind the statements and careful selection of the words used – not just what's said.

Then what are rhetorical techniques?

The techniques used in rhetoric are the same things students have been told for years that good essays will answer – who, what, how – as well as the way information is delivered, the actual content, and the method used to convey the message. Two main techniques, or devices, are tropes and schemes.

Tropes are figures of speech that provide an unexpected twist in the meaning of words, and is used when there is a change in words that embellishes or energizes a phrase. The four most frequently used tropes (and the basic, or most essential ones) are metaphor, metonymy, synecdoche, and irony. We define these for you below, so you have a quick reference list. Schemes are the pattern and format of words.

A trope is also sometimes called a "figure of thought" where as when the pattern changes for schemes, it may be called "figure of speech."

How is rhetoric created or used?

There are different ways that people use words to get a point across, as they are trying to persuade listeners to believe in what they are saying. It includes the pace or speed of their delivery, the tone of voice of the speaker (or author) and the interaction with body language as the words are spoken. You can see that rhetoric likely does not work very well on the phone (where other distractions can pull a listener away from a speaker's delivery and there is no way to see the body language); similarly, to be understood well in writing, the author must be very accomplished indeed.

The way to achieve good writing and speaking is through a rhetorical device. It's how the speaker persuades the listener to understand and convert to a different perspective. The primary purpose is for the listener to believe in the argument, though side effects (of emotional response or reaction) are likely to occur depending on the method used by the speaker.

Rhetorical Devices Help Explain Words In Context

Devices or different "mechanisms" are used to convey ideas, and they are very important in successful rhetoric. Here is a partial list of rhetorical devices in alphabetical order, including the most common (the most likely to be used or asked in definitions on the exam). You need to know the definitions as well as be able to identify/create examples and to help you on the multiple choice section. If you understand these – and don't just memorize them – you will be able to consider the provided answers faster in context with the reading selection, ruling out one if not two answers immediately, then you will be able to select the most appropriate answer from the ones remaining.

Some of these are called "sonic" because they depend on sound and they are marked by (s) to help you distinguish them. Others classified as "imagery" because they conjure visions and they are marked by (i) for ease in identification.

Adynaton: a ridiculous over-exaggeration, much more than "just" hyperbole; "when donkey's fly" was a quote from an old television show when a waitress didn't believe something would happen

Alliteration(s): repetitive initial consonant sounds, usually with an overtone of humor or nonsense; she sells sea shells by the sea shore. Assonance (s) would be the same, though with vowel sounds.

Allusion: a reference to an event, literary work or person; "he's as fast as The Flash"

Antanagoge: places a criticism and compliment together

Antonomasia: using an epithet or nickname instead of a person's true name; "The Lionheart"

Epithet(i): using an adjective or adjective phrase to describe, and it can be metaphorical or transferred (adjective modifying something it normally doesn't); "lazy road" and "blind mouths", respectively

Euphemism: replacing a harsh plain phrase with a less offensive one; "her elevator doesn't go to the top"

Hypocatastasis(i): labelling far beyond metaphor or simile; "that snake"

Irony: saying something contrary to make a point – but in rhetoric, it's most often used a a device of humor to reduce an option for a course of action; Abraham Lincoln said about an adversary that he "died down deeper into the sea of knowledge and come up drier than any other man he knew."

Metaphor(i): compares two things without "as" or "like"; "she is a lion"

Metonymy: when a similar word is substituted for the actual or typical word and it can also be when you describe something or a person by describing what's around the item being depicted; like "redneck" to describe someone who lives in a rural area (in a negative way)

Onomatopoeia(s): words that sound like what they describe; "bang"

Oxymoron: a two word paradox; "near miss"

Simile(i): compares one object to another with "like" or "as"; "strong as the sun"

Synecdoche: when parts are used to describe a whole (can be a subvarient of metonymy; "a new set of wheels" to describe a new car

Presentation of Information and Ideas_____

The philosopher, Cicero, was very effective in persuading listeners to his point of view using various styles, called rhetoric canons. This CLEP exam will test your understanding of how authors express their points of view – or how their characters present their ideas. These styles, or categories, provide a template of the author's argument as well as a pattern for training in that style.

There are other various styles, but these are the five examples for structure (the canons) that The College Board may use in the selecting the passage for multiple choice question/answer options. While you don't need to memorize the different methods, recognizing the differences may help you on the exam answer questions about the passage.

a) **Invention**: a derivative of Aristotle's theory, this is when the author finds (or "invents") something to say and bases the points on logic. It may include an "if…then" sort or progress to explain cause and effect or compare different aspects to get to the author's conclusion. This is generally a brainstorming phase, where the author must consider the audience, what facts are available to use in the presentation, the best Aristotelian method to present those facts, and the time you have to deliver the argument.

b) **Arrangement**: in this process, Cicero uses all of the tools from Aristotle, beginning with an introduction (using ethos, and appeal to ethics); the next sections of facts, division, proof, refute (employing logos, or logic); the conclusion uses pathos (meaning emotion).

c) **Style**: refreshingly, Cicero named this exactly what he intends – the style of how something is said – and it's no surprise, with the original root of Latin meaning "elocution." Style is very intentional in rhetoric and should be remembered that the style gives clues to the meaning and position of the author. Style includes grammar, consideration of audience, address of appeal, decorum (appropriateness and "situation"), and ornamental language. Style is more than pathos – it incorporates ethos as well, or persuasion effect.

d) **Memory**: Cicero often had to improvise and respond or interact with his audience, and thus this style was intended to continue a path of the speech but giving sensitivity to "input" (verbal or other visual cues) from an audience. It is a psychological component of the rhetoric in addition to the formality of a speech, especially since the most effective speeches in ancient times were totally memorized. (In fact, ancient orators were scorned if they used notes; memorization was a must.)

e) **Delivery**: very important, though frequently not considered as important as word choice, is the how something was said; this is what Cicero termed delivery. As you may have experienced yourself, the way a teacher presents a topic can get you engaged… or not. Delivery can significantly alter the way something is interpreted, thus pathos is integral to the successful delivery. Today, people are very skeptical of someone who has a speech memorized and polished – they almost prefer a little authenticity and "humanness" in a composition (though too rough and the speaker will get criticized for that, too!)

Why Is Any Of This Important?

By identifying the various facets of rhetoric in the multiple choice section and then using the tools of successful experts in rhetoric within your essay responses (if you chose to do the essays), you will be able to achieve your highest possible score.

Strategy for Points: Techniques for comprehension

1. Remember that rhetoric is an author or speaker attempting to persuade a reader or listener to his/her point of view.
2. You don't need to know all of the words for rhetorical devices – some lists have more than 160 options! Remember the main definitions as multiple choice questions frequently are given with a statement and you must select the correct answer.
3. It is a good idea to know the difference between sonic and imagery – it will likely come in handy during your composition section (though you will not be able to look back at the multiple choice section). Use them at the appropriate times.

4. Understanding the uses of rhetoric will help in reading comprehension, to know when there is a play on words or which of the three efforts is being put forth by the author (or speaker) and why.
5. The CLEP uses these rhetorical devices to ask more questions about reading comprehension and literature, but the example passages used will have various types of literature from different eras.

Chapter 2: Vocabulary

The English language has a more extensive vocabulary than any other language. English is a language of synonyms, words borrowed from other languages, and coined words – many of them introduced by the rapid expansion of technology. It is important to understand that language is in constant flux, and the English language in particular is constantly evolving with words that are created based on societal trends. Improvements in your vocabulary will increase your ability to correctly identify answers in the CLEP Analyzing and Interpreting Literature exam.

Register (informal and formal language) is a distinction made on the basis of the occasion and the audience. In written English, a formal register would be used for scholarly works, research papers, literary criticisms, professional conference presentations, and other serious works. When the register is formal, longer sentences, more complex and exact syntax are used, as is more complex vocabulary. Slang is frowned upon, as are common expressions or colloquialisms and contractions. Informal works or occasions call for a less formal use of language. In informal setting (such as texting or emailing friends), vocabulary is more casual; slang, colloquialisms, and contractions are used freely. Syntax is more relaxed; sentences are shorter in informal discourse. Informal written communications would include newspaper and magazine articles, popular books, and everyday conversations.

When preparing for the exam, practicing different tones and incorporating vocabulary will give you to opportunity to familiarize yourself with the proper register. Given your audience (experienced professors), you can be certain that formal language will be used throughout the exam. You will need to analyze writing using a formal tone and be able to correctly interpret meanings given the context of the selection.

A few strategies to read unfamiliar words and to build vocabulary include:
- expand vocabulary through wide reading, listening, and discussing;
- rely on context to determine meanings of words and phrases such as figurative language, idioms, multiple meaning words, and technical vocabulary;
- apply meanings of prefixes, roots, and suffixes in order to comprehend new words;

- research word origins, including Anglo-Saxon, Latin, and Greek words;
- use reference material such as glossary, dictionary, thesaurus, and available technology to determine precise meanings and usage; and
- identify the relation of word meanings in analogies, homonyms, synonyms/antonyms, and connotation/denotation.

Root, Base, and Compound Words

Structural elements within words can be used independently to determine meaning. Often including a historical element, root words commonly stem from Latin or Greek origins. Base words are considered language in the simplest form. Compound words create meaning through the combination of two words that are able to stand alone.

Root words: A root word is a word from which another word is developed. The second word can be said to have its "root" in the first. This structural component lends itself to an illustration of a tree and its roots, which can concretize the meaning for students. Typically, root words cannot stand alone.

Aphostrophe (apho = separate)

Submerge (sub = under)

Junction (junct = connect)

Base words: Unlike root words, base words are stand-alone linguistic units that cannot be deconstructed or broken down into smaller words. Prefixes and suffixes are connected to base words to create meaning.

Retell (base = tell)

Instructor (base = instruct)

Sampled (base = sample)

Compound words: Compound words occur when two or more base words are connected to form a new word. The meaning of the new word is in some way connected to the meanings of the base words.

Everything (every + thing)

Backpack (back + pack)

Notebook (note + book)

Prefixes and Suffixes

Prefixes are beginning units of meaning that can be added (affixed) to the beginning of a base word or root word. They are also known as bound morphemes, meaning that they cannot stand alone as words.

Prefix	Meaning	Example
Re-	To do again	Reread
Anti-	Against	Anticlimactic
Uni-	One	Unibrow
Mis-	Incorrect	Misunderstood

Suffixes are ending units of meaning that can be affixed to the end of a base word or root word. Suffixes transform the original meanings of base and root words. Like prefixes, they are also known as bound morphemes because they cannot stand alone as words.

Suffix	Meaning	Example
-able	Ability	Likeable
-er	One who	Teacher
-less	Without	Careless
-est	Comparative	Smartest

Inflectional endings: Inflectional endings are types of suffixes that impart a new meaning to the base word or root word. These endings change the gender, number, tense, or form of the base or root word. Just like other suffixes, these are bound morphemes.

Ending	Original Word	New Word
-s	Road	Roads
-es	Mix	Mixes
-ing	Write	Writing
-ed	Sample	Sampled

Connotation and Denotation _____

Denotation is the literal meaning of a word, as opposed to its connotative meaning. **Connotation** refers to the ripple effect surrounding the implications and associations of a given word, distinct from the denotative or literal meaning. Connotation is used when a subtle tone is preferred. It may stir up a more effective emotional response than if the author had used blunt, denotative diction. For example, "Good night, sweet prince, and flights of angels sing thee to thy rest," a line from Shakespeare's Hamlet, literally refers to death; connotatively, it renders the harsh reality of death in gentle terms such as those used in putting a child to sleep.

Informative connotations are definitions agreed upon by the society in which the learner operates. A skunk is "a black and white mammal of the weasel family with a pair of pineal glands which secrete a pungent odor." The Merriam-Webster Collegiate Dictionary adds "...and offensive" odor. The color, species, and glandular characteristics are informative. The interpretation of the odor as offensive is affective.

Affective connotations are the personal feelings a word arouses. A child who has no personal experience with a skunk and its odor will feel differently about the word skunk than a child who has smelled the spray or been conditioned vicariously to associate offensiveness with the animal denoted skunk. The fact that our society views a skunk as an animal to be avoided will affect the child's interpretation of the word. In fact, it is not necessary for one to have actually seen a skunk (that is, have a denotative understanding) to use the word in either connotative expression. For example, one child might call another child a skunk, connoting an unpleasant reaction (affective use) or, seeing another small black and white animal, call it a skunk based on the definition (informative use).

Figurative Devices _____

Figurative language allows for the statement of truths that more literal language cannot. Figures of speech add many dimensions of richness to our writing and allow many opportunities for worthwhile analysis. Skillfully used, a figure of speech will help a reader see more clearly and focus upon particulars. Listing all possible figures of speech is beyond the scope of this list. However, for purposes of building vocabulary and increasing your reading comprehension, a few are sufficient.

Parallelism: The arrangement of ideas in phrases, sentences, and paragraphs that balance one element with another of equal importance and similar wording. Here is an example from Francis Bacon's Of Studies:

> "Reading maketh a full man, conference a ready man, and writing an exact man."

Euphemism: The substitution of an agreeable or inoffensive term for one that might offend or suggest something unpleasant. Many euphemisms are used to refer to death to avoid using the word, such as "passed away," "crossed over," or "passed."

Hyperbole: Deliberate exaggeration for dramatic or comic effect. Here is an example from Shakespeare's The Merchant of Venice:

> Why, if two gods should play some heavenly match
> And on the wager lay two earthly women,
> And Portia one, there must be something else
> Pawned with the other, for the poor rude world
> Hath not her fellow.

Bathos: A ludicrous attempt to portray pathos – that is, to evoke pity, sympathy, or sorrow. It may result from inappropriately dignifying the commonplace, using elevated language to describe something trivial, or greatly exaggerating pathos.

Oxymoron: A contradiction in terms deliberately employed for effect. It is usually seen in a qualifying adjective whose meaning is contrary to that of the noun it modifies, such as "wise folly."

Irony: Expressing something other than and often opposite of the literal meaning, such as words of praise when blame is intended. In poetry, it is often used as a sophisticated or resigned awareness of contrast between what is and what ought to be and expresses a controlled pathos without sentimentality. It is a form of indirection that avoids overt praise or censure. An early example is the Greek comic character Eiron, a clever underdog who by his wit repeatedly triumphs over the boastful character Alazon.

Malapropism: A verbal blunder in which one word is replaced by another similar in sound but different in meaning. This term comes from Sheridan's Mrs. Malaprop in The Rivals (1775). Thinking of the geography of contiguous countries, she spoke of the "geometry" of "contagious countries."

Other Syntax Devices _____

Synonyms and antonyms

A synonym is an equivalent of another word and can substitute for it in certain contexts. Diversifying vocabulary in your writing by incorporating synonyms will improve your writing, giving you the best chance for a high score on the multiple choice section for the exam.

Original word	Synonyms
Required	Necessary, mandatory, needed, essential
Many	Numerous, several
Smart	Intelligent, bright, intellectual

An antonym represents the opposite meaning for a word.

Original word	Antonym
Before	After
Optional	Required
Complex	Simple

Analogies _____

A comparison between two things, an analogy illustrates an idea by means of a more familiar idea that is similar or parallel to it. These are commonly found on CLEP exams, and studying vocabulary and literary devices will help you in breaking down meaning to find the correct answers. As you read through options for analogies in the multiple choice sections, it's important to keep in mind that you're looking for the most logical answer. Beware of questions that have multiple options that make sense, and try to zero in on the "best" answer. Also, it's best to go with your gut answer while determining the correct option for analogies; overthinking will lead to second guessing, and you could waste valuable test time if you continue to run through the possibilities.

Most commonly, direct analogies would be laid out like this:

An apple is to fruit as _____ is to vegetable.
  (A) Celery
  (B) Water
  (C) Organic
  (D) Hydroponic

The answer is Celery A..

You may find analogies on exams that stem from cause/effect, part of a whole, and characteristics (similar or complete opposite).

Idioms

An idiom is a word or expression that cannot be translated word for word in another language, such as "I am running low on gas." By extension, writers use idioms to convey a way of speaking and writing typical of a group of people. Some idioms are passed down from one generation to the next, but not all. Because language is constantly evolving, some idioms are left behind while new phrases are used to parallel the common society. For example, the saying "burn the midnight oil," meaning, working late into the night, has died off. This may have been a common saying around the time oil lamps were used, but technology has evolved to the point this saying would be arbitrary to our current society.

Examples:

Birthday suit	Play it by ear
Down the drain	Raining cats and dogs
Show off	An arm and a leg
At the drop of a hat	Sick as a dog
Taste of your own medicine	Silver lining
Piece of cake	Last straw
Keep an eye on it	Get the ball rolling
Long shot	

Dialect

Dialect, also referred to as regionalism, includes usages that are peculiar to a particular part of the country. A good example is the second-person plural pronoun you. Because the plural is the same as the singular, speakers in various parts of the country have developed their own vocabulary solutions to be sure that they are understood when they are speaking to more than one "you." In the South, "you-all" or "y'all" is common. In the Northeast, one often hears "youse." In some areas of the Midwest, "you'ns" can be heard. Similar to idiomatic expressions, dialect evolves to incorporate societal trends and expands from year to year.

Jargon

Jargon is a specialized vocabulary. It may be the vocabulary peculiar to a particular industry such as computers or of a field such as religion. It may also be the vocabulary of a social group. The jargon of bloggers comprises a whole vocabulary that has even developed its own dictionaries. The speaker must be knowledgeable about and sensitive to the jargon peculiar to the particular audience. That may require some research and some vocabulary development on the speaker's part. For example, technical language is a form of jargon. It is usually specific to an industry, profession, or field of study. Sensitivity to the language familiar to the particular audience is important.

Strategy for Points: Avoiding Vocabulary Errors

1. Avoid using the pronunciation of a word, which often results in improper spelling. Test day is not a great time to incorporate vocabulary words that you are not 100% confident in; therefore, if you find yourself trying to sound a word out, skip that word and try using something you're more familiar with.

2. Varying vocabulary is a great way to diversify your writing. Because you will be developing a written response to portray concise, strong writing, you do not want to take away from your message by using the same words over and over again. Look back over the synonym and antonym section to refresh your memory for substituting and expanding the words used in your written responses. Switching up words, phrases, and methods of emphasizing will give you the best opportunity for a high score.

3. Stick to words that you know. Now is not the time to try to add in a fancy word to make your writing seem college ready. It's best to use words that you are familiar with (in both meaning and usage) than to take a risk and end up losing points because you have used a word incorrectly.

4. Use context clues to define words that are unknown. This will assist you when reading multiple choice questions, particularly definitions and analogies, as well as poetry selections that you may not be familiar with.

5. Flashcards can be a great way to prepare you for unknown words. You may pick up on a root, or a common prefix or suffix that will help you in selecting correct answers on the day of the test.

Chapter 3: Literary Periods

All throughout history, the politics of each culture are reflected in its literature. Developments in technology, philosophy, and language can be charted through familiarity with each culture's body of work. The CLEP Analyzing and Interpreting Literature test has a focus on English language literature, specifically that of the United States and the British Isles, but an understanding of major developments in world literature is also essential. By knowing the major works, authors, and themes of each literary period, you can demonstrate a fuller understanding of the literary canon that shaped the world we live in today.

This chapter can act as a refresher to each literary period throughout world literature, but it's also important to do more in-depth research of specific literary works as you study for the test. An understanding of the historical context of these works is also important.

American Literature

The earliest literature to come out of North America was produced by the various indigenous tribes that inhabited the continent before European settlers appeared. These stories were almost always oral tellings, passed down from generation to generation, dealing with themes such as the interconnectedness of nature and a reverence for family and tradition. After European colonization began, Native American stories took on somber tone as they lamented the destruction of their people and culture.

The **Colonial Period** of American literature, by contrast, was written down instead of told orally, and was deeply Christian and neoclassical in style. In the 1630s, the first printing presses were built by colonists in the New World, and they created writings that borrowed heavily from British literary canon. Colonists were often taught proper English grammar and spelling, and their works depicted the struggles of early colonial life, always with an emphasis on order, family, and religion. William Bradford's *Mayflower Compact* recounted the daily hardships of colonization during the harsh winter in Massachusetts, whereas Anne Bradstreet explored colonial daily life through poetry. Captain John Smith is sometimes considered the first author of the New World due to his journals recalling his earliest days on the new continent.

Values at this time were distinctly Puritan, emphasizing the church as the center of all daily life. Indeed, much of the writing produced at this time was intended simply to be read aloud during sermons. It wasn't until the **Revolutionary Period** in the mid-1700s that works of a more political nature began to appear.

In 1775, Thomas Paine, a philosopher and agitator, wrote a pamphlet that would go on to become the top-selling piece of American literature of all time. *Common Sense* was an incendiary piece of writing, detailing in clear, simple prose the need for rebellion against British rule. The pamphlet's fierce rhetoric stirred the hearts of the colonial upper class, and its concise style meant it could be read aloud in taverns and town squares so that even the illiterate could hear Paine's words. John Adams would later say, "Without the pen of the author of *Common Sense*, the sword of Washington would have been raised in vain." *Common Sense* epitomized this period of American literature, emphasizing freedom from Britain and the need to forge a new identity as Americans.

Among the educated elite, Enlightenment was the watchword of the day. Enlightenment thinkers criticized the religious and political dogma they had been raised with, insisting a new social order based on reason was necessary to modernize the human race. Some Enlightenment thinkers, like Benjamin Franklin, explored new concepts of morality outside of Puritanism — Franklin's *Poor Richard's Almanack* was a collection of wit and wisdom that detailed Franklin's concepts of common virtue in an entertaining style. Many of Franklin's aphorisms from this book ("A penny saved is a penny earned") survive to this day.

The Revolutionary Period also produced stirring oration — Patrick Henry's "Speech to the Virginia House of Burgesses" produced the timeless quotation "Give me liberty or give me death!" This directness was a necessary component of Revolutionary writing, as it needed to be accessible to even the uneducated and illiterate citizens the upper class wished to recruit.

Even the *Declaration of Independence* exhibits characteristics of good Revolutionary literature. Written by Thomas Jefferson, it offers neoclassical style, direct prose, and plenty of irresistible quotations that deliver a unified political message.

The 1800s saw the rise of the **Romantic Period** in American literature. Romanticism was considered very liberal and radical for its time, a reaction to the Industrial Revolution and the increasing scientific rationalization of nature. Romanticism focused on intense emotions, such as awe, horror, love, lust, and depression, and found artistic beauty in the wonders of nature. American Romanticists also lionized their own exploits – the trials against the Indians, Manifest Destiny, and the triumphs of Revolutionary heroes like George Washington. Later critics would characterize Romanticism as naïve, but the influence of the movement on world literature was indelible.

Washington Irving was an early American Romantic, creating folk tales like "The Legend of Sleepy Hollow" and "Rip Van Winkle", which largely rejected British influence in favor of a new American consciousness. The Romantic period also saw a rise in poetry intended to be read as cozy fireside entertainment. "Fireside Poets" such as James Russell Lowell, Oliver Wendell Holmes, and John Greenleaf Whittier wrote of scenarios familiar to Americans at the time, such as the harshness and beauty of New England winters. Henry Wadsworth Longfellow wrote longer poetic epics like The *Song of Hiawatha* and *The Courtship of Miles Standish* which could thrill as well as educate.

Another prominent American Romantic author is Edgar Allan Poe. Among the first authors to make his living solely by writing, Poe's influence has been felt around the world. With short stories like "Murders in the Rue Morgue", Poe invented the genre of detective fiction, and works like "The Cask of Amontillado" pioneered in the genre of horror. His works explored topics of depression and family strife, drawing heavily upon his own struggles. He had a major influence on other genres like science fiction and mystery, and he's considered one of the all-time masters of the short story, helping to establish it as a major literary form.

Meanwhile, Nathaniel Hawthorne offered some of the first true criticisms of the Puritan lifestyle that had been so prominent in Colonial times. *The Scarlet Letter* is considered his masterwork, depicting the public shaming and ostracization of Hester Prynne, a Puritan woman accused of adultery. Though a fundamentally Romantic book, it eschews much of the wide-eyed naiveté common to the movement, focusing more on the grim realities of human nature.

This political bend in Romantic literature was pushed further by the "Transcendentalists" – Henry David Thoreau and Ralph Waldo Emerson created this subgenre of Romanticism which sought beauty in the simplicity of nature and freedom from the struggles of society. Both authors were intensely political and anti-government, this being reflected in the works *Walden* and the anti-authoritarian screed "On the Duty of Civil Disobedience". In *Walden*, Thoreau painted an attractive portrait of his time living simply in the bounty of nature. The book mixes social commentary, satire, and observations of the natural world to great effect.

But perhaps the single most prominent work of American Romantic literature is Herman Melville's *Moby Dick*. The timeless story pits mad Captain Ahab against the whale that took his leg, casting their struggle as a battle between man and nature, or perhaps man against the very universe itself. Melville explores a heightened dialect in the book, harkening back to the works of Shakespeare or the ancient Greeks, which rejects realism in favor of operatic emotion. Though unappreciated in its time, the story is now considered among the best novels ever produced by an American.

As the Romantic Period faded in the 1850s with the American Civil War, a new **Realist Period** began to take hold. Americans felt Romantic writings no longer reflected the grim realities of life during wartime, and so began producing simpler, more grounded literature, replete with imagery and often expressing cynicism and dissatisfaction.

Walt Whitman was among the early Realist pioneers. His poetry made use of simple images, and was very prose-like. He's considered the "Father of Free Verse" for his influential style, which shirked much of the established rules of poetry for the time. Emily Dickinson is also sometimes considered a Realist. A reclusive woman, Dickinson's body of work is deeply introspective, focusing on intense sensory input and attention to detail which reflects her apprehension of the outside world.

But no one captured the sentiment of post-Civil War America quite like Mark Twain. The pen name of Samuel Longhorn Clemens, Twain is considered by many to be America's first great humorist, penning works of staggering wit that oozed nostalgia, appealing to both young readers and old. His works explore the American South during the Reconstruction period, drawing on his own childhood and adventures as a river boat worker for inspiration. His works, like *The Adventures of Huckleberry Finn*, also explore racial themes and are considered controversial to this day.

Other authors of note include Stephen Crane, whose book, *The Red Badge of Courage*, offered a realistic depiction of a soldier's life during the Civil War. He also wrote *Maggie: A Girl of the Streets*, a cynical tale of a poor woman who turns to prostitution. Upton Sinclair's work is similarly unromantic, with books like *The Jungle* exposing the deplorable working conditions of Chicago meat packers. Sinclair was considered a major agitator in his time. He also wrote *Oil!*, which criticized the greed of American oilmen and proved extremely controversial due to its depiction of a sexual encounter in a motel.

20th Century literature is very diverse due to the rise of mass media, and can be divided into the realms of fiction, poetry, and drama. Among the greatest American dramatists is Eugene O'Neill, who won an unprecedented four Pulitzer Prizes for Drama for his works. Deeply personal, O'Neill's works reflect his own struggles with depression, alcoholism, and family dysfunction that bordered on abuse. His masterpiece is *Long Day's Journey Into Night*, a semi-autobiographical tale of a family being slowly torn apart by substance abuse and their own incompatible egos. Tennessee Williams is another giant of American drama, penning classics like *Cat On a Hot Tin Roof* and *A Streetcar Named Desire*, which deal with issues of sexuality, gender, and mental illness. Both dramatists evoked the Realist style from decades earlier, creating terse and sometimes pessimistic deconstructions of modern American life through the lenses of volatile families and failed careers.

Of poetry, the 20th masters would be Maya Angelou, Langston Hughes, and Robert Frost. Angelou was a Civil Rights activist who wrote stunning poems and memoirs on themes of racism and gender, with the autobiographical *I Know Why the Caged Bird Sings* detailing her growth from an insecure and abused young woman into an independent firebrand. Hughes, likewise, wrote detailed accounts of the African-American experience. He was a leading figure in the Harlem Renaissance, a movement in the 1920s that gave a voice to black writers in New York City, many of whom would go on to become massively influential. Meanwhile, Frost's poems are more traditional, detailing the beauty of the natural world he experienced growing up in rural New England and the joys of simple living. His work "The Road Less Traveled" is among the most well-known and acclaimed poems of all time.

But prose fiction has always had the largest reach and biggest influence, and many 20th century American authors have penned works that continue to change the world. In 1925, F. Scott Fitzgerald published *The Great Gatsby*, considered by many to be perhaps the greatest American novel. The book follows wealthy socialite Jay Gatsby as viewed through the eyes of his friend and confidante Nick Carraway, as Gatsby tries in vain to leverage his vast wealth and influence towards winning back the woman of his dreams. The book is considered the ultimate satire on the American Dream, exploring the vacuity of wealth and material gains that so many Americans strive for.

Meanwhile, the works of Ernest Hemingway and John Steinbeck explored the struggles of the lower classes. *Steinbeck's The Grapes of Wrath* follows the doomed Joad family during the Great Depression as they try time and again to carve out a better future for themselves, being stopped at every turn by greedy opportunists and exploitative businessmen. Steinbeck wrote in a very colloquial dialect that made his works extremely popular, but Hemingway took it even farther, pioneering a new style involving simple words and short declarative sentences that emphasized action and image rather than introspection. He wrote philosophical tales of fate like *The Old Man and the Sea* and also wartime narratives like *A Farewell to Arms* and *The Sun Also Rises*, which were inspired by his own experiences in WWI.

And lastly, William Faulkner pioneered in the Southern Gothic genre, exploring grotesque scenarios involving poverty, mysticism, or outcast characters in the American South. Faulkner's work described the lingering effects of slavery and the erosion of traditional Southern institutions in an absurdist and experimental style. *As I Lay Dying* and *The Sound and the Fury* are considered his masterpieces.

Since the beginning, American literature has focused largely on issues of class, race, religion, and the struggle for independence, be it from oppressive institutions, economic inequality, or bigotry. The so-called "pioneer spirit" can still be found in contemporary American iconography, the cowboys and superheroes that Americans enjoy reflect a fierce belief in the power of the individual and the need to struggle against life's unfairness. Much world literature focuses on groups, on collectives or movements, but it is not uncommon for American stories to focus on one character only and tell a more universal tale through their experiences. From the earliest pioneer tales to modern stories of the empty promises of the American Dream, the United States has proved itself a powerhouse in the world of literature.

British Literature

The myriad varieties of literature found throughout the world are too numerous to explore in any book, but for the purposes of CLEP study, some of the most significant literary accomplishments can be summarized. Remember, there is no substitute for in-depth research. Read reviews, summaries, criticisms, or even the works themselves to get a fuller understanding of the power these stories have held in whatever culture they may have sprung from.

The most significant direct influence on American literature comes from our neighbors across the Atlantic in the British Isles. During the Anglo-Saxon period between the 8th and 11th centuries, the English language was still coming into its own as a unique dialect separate from Latin or German. Among the earliest works in the English language is *Beowulf*, an epic poem describing the exploits of its titular hero as he attempts to slay the monstrous creature, Grendel. *Beowulf's* author is not known, and the story likely originated as an oral telling that distorted real historical events into the realm of fairy tale.

The medieval period lasted until the 15th century and introduced many other stories that have become an essential part of British consciousness. Thomas Malory's *La Morte D'Arthur* is one of the first Arthurian legends, describing the exploits of King Arthur, Guinevere, Sir Lancelot, and the rest of the Knights of the Round Table which have made an indelible mark on world literature. But Geoffrey Chaucer's *Canterbury Tales* is the true apex of Medieval British literature. The book, which follows a group of pilgrims engaged in a storytelling contest as they travel to a famous shrine, featured an unprecedented mastery of common language and a massive cast of characters from all walks of life who painted an ironic and critical view of English life. Chaucer introduced many new words and phrases into the English language with *Canterbury*, and his view of English life as seen through the eyes of worldly lower class laborers has proven invaluable to historians ever since.

Of course, no mention of British literature is complete without Shakespeare and his contemporaries who worked during the **Renaissance Era** of the 14th through 17th centuries. Considered by many to be the greatest writer in the English language, William Shakespeare produced thirty-nine plays and over one hundred sonnets, ranging from broad comedies to heartfelt tragedies and bloody historical tellings. Shakespeare was a master of iambic pentameter, a poetical meter with each line having five iambs or "feet", each containing a stressed and unstressed syllable. This style of verse was said to mimic the beating of the human heart, and it leant Shakespeare's prose much lively energy that has proved attractive to actors and readers for centuries. Shakespeare was also a great wit and an incredible craftsmen of language. No other author has contributed more words to the English language than Shakespeare. His contemporaries, such as Christopher Marlowe and John Webster, also experimented wildly with new forms of vernacular storytelling, often repackaging ancient Greek tales for popular consumption.

In the 17th century, British literature largely focused on religious concerns. John Milton, a staunch Puritan, gave *Paradise Lost* to the world. The epic poem details the fall of the archangel Lucifer from heaven and his subsequent rebellion against God. The work proved so influential that it is sometimes mistaken for Biblical canon. John Bunyan's *The Pilgrim's Progress* is also staunchly religious, telling of a man's journey towards heaven after death. For many years, the book was second only to the Bible in terms of sales. John Donne's poetry, meanwhile, was more personal and satirical. Common turns of phrase like "for whom the bell tolls" and "no man is an island" come from his works.

18th century British literature became even more intensely political following the revival of the monarchy under Charles II. **Neoclassical** writing was the rule at this time, as British citizens sought to elevate and reconnect with their past. Notable authors include Alexander Pope, a poet who dabbled in a variety of neoclassical forms, and Robert Burns, a Scotsman who explored common Scottish brogue in his poems such as "To A Mouse". But William Blake came to be viewed as the eminent voice of this generation – a notably progressive thinker with decidedly anti-church politics, Blake's work fought for the dissolution of gender roles and more critical views towards religion. He was a friend and contemporary of Thomas Paine, and the two shared many views popular amongst Enlightenment figures at this time.

The works of Blake help usher in an era of **Romanticism** in British literature in the 1800s. The "First Generation" of Romantics included William Wordsworth and Samuel Taylor Coleridge, who collaborated *Lyrical Ballads*, a collection of experimental poems like "Rime of the Ancient Mariner" which epitomized the Romantic style and essayed Wordsworth's philosophical belief that men are inherently good but often become corrupted by society. The Second Generation of Romantics include John Keats, Lord Byron, and Percy Bysshe Shelley, who churned out sonnets, epics, and narrative poems featuring gorgeous prose and keen wit. Byron's *Don John* is a masterpiece of British satire, and his autobiographical *Childe Harold's Pilgrimage* is exceedingly self-deprecating. Shelley's works feature remarkable sensory detail – his poem "Ozymandias" describes a traveler who discovers a monument to some forgotten king whose grand empire has crumbled to dust. Keats' works display maturity far beyond his years, as the poet died at the tender age of 25.

The Romantic era also saw the rise of the some of the first prominent female authors in British history, creating a feminist perspective that was often missing from literature until that point. Jane Austen is the most popular author from this time, and her works, such as *Pride & Prejudice* and *Mansfield Park*, provided realistic characters and cutting social commentary that have endured in popularity even to the present day. Charlotte and Emily Bronte were sisters and professional rivals, who wrote Jane Eyre and *Wuthering Heights* respectively, two grand Romantic novels focusing on duplicity and unrequited love amongst the landed gentry of England. All of these authors struggled against societal expectations of women during this time, and many critics less were than generous with their reviews, leading another prominent author of this time, Mary Ann Evans, to write under the alias of George Eliot to get a fairer appraisal of her work.

The rise of printed media in the 1800s created a diverse range of literature in Britain, ranging from the sharply **satirical** to the proudly **adventurous**. Great satirists like Oscar Wilde skewered the manners and customs of the upper class to a greater degree than ever before, earning scorn from censors and traditionalists while keeping readers enraptured. It was also a great time for young adult literature – Robert Louis Stevenson's *Treasure Island* and *20,000 Leagues Under the Sea* wove action-packed tales of high adventure that appealed to young readers. Still other authors focused their attentions on social commentary, such as Rudyard Kipling, who crafted many fables and parables that taught valuable lessons in *The Jungle Book*. Charles Dickens's works were more critical, deconstructing Victorian values of greed and decadence, focusing his attentions on the downtrodden orphans and lower class laborers who suffered during the Industrial Revolution. He also wrote immensely popular potboilers such as *A Christmas Carol*, which helped re-popularize the Christmas holiday and has never once been out of publication since its first printing.

This experimentation and variety has continued in the 20th century, in which Britain has firmly established itself as a major force in world literature. Irish authors James Joyce and Samuel Beckett pioneered **Modernist** literature, which remixed and recontextualized existing dramatic forms in absurd, experimental new ways. Beckett's *Waiting for Godot* is among the most influential plays ever written, examining the tragedy and comedy of the human condition via two clownish vagabonds contemplating their own inability to accomplish anything of note. The play is a landmark work of Absurdist and Post-Modern theater, two experimental styles that pushed the limits of what audiences could expect from the stage.

Joyce's *Ulysses* is considered by many critics to be perhaps the greatest English language novel – it experiments and invents in nearly every literary style, using a dreamlike stream-of-consciousness narrative of a man's madcap journey through Dublin on a single day. The works of George Orwell are more political. A former police officer in English-occupied Burma, Orwell's works are fiercely anti-fascist, providing stark warnings about the dangers of totalitarianism. His science-fiction/dystopian novel *1984* is considered his masterpiece, telling the tale of a common man's struggle against his brutally conformist society led by the mysterious dictator, "Big Brother".

British literature has flitted between proud lionization of their own accomplishments and self-deprecating laughter at their failings. Traditions of satire and wordplay run deep in English writings, from the comedies of Shakespeare with their puns and double entendres, to the biting, controversial ironies of Oscar Wilde. Still other authors have sought to elevate institutions of British life, such as religion or the monarchy. British writings owe a strong debt to the works of the ancient Greeks, whose tragedies and philosophical writings inspired countless English-language works. The body of work produced by these small island nations continues to grow and develop, further establishing their place as a force to be reckoned with in world media.

The CLEP Analyzing and Interpreting Literature test focuses largely on American and British writings, but a familiarity with other figures of world literature is also useful.

World Literature

Among the most important authors from the rest of the European continent, **ancient Greek** philosophers such as Sophocles, Euripedes, and Aeschylus wrote many tragedies that have formed the backbone of much of Western literature. Greek tragedies focus largely on the failings of the main character, on their pride (or "hubris") that causes them to subvert the natural order of things and earn the ire of the gods, which eventually leads to their downfall (a "catharsis" or cleansing). Most plays contain a mythic or religious component, and many end with direct intervention from the gods themselves (termed a "deus ex machina", a sudden ending where a godlike figure appears and re-establishes order). Important Greek tragedies include *Oedipus Rex, Medea,* and *Antigone.* The epics of Homer are also noteworthy, which include *The Iliad* and *The Odyssey,* epic poems that described the exploits of brave Greek warriors and their struggles against each other and the gods themselves. Homer is sometimes considered the first great European author, and his influence cannot be overstated.

French literature has also proven massively influential to American writers, with much of their work being deeply Romantic and socially conscious, exploring the country's long history of revolution, monarchy, and military triumph. Victor Hugo is considered to be perhaps the premiere French author, penning heartbreaking tragedies like *The Hunchback of Notre Dame* and *Les Miserables* that explored the suffering of outcasts and the lower class, in a similar manner to Charles Dickens across the English Channel. The works of Alexandre Dumas are more pulpy and readable, often classified as swashbucklers or tales of high adventure. Dumas' works include *The Three Musketeers* and *The Count of Monte Cristo,* focusing on tales of revenge, rebellion, and complex love triangles. His works have been translated into over 100 languages and have formed the basis for countless adaptations into film and theater.

The greatest author from the **Slavic** nations would have to be Franz Kafka. Though largely unnoticed during his lifetime, Kafka is now considered one of the most important figures in 20th century literature, writing accounts of depression, anxiety, and isolation that blended the realistic and surreal. He was among the first authors to criticize bureaucratic institutions, with works like *The Trial* and *In the Penal Colony,* which feature characters being tormented by shady government figures for reasons that are never fully explained. He also delved into more fantastical subject matter with works like *The Metamorphosis*, a tale of a traveling salesman who awakens one day to find he has been transformed into a massive bug. The term "Kafkaesque" is common in literary criticism today, describing situations in which a main character is being persecuted for unclear reasons and has no clear method of rectifying their terrible situation.

Russian literary greats include Leo Tolstoy, who described Napolean's capture of the city of Moscow in *War and Peace*, and Fyodor Dostoyevski, who wrote *The Brothers Karamazov*, a satirical and philosophical depiction of the dissolving relationship between three brothers and their father which eventually culminates in murder. Tolstoy also wrote *Anna Karenina*, a prime example of Realist fiction, following the exploits of its titular heroin as she pursues a doomed affair with a wealthy count. The 20th century gave Vladimir Nabokov to the world, the controversial author of such works as *Lolita*, which describes the relationship between a literarily-minded pedophile and his stepdaughter. Nabokov's works are replete with sensory detail and are sharply ironic, offering many cutting observations about the American culture that Nabokov gradually assimilated into. Anton Chekov is considered Russia's prime dramatist, giving the world stories like *Uncle Vanya* and *The Cherry Orchard* which stretched the limits of actors' abilities and paved new ground for concepts like subtext and psychological realism in theater.

These works form much of the basis for the Western canon of literature. One can study these works for a lifetime and not scratch the surface of the stories available, but for the purposes of the CLEP Analyzing and Interpreting Literature exam, and a functional understanding of Western literature, a good comprehension of the primary titles and authors will suffice.

Strategy for Points: Literary Periods: _____

1. If nothing else, understand the following literary periods – Colonial, Revolutionary, Romantic, Realist, and Contemporary or 20th Century. Most of these periods contain numerous sub-movements as well.

2. Know how these movements affected and were affected by major events in American history. The Colonial era inspired literature that was religious and orderly, the Revolution created an era of political agitation. Romanticism harkened back to simpler times before industry and reason removed much of the wonder from life, and Realism reminded us of

the grim realities of the Civil War. Literature is always a reflection of the time period that creates it.

3. Familiarize yourself with the works of the major names in American literature, such as Hemingway, Faulkner, Poe, Melville, Fitzgerald, or Twain. Even if the test does not require you to analyze these authors directly, a familiarity with their work will prove useful for comparisons, and it will demonstrate your broader knowledge of literary history.

4. It's not enough to merely state that a work belongs in a certain literary period. You must demonstrate why, often with explicit references to the text.

5. Most great works of literature are considered to have pioneered in some respect, to have shirked what came before and created something innovative and new. Knowing what literary period preceded a work can help you make your case as to why the piece is a work of genius.

Chapter 4: Drama

Drama is the primary expression of narrative in performance. Any type of creative display involving performers and an audience could be said to have its roots in drama. In Greek, the word ***drama*** means "action", derived from the verb form *dran*, meaning "to do" or "to act". More specifically, "drama" often refers to a composition of verse or prose, delivered to a live audience, involving characters and a conflict of some sort. Thus, things that are not true drama, such as poems, songs, or real-life situations that contain elements of conflict and high emotion are often said to be dramatic.

Drama is also a unique artform in that is, by necessity, collaborative – an author needs only a pen and paper to write a story, but a drama requires multiple voices, such as actors, authors, and directors of some kind, to deliver the performance, as well as an audience to receive it. Drama is a fundamental understanding of storytelling that stretches back to the earliest creations in the western canon.

Ancient Greek Drama

The first Western dramatists to record their works were the Greeks, and it is from their experiments that much of our modern dramatic structures are derived. It was the understanding of Greek dramatists like Sophocles, Aeschylus, and Euripides, that drama was governed by the laws of comedy and tragedy, represented by the famous grinning and weeping masks. The Greeks saw a clear delineation between comedy and tragedy, deciding that essentially, a comedy could be defined as a drama with a happy ending whereas a tragedy would have a sad one. This terminology continued up through the Renaissance, where even the works of Shakespeare and Marlowe can be clearly separated into comedies and tragedies. Comedies, to the Greeks, were life-affirming romps, often containing satire, clowning, and jokes involving scatological references and innuendo.

Tragedies, on the other hand, were serious business. The "Greek Tragedy" is considered the most enduring gift of the ancient Greeks. The most famous of these is the *Oedipus The King*, Sophocles' magnum opus, describing the rise and fall of the mighty Oedipus, doomed by fate to slay his father and marry his mother. A common trope in Greek tragedy is the prophecy, delivering the will of the gods to the hero via an oracle, which the hero ignores or seeks to defy more often than not. This reveals the hero's *hamartia*, his fatal flaw that brings about his downfall. For Oedipus, this is *hubris*, a great pride that sets him above the will of the gods and thus incurs their wrath. In the play, Oedipus was a brilliant man, able to solve the Sphinx's riddle and become king of Thebes, but even his vaunted intellect could not save him from his prophecy. In a fit of blind rage, King Oedipus slays a traveler he meets on the road, later revealed to be his father, Laius. He also unwittingly took his mother, Jocasta, to bride, who bore him four children before their true relationship was uncovered. In true tragic form, the play ends with a *catharsis*, a cleansing act brought on by extreme emotion: Jocasta hangs herself due to shame, and Oedipus, upon finding the body, takes the pins from her dress and plunges them into his eyes.

These concepts as outlined by the Greeks would go on to define Western drama for millennia, even as drama declined in relevance over the centuries as European languages evolved and borders were drawn. Most performance in Europe up to the Middle Ages was strictly religious in nature: drama amongst the working classes amounted to little more than campfire stories and folk songs, whereas the church dabbled in live re-enactments, feeling they could be a useful imparting Biblical tales to the illiterate masses. High drama for the purposes of entertainment or art was little known. This changed in the 16th century with the rise of vernacular English, or "Middle English", and the flowering of literary giants like Christopher Marlowe, John Webster, and William Shakespeare.

British Dramatists

Considered perhaps the greatest and most influential author in the English language, **William Shakespeare** wrote 39 plays, 154 sonnets, and two long-form poems, displaying a mastery of language that has a larger influence on the Western canon of drama than any other figure. He invented or popularized roughly 1700 words that are in common use to this day (only Geoffrey Chaucer can claim to have created nearly as many), and displayed a stunning deftness with the tropes and forms common in Greek tragedy, immortalizing their styles for centuries to come.

Like the Greeks, Shakespeare divided his works into comedies and tragedies, with a few historical plays belonging to neither category.

Shakespeare's tragedies exhibit many Greek forms: in the tragedy of *Macbeth*, for instance, the plot is set in motion by supernatural forces, though Shakespeare substitutes three meddlesome witches for an oracle. Macbeth, our protagonist, possesses the hamartia of ambition – he seeks to become king of Scotland, and is driven to commit many terrible crimes in this pursuit. In the end, this destroys him, as the honorable MacDuff avenges the deaths of his family by beheading Macbeth in single combat, thus bringing peace and order back to the realm, albeit at a terrible cost. The comedies of Shakespeare, likewise, are light-hearted romps involving romance, wordplay, physical comedy, and numerous innuendos.

Shakespeare dabbled in satire and social commentary, but his works are still fundamentally religious and pro-status quo. More often than not, order is restored through royal decree or divine intervention. Conflicts have a tendency to resolve themselves or peter out entirely, as is the case in *Much Ado About Nothing*, where the villainous Don John is captured by unnamed soldiers with no help from the main characters. This kind of abrupt conclusion harkens back to another term coined by the ancient Greeks: the **deus ex machina**, a sudden conclusion brought on by forces not previously established in the play. In Greek plays, it was not uncommon for the action to be resolved by the appearance of a literal god onstage. Zeus may appear, brandishing thunderbolts, to destroy the wicked, punish the prideful, and restore the natural order of things, before disappearing just as suddenly. Even the Greeks considered the deus ex machina to be a hallmark of lazy writing, Aristotle being one of the trope's most famous critics, but the plot device endured in the works of Shakespeare, sometimes as tongue-in-cheek parody, and other times as an earnest expression of the belief that godly order will naturally assert itself, even in bizarre or dangerous situations.

Stylistically, Shakespeare's works reveal an astounding command of the nascent English language. Though he invented many words and phrases that became common to English speakers, his dialogue was intentionally heightened and unrealistic for dramatic effect. Shakespeare wrote in **blank verse**, a type of poetic style involving regular metrical lines with only occasional rhymes. Each line in blank verse has the same poetic meter, consisting of equal syllables on each line. More specifically, Shakespeare's style of blank verse made use of **iambic pentameter**, a style innovated by Shakespeare's contemporary Christopher Marlowe, which uses ten syllables per line divided into five "feet" consisting of a stressed and unstressed syllable. This creates sort of a galloping or heartbeat cadence for each line, a *buh-BUM buh-BUM buh-BUM* rhythm that has proved attractive to actors for centuries. The limitations imposed by iambic pentameter are numerous, but Shakespeare mastered the form, creating dialogue that was heightened enough to be dramatic yet witty and ribald enough to be understood and enjoyed by the common listener.

The styles of Renaissance artists like Shakespeare and Marlowe, as well as the Greeks who inspired them, provided much inspiration for English and American dramatists in the centuries to come. The first professional theater company to perform in America, the Lewis Hallam troupe, staged Shakespeare's *The Merchant of Venice* in Williamsburg, Virginia in 1752. Their run in the colonies was a mild success, though theater companies struggled to find an audience in more conservative areas where Puritan communities considered theater to be, at best, a frivolous distraction and at worst, blasphemy. It was not until after the Revolutionary War, where the populace had been inspired by the fiery orations of leaders like Patrick Henry ("Give me liberty or give me death!") and the lean, aggressive prose of authors like Thomas Paine, that American drama would find its own identity.

American Dramatists

William Dunlap is considered the father of American theater. A painter, historian, and artist, Dunlap produced over sixty plays in his career, many of them being translations of German or French works displaying a broad knowledge of politics and a fierce loyalty to the newly minted American identity. His most famous works include *Andre*, a tragedy that dramatizes the trial of Major John Andre, a British soldier who was hanged as a spy for his support of Benedict Arnold, and *The Italian Father*, a comedy which borrowed heavily from the works of English dramatist Thomas Dekker.

In the 19th century, American theater was largely melodramatic. American authors mimicked the style of the classical greats who inspired them, creating broad and operatic pieces dealing with issues of class, race, and the American dream. *Uncle Tom's Cabin* was by far the most popular American play of the 1800s. Due to sparsely-enforced copyright laws and the immense popularity of **Harriet Beecher Stowe**'s source novel, many "Tom shows" were performed throughout the United States and England, incorporating elements of heightened soap opera and blackface minstrelsy. Though the novel is staunchly anti-slavery, it resorts heavily to stereotypes, and theaters portrayed these with varying degrees of sensitivity and clownishness. It was not uncommon at this time for white actors to portray black characters, complete with darkened faces and exaggerated African-American dialects, and the various "Tom shows" and minstrel shows this spawned dominated the American theatrical scene for some time. These shows often validated the racist attitudes of Americans instead of challenging them, and they became symbolic of the American South's troubled history with race.

The 20th century saw a flowering of American theater. The Civil War, the Depression, and the rise of mechanization and industry left many Americans nostalgic for simpler times and confused about the modern world they lived in, with its promises of a mythical American Dream. The early quarter of the century was dominated by vaudeville revues featuring circus acts, burlesque, music, and fast-paced comedy. After WWII, American drama would finally discover its own voice in the works of Eugene O'Neill, Tennessee Williams, and Arthur Miller, each of whom would explore distinctly American themes relating to family, individuality, sexuality, and the failings of a capitalist system.

Eugene O'Neill was born into a family with deep ties to the theater. His father, James O'Neill, was considered one of the greatest actors of his generation, at least until he squandered his career playing in a successful production of *The Count of Monte Cristo* for a full six thousand performances, causing many critics to label him a sell-out. The family James built with his wife, Mary Ellen Quinlan, was rife with dysfunction, alcohol abuse, and emotional manipulation. Eugene dropped out of school at a young age and spent several years at sea, struggling with alcoholism and depression. He became a popular fixture in Greenwich village's literary scene before writing his first play, *Beyond the Horizon*, in 1920. The play would win the young author a Pulitzer Prize for Drama. O'Neill would earn three more of the prizes over his vaunted career, an unprecedented accomplishment for any author.

Other great works by O'Neill include *Strange Interlude*, *Anna Christie*, *The Hairy Ape*, and his masterpiece, *Long Day's Journey Into Night*, which depicts in brutal detail the emotional manipulation and substance abuse that turned his childhood into a living hell. O'Neill was among the first authors to explore American vernacular as a legitimate dialect of the theater. His works often dealt with alcoholism and masculinity, and his plays often featured characters who lived on the fringes of society, such as prostitutes, addicts, and homeless people. O'Neill was also the first author to write a major play starring an African-American in a serious role: *The Emperor Jones*, which was influential in the black literary community despite resorting to stereotypes to get its message across. O'Neill died in 1953 after years of declining health, with his final play, *Long Day's Journey*, being considered one of the greatest dramatic achievements of all time.

Like his contemporary, **Tennessee Williams** struggled with various addictions and depression throughout his life, channeling these struggles into his plays. Williams was also a closeted homosexual – this revelation, an open secret during much of Williams' career but not formally acknowledged until after his death, has caused many critics to re-evaluate Williams' works from a new perspective. The machismo and violence of many of his male characters, such as the brutish Stanley Kowalski from *A Streetcar Named Desire*, represents a stern commentary by Williams on the strict gender roles that had caused him to hide his sexuality for much of his life. Williams' was also very close with his sister, Rose, who was diagnosed with schizophrenia at a young age and spent much of her life in institutions. Williams used her as an inspiration for many similar characters, such as the disabled Laura in *The Glass Menagerie* and even in *Streetcar's* Blanche Dubois, who suffers a mental breakdown at the end of the play after being preyed upon by the overly masculine Stanley.

Williams other works deal with the identity of the American South and the notion of the "fading Southern belle", an upper class woman struggling with new realities after her money runs out and her looks begin to go. This trope is explored in some of Williams' best works, such as *Cat on a Hot Tin Roof, Orpheus Descending,* and *The Glass Menagerie,* in which the mother, Amanda, wishes to recapture her glamorous youth by living vicarious through Laura, whose illness prevents her from socializing. Williams was also instrumental in advancing the careers of great talents like director Elia Kazan, and actors Kate Hepburn and Marlon Brando, the latter of whom originated the role of Stanley Kowalski, considered by many to be one of the great stage performances of all time.

Arthur Miller's output was largely concerned with the social upheaval of the 1950s. He was forced to testify in front of Senator Joseph McCarthy's House UnAmerican Activities committee to ascertain his supposed communist sympathies, and he became a controversial voice during the period known as the Red Scare. This formed the basis for his classic play, *The Crucible*, which explores the paranoia of the time by transplanting it back to the Salem Witch Trials. His other great works include *All My Sons*, a tragic play centering around a family business and WWII, and *Death of a Salesman*, which follows fading businessman Willy Loman as he slides into obscurity and purposelessness. Miller's works were harshly critical of the American Dream, prompting Sen. McCarthy's interest in attacking Miller's reputation. Miller's career survived the hearings, though he did out several of his contemporaries as communist sympathizers.

Modern American Drama

In the latter half of the 20th century, American theater became a dominant cultural force, even as the popularity of the art form was long-since eclipsed by film. The Civil Rights movement of the 1960s spurring many new plays dealing with issues of race, such as Lorraine Hansberry's *A Raisin in the Sun*, which followed the struggles of a black family in Chicago. The play won a Pulitzer Prize, making Hansberry the first African-American to win the award. Her works were heavily influenced by the Harlem Renaissance of the 1920s, a movement amongst black intellectuals such as Langston Hughes and Zora Neale Hurston to forge a new African-American identity in the United States through artistic and political action in the Harlem neighborhood of New York.

In recent years, American drama has proven to be experimental and uncompromising, displaying a facility with both naturalistic and heightened dialogue as well as finding strong humanity in characters from all walks of life. Dominant theatrical voices since the 1950s include David Mamet (*Glengarry Glen Ross, Speed-The-Plow*), Neil Simon (*Lost in Yonkers, The Odd Couple*), Henry David Hwang (*M. Butterfly*), and Tony Kushner (*Angels in America*). American drama continues to explore themes of sexuality, race, class, and gender as they affect all walks of life. The forms and styles owe a heavy debt to Renaissance artists like Shakespeare and the Greek forerunners that inspired them, but the soul is distinctly American.

Strategy for Points: Drama

1. Know the fundamental aspects of drama: the role of hamartia, hubris, and catharsis as they appear in classical works, as well as more contemporary dramas. These forms appear in nearly all western drama in some form or another.

2. Theater has always been closely tied to the culture that creates it. Try to connect theatrical works to the social issues of its time. The works of Williams and O'Neill are concerned with money, important to a generation that survived the Great Depression. The works of Hansberry and Hurston deal with race, just as Civil Rights came into its own.

3. Understand the styles of classical artists like Shakespeare and Marlowe. Familiarize yourself with Iambic pentameter, blank verse, and the relationship between poetic language and dialogue they created.

4. Many authors drew from elements of their own life. For instance, Williams explored issues of mental illness and strict gender roles, whereas O'Neill dramatized his own struggles with alcohol and family dysfunction.

5. Be prepared to analyze text directly. You must offer quotations to support your point.

Chapter 5: Prose

Unlike Poetry (covered in the next chapter), prose does not contain metrical structure. While it follows the normal grammatical rules for the language, prose includes a more literal, natural way of speaking. It's straightforward and does not follow a rhyme scheme.

It is very likely that an excerpt from a famous work of prose will be included in the multiple portions of your CLEP exam. By familiarizing yourself with the difference between poetry and prose and the various styles of each, you will set yourself up for the best probability of a high score. Being familiar with the context from the time period and the author's background will be instrumental in creating strong support for your responses.

Poetry Versus Prose

Poetry follows a structure with metric or rhyme scheme, while prose does not have a standard style of writing. In addition, poetry often leads the reader to read between the lines, while prose has a much more literal approach. There is minimal critical thinking involved when it comes to reading a piece of prose- you are simply reading a story. You do not have to continuously question the author's intention or the intended meaning of the piece.

Poetry	Prose
Written in verse	Written in narrative form
Contains poetic meter	Contains paragraphs
It's up to the reader to determine the author's intention	Includes a setting, characters, plot, and point of view
Metaphorical	Literal

If you were to write a piece in both poetry and prose formats and put them beside one another, they would represent the same idea using extremely different formats. Take a look at the two examples below, Emily Dickinson's famous poem The Carriage, and Life by Charlotte Brontë.

Example 1: The Carriage

Petry

Because I could not stop for Death –
He kindly stopped for me –
The Carriage held but just Ourselves –
And Immortality.

We slowly drove – He knew no haste
And I had put away
My labor and my leisure too,
For His Civility –

We passed the School, where Children strove
At Recess – in the Ring –
We passed the Fields of Gazing Grain –
We passed the Setting Sun –

Or rather – He passed us –
The Dews drew quivering and chill –
For only Gossamer, my Gown –
My Tippet – only Tulle –

We paused before a House that seemed
A Swelling of the Ground –
The Roof was scarcely visible –
The Cornice – in the Ground –

Since then – 'tis Centuries – and yet
Feels shorter than the Day
I first surmised the Horses' Heads
Were toward Eternity –

-Emily Dickinson

Prose

As I look back on my life, I cannot help but think about lost opportunity and what it will be like when I leave this world. (She dies and is buried in a cemetery where she will stay for eternity.)

Example 2: Life

Poetry

Life, believe, is not a dream
So dark as sages say;
Oft a little morning rain
Foretells a pleasant day.
Sometimes there are clouds of gloom,
But these are transient all;
If the shower will make the roses bloom,
O why lament its fall?

Rapidly, merrily,
Life's sunny hours flit by,
Gratefully, cheerily,
Enjoy them as they fly!

What though Death at times steps in
And calls our Best away?
What though sorrow seems to win,
O'er hope, a heavy sway?
Yet hope again elastic springs,
Unconquered, though she fell;
Still buoyant are her golden wings,
Still strong to bear us well.

Manfully, fearlessly,
The day of trial bear,
For gloriously, victoriously,
Can courage quell despair!

-Charlotte Bronté

Prose

I think it's critical to understand that even if you're having a bad day, your outlook and attitude can help you be happy. Everyone should strive to live life in the moment and enjoy the good times because time passes by faster than you'd expect.

Prose Categories

Fictional prose

The most common example of fictional prose is a novel. Using a narrative form of writing, fictional prose has been used to tell tales of adventure, erotica, and mystery. Other examples include romance and short story.

Nonfiction prose

Nonfiction prose is based on facts, but it may also include fictional elements. It is used to be informative and persuasive, yet it does not include any scientific evidence to support its claims. Examples include: journal entry, biography, and essay.

Heroic prose

Also written in the narrative form, heroic prose has a dramatic style that allows for the works to be recited or performed. The most common form of heroic prose is the legend.

Rhymed prose

The difference between prose and poetry is not always clear. Rhymed prose is written with rhymes that are not metrical and is considered to be an artistic, skilled form of writing across the world. Examples include Rayok in Russian culture, Saj' from Arabic culture, and Fu from Chinese culture.

Prose poetry

Prose poetry can be considered a combination, or fusion, of both poetry and prose. It uses extreme imagery, yet does not include the typical metrical structure or rhyme scheme found in a poem.

Types of Prose

Allegory: A story in verse or prose with characters representing virtues and vices. An allegory has two meanings: symbolic and literal. John Bunyan's The Pilgrim's Progress is the most renowned of this genre.

Epistle: A letter that was not always intended for public distribution, but due to the fame of the sender and/or recipient, becomes widely known. Paul wrote epistles that were later placed in the Bible.

Essay: Typically a relatively short prose work focusing on a topic, propounding a definite point of view and using an authoritative tone. Great essayists include Carlyle, Lamb, DeQuincy, Emerson, and Montaigne, who is credited with defining this genre.

Legend: A traditional narrative or collection of related narratives, popularly regarded as historically factual but actually a mixture of fact and fiction.

Novel: The longest form of fictional prose containing a variety of characters, settings, local color, and regionalism. Most have complex plots, expanded description, and attention to detail. Some of the great novelists include Austen, the Brontë sisters, Twain, Tolstoy, Hugo, Hardy, Dickens, Hawthorne, Forster, and Flaubert.

Romance: A highly imaginative tale set in a fantastical realm dealing with the conflicts between heroes, villains, and/or monsters. "The Knight's Tale" from Chaucer's Canterbury Tales, Sir Gawain and the Green Knight, and Keats' "The Eve of St. Agnes" are representatives.

Short story: Typically a terse narrative, with less development and background about characters; may include description, author's point of view, and tone. Poe emphasized that a successful short story should create one focused impact. Some great short story writers are Hemingway, Faulkner, Twain, Joyce, Shirley Jackson, Flannery O'Connor, de Maupassant, Saki, Edgar Allen Poe, and Pushkin.

Analyzing Prose

The analysis of prose, similar to the analysis of poetry, also calls for attention to structural elements so as to discern meaning, purpose, and themes. The author's intentions are gleaned through the elements he or she uses and how they are used. As you read the passages in the multiple choice section, it is important to deeply analyze all structural elements (plot, characters, setting, and point of view). This will assist you in answering the multiple choice questions wisely – and quickly.

Plot

The plot is the sequence of events (it may or may not be chronological) that the author chooses to represent the story to be told--both the underlying story and the externals of the occurrences the author relates. An author may use "flashbacks" to tell the back story (or what went before the current events begin). Often, authors begin their stories in media res, or in the middle of things, and, over time, supply the details of what has gone before to provide a clearer picture to the reader of all the relevant events.

In good novels, each part of the plot is necessary and has a purpose. For example, in *Anna Karenina*, a chapter is devoted to a horse race Count Vronsky participates in. This might seem like mere entertainment, but, in fact, Count Vronsky is riding his favorite mare, and, in a moment of carelessness in taking a jump, puts the whole weight of his body on the mare's back, breaking it. The horse must be shot. Vronsky loved and admired the mare, but being overcome by a desire to win, he kills the very thing he loves. Similarly, Anna descends into obsession and jealousy as their affair isolates her from society and separates her from her child, and ultimately kills herself. The chapter symbolizes the destructive effect Vronsky's love, coupled with inordinate desire, has upon what and whom he loves.

Other authors use repetitious plot lines to reveal the larger story over time. For example, in Joseph Heller's tragic-comedy *Catch-22*, the novel repeatedly returns to a horrific incident in an airplane while flying a combat mission. Each time the protagonist, Yossarian, recalls the incident, more detail is revealed. The reader knows from the beginning that this incident is key to why Yossarian wants to be discharged from the army, but it is not until the full details of the gruesome incidents are revealed late in the book that the reader knows why the incident has driven Yossarian almost mad. Interspersed with comedic and ironic episodes, the book's climax (the full revealing of the incident) remains powerfully with the reader, showing the absurdity, insanity, and inhumanity of war. The comic device of *Catch-22*, a fictitious army rule from which the title is derived, makes this point in a funny way: *Catch-22* states that a soldier cannot be discharged from the army unless he is crazy; yet, if he wants to be discharged from the army, he is not crazy. This rule seems to embody the insanity, absurdity, and inhumanity of war.

Characters

Characters usually represent or embody an idea or ideal acting in the world. For example in the *Harry Potter* series, Harry Potter's goodness, courage and unselfishness as well as his capacity for friendship and love make him a powerful opponent to Voldemort, whose selfishness, cruelty, and isolation make him the leader of the evil forces in the epic battle of good versus evil. Memorable characters are many-sided: Harry is not only brave, strong, and true, he is vulnerable and sympathetic: orphaned as a child, bespectacled, and often misunderstood by his peers, Harry is not a stereotypical hero.

Charles Dickens's *Oliver Twist* is the principle of goodness, oppressed and unrecognized, unleashed in a troubled world. Oliver encounters a great deal of evil, which he refuses to cooperate with, and also a great deal of good in people who have sympathy for his plight. In contrast to the gentle, kindly, and selfless Maylies who take Oliver in, recognizing his goodness, are the evil Bill Sykes and Fagin – thieves and murderers – who are willing to sell and hurt others for their own gain. When Nancy, a thief in league with Sykes and Fagin, essentially "sells" herself to help Oliver, she represents redemption from evil through sacrifice.

Setting

The setting of a work of fiction adds a great deal to the story. Historical fiction relies firmly on an established time and place: *Johnny Tremain* takes place in revolutionary Boston; the story could not take place anywhere else or at any other time. Ray Bradbury's *The Most Dangerous Game* requires an isolated, uninhabited island for its plot. Settings are sometimes changed in a work to represent different periods of a person's life or to compare and contrast life in the city or life in the country.

Point of View

The point of view is the perspective of the person who is the focus of the work of fiction: a story told in the first person is from the point of view of the narrator. In more modern works, works told in the third person usually concentrate on the point of view of one character or else the changes in point of view are clearly delineated, as in *Cold Mountain* by Charles Frazier, who names each chapter after the person whose point of view is being shown. Sudden, unexplained shifts in point of view – i.e., going into the thoughts of one character after another within a short space of time – are a sign of amateurish writing.

Strategy for Points: Prose _____

1. Review prose written by different authors in different eras so you understanding how the context and time period will assist you in identifying pieces in multiple choice questions.

2. When reviewing a passage, pay close attention to the point of view in the work that is being used. This will help you in depicting the author's intended message.

3. Analyze pieces for rhyme scheme and rhythm when trying to determine if it's poetry or prose, and familiarize yourself with the "poetry vs prose" section at the start of this chapter.

4. Cite specific examples from the prose passage if you do the optional essay in order to support your claims in your written responses. (And don't forget to use quotations while citing.)

5. Build your familiarity with prose pieces that are most likely to appear on the SAT exam, but remember that the most important component is answering the questions within the context of what appears in the exam itself.

Chapter 6: Poetry

Poetry is the use of words to convey image and emotion. Poetry is often less explicit than prose, relying on implication and suggestion rather than overt statement of fact. Poetry is not always concerned with "realism", often shirking basic tenets of grammar and syntax for better artistic effect. There are few true "answers" in poetry, as poems are often interpreted in a variety of ways, but certain conclusions can be drawn from a close reading of the text. This is an important skill for the CLEP Analyzing and Interpreting Literature exam, which will ask questions about general poetic forms, styles, and nomenclature as well as interpretation of meaning, tone, and intent.

Poetic Terminology

Rhyme: Indicates a repeated end sound of lines or words within a poem. Rhymes usually occur at the ends of lines, though they can also be internal.

Example:

"Because I could not stop for Death
He kindly stopped for me
The Carriage held but just Ourselves
And Immortality."
– *Emily Dickinson, "Because I could not stop for Death"*

"Me" and "Immortality" rhyme in this poem, lending a sense of finality to the last line and giving it a pleasing rhythm.

Rhyme scheme: The pattern of rhymes in each line of a poem. Rhyme schemes are usually indicated with letters. Some poets follow strict rhyme schemes, some shirk them entirely, but most employ repetitive rhyme schemes when aesthetically appropriate and then subvert them for stronger effect.

Example:

"A wonderful bird is the pelican;
His beak can hold more than his belly-can.
He can hold in his beak

Enough food for a week,
Though I'm damned if I know how the hell-he-can!"
— *Dixon Lanier Merritt*

This is an example of a Limerick, a short, humorous poem employing a five line rhyme scheme. Limericks always follow an AABBA rhyme scheme – the first two lines rhyme, the next two shorter lines have a different rhyme, and the fifth line calls back to the original rhyme. Limerick structure is intentionally simplistic, highlighting the absurdity of the subject matter and allowing the poet to focus more on wordplay. The B rhymes of the third and fourth lines build anticipation for the final reveal on the fifth line, where the author can reveal a witty subversion.

Slant Rhyme: A slant rhyme is also known as a "near rhyme", "half rhyme" or "lazy rhyme". Slant rhymes sometimes have the same vowel sounds but different consonants, or the reverse. Slant rhymes are sometimes considered childish or uncreative, but many poets of have made use of them in order to avoid clichés, to create disharmony in a piece, or to draw unusual connections between words.

Example:

"WHEN have I last looked on
The round green eyes and the long wavering bodies
Of the dark leopards of the moon?
All the wild witches, those most noble ladies"
– *W. B. Yeats, "Lines Written in Dejection"*

"On" and "moon" are slant rhymes, as are "bodies" and "ladies". This could be said to suggest the author's discordant, dejected state of mind. Perfects in a happier poem these rhymes would be clearer and more musical. But not here.

Stanza: A group of lines, offset by punctuation or spacing, forming a metrical unit or verse in a poem.

Example:

"Do not go gentle into that good night,
Old age should burn and rave at close of day;
Rage, rage against the dying of the light.
Though wise men at their end know dark is right,

Because their words had forked no lightning they

Do not go gentle into that good night."

– Dylan Thomas, "Do not go gentle into that good night".

Each short stanza contains three lines and ends with either "do not go gentle into that good night" or "rage, rage against the dying of the light". This ending rhyme repeats throughout the entire poem, ensuring that each stanza delivers the essential message in a profound and affecting way.

Meter: The basic rhythmic structure of a poem, the "music" of it. Some poetic forms prescribe their own metrical structure, but other poets invented or modified their own.

Example:

"Shall I compare thee to a summer's day?

Thou art more lovely and more temperate

Rough winds do shake the darling buds of May,

And summer's lease hath all too short a date."

– William Shakespeare, "Sonnet 18"

Almost any poem could be said to have some form of meter, but Shakespeare's "iambic pentameter" is among the most famous styles. This metrical style is divided into "iambs", five of them per line, each containing a stressed and unstressed syllable. The pattern could be described as "ba-BUM, ba-BUM, ba-BUM", not unlike the beating of a heart. This metrical rhythm permeates Shakespeare's work, proving very attractive to actors who appreciate the clear, emphatic delivery.

Alliteration: the use of repeated sounds at the start of words in quick succession. Alliteration is often used to draw attention to specific words or sounds, to lend emphasis to specific aspects of the poem. It can also be used to provide an entertaining and engaging voice to a poem.

Example:

"One short sleepe past, wee wake eternally,

And death shall be no more; death, thou shalt die."

– John Donne, "Death Be Not Proud

In this poem, the alliterative W and D sounds draw parallels between their respective words, and creating sort of a vocal punctuation for the line. A D sound begins the last line and a D sound ends it, creating a sense of urgency, of continuity and finality in the line.

Assonance: similar to alliteration, except that the repeated sounds are contained within certain words.

Example:

> "And miles to go before I sleep,
> And miles to go before I sleep."
> – *Robert Frost, "Stopping by Woods on a Snowy Evening".*

The repeated O sounds create a sense of speed and urgency. The sound carries us through the line, creating contrast with the E sound in "sleep", where both the narrator and reader finally rest.

Enjambment: An enjambed line flows into the next without a break. No punctuation divides one line from the next, it simply continues.

Example:

> "April is the cruellest month, breeding
> Lilacs out of the dead land, mixing
> Memory and desire, stirring
> Dull roots with spring rain."
> – *T. S. Eliot, The Waste Land.*

Eliot's use of enjambment in The Waste Land creates a sense of suspense in the poem. The action of breeding, mixing, and stirring are lent equal or superior importance to the actual subjects these actions are done to. The enjambment also creates a slant rhyme as well, with each line ending on an "-ing" until we arrive at "rain".

Free Verse: Poetry that avoids an identifiable meter or rhyme scheme could be said to be "free". The style became more popular amongst avant-guarde, modern, and post-modern poets. It was comparatively rare in classical poetry.

Example:

> i carry your heart with me(i carry it in
> my heart)i am never without it(anywhere
> i go you go,my dear;and whatever is done
> by only me is your doing,my darling)
> – *e e cummings, "i carry your heart with me"*

Cummings' style shirked literary conventions, creating poems that challenged traditional assumptions about form and aesthetic appeal through his use of strange capitalization, heavy enjambment, and free verse. Cummings' poems defy clear explanation, but some critics suggest he wrote in this manner to evoke a childish, earnest state of mind.

Metaphor: An indirect comparison between two things, denoting one object or action in place of another to suggest a comparison between them. This is distinct from a simile, which directly compares two things using words such as "like" or "as".

Example:

"I'm a riddle in nine syllables,
An elephant, a ponderous house,
A melon strolling on two tendrils.
O red fruit, ivory, fine timbers!"
– *Sylvia Plath, "Metaphors"*

Appropriately enough, Sylvia Plath's "Metaphors" contains several playful metaphors used to describe her pregnancy. Plath uses herself as a subject, comparing her pregnant state to an elephant, a melon, and in several ways to a shelter for the life growing inside her. At first the metaphors seem self-deprecating and humorous, but later in the poem, where she calls herself a "means, a stage" and mentions how she's "boarded the train there's no getting off", the metaphors take on darker connotation as they reflect her dehumanization and resigned acceptance that she's become merely an incubator for the child she now carries.

Sonnet: A poetic form that originated in Italy, consisting of fourteen lines which follow a clear alternating rhyme scheme. Conventions of sonnets have shifted through the centuries, and the form has proved popular in England, Italy, and France.

Example:

Do not stand at my grave and weep:
I am not there; I do not sleep.
I am a thousand winds that blow,
I am the diamond glints on snow,
I am the sun on ripened grain,

I am the gentle autumn rain.
When you awaken in the morning's hush
I am the swift uplifting rush
Of quiet birds in circling flight.
I am the soft starshine at night.
Do not stand at my grave and cry:
I am not there; I did not die.
– *Mary Elizabeth Frye, "Do not stand at my grave and weep"*

This sonnet showcases much of what is attractive about the form to poets. The simple rhyme scheme is unpretentious and readable, and the poem's format lends itself well to repetition. The repeated "I am's" creating a soothing rhythm, sort of a lullaby quality. The subject matter is bittersweet, as with many sonnets that have explored romance, mortality, or spirituality. The first and last two lines mirror each other, suggesting change and finality. The poem's subject matter insists we not fear the end, and this is reflected in the sonnet's form.

Imagery: Any sequence of words that refers to a sensory experience can be considered imagery. Rather than merely describing the visual aspect of something, imagery often relies on taste, touch, smell, or sound to draw a fuller portrait of the subject.

Example:

"Whirl up, sea—
Whirl your pointed pines,
Splash your great pines
On our rocks,
Hurl your green over us—
Cover us with your pools of fir."
– *Hilda Doolittle, "Oread"*

Doolittle's poem neatly encapsulates a style known as Imagism, a short-lived movement in the early 20th century that sought to reduce poetic language to its barest components. Each line, each word in this poem reveals something new – Doolittle likens a forest to a sea (or perhaps a sea to a forest), encouraging us to imagine green trees like torrential waves, evoking sound, color, and texture to maintain this dual metaphor. The poem is unique in that there is no "correct" image. Both the sea and the forest are equally valid interpretations of this poem, drawn together by their shared sensory features.

Onomatopoeia: A "sound effect", a word that imitates that actual sound it describes. "Buzz" or "hiss" both sound like the actions of buzzing or hissing.

Example:

"I chatter over stony ways,
In little sharps and trebles,
I bubble into eddying bays,
I babble on the pebbles."
— *Alfred, Lord Tennyson, "The Brook"*

The onomatopoeia in Tennyson's "The Brook" evoke the sounds of its subject. The assonant B and T sounds suggest the burbling of a river.

Personification: When human qualities are applied to a non-human entity, such as an animal, an emotion, an object, or something more esoteric.

Example:

"Let the rain kiss you
Let the rain beat upon your head with silver liquid drops
Let the rain sing you a lullaby"
— *Langston Hughes, "April Rain Song"*

In this poem, Hughes suggests that the rain has the human ability to kiss and to sing. Rather than merely describing pleasant, "realistic" aspects of rain, he personifies it as a friendly, motherly figure to better describe his feelings towards rain.

Couplet: A pair of rhyming lines with the same meter. A "heroic couplet" is a couplet in iambic pentameter that is "self-contained" and not enjambed. Shakespeare often ended his sonnets with a heroic couplet, allowing the piece to build towards a climactic, self-contained final rhyme that delivered the sonnet's chief message.

Example:

"Sol thro' white Curtains shot a tim'rous Ray,
And op'd those Eyes that must eclipse the Day;
Now Lapdogs give themselves the rowzing Shake,
And sleepless Lovers, just at Twelve, awake:"

— Alexander Pope, "Rape of the Lock"

Pope's "Rape of the Lock" is a satirical narrative poem written entirely in heroic couplets. The subject matter of the piece, regarding a baron's attempts to gain a lock of a woman's hair, is silly and banal. Thus, the constant use of triumphant, heroic couplets renders the whole thing a bizarre parody.

Narrative poem: Appropriately enough, a narrative poem is a poem that tells a story. It can make use of narrators, characters, plot, setting, and other literary devices, though they often contain more poetic features, such as rhyme, meter, and metaphor. An "epic poem" is a type of narrative poem that's usually lengthy and recounts heroic deeds and mythology.

Example:

"By the shore of Gitche Gumee,
By the shining Big-Sea-Water,
At the doorway of his wigwam,
In the pleasant Summer morning,
Hiawatha stood and waited."

— Henry Wadsworth Longfellow, "The Song of Hiawatha"

Longfellow's epic poem, "The Song of Hiawatha", recalls the mythologized exploits of the titular Native American hero. Hiawatha is based on a few historical persons, but as with much epic poetry, his exploits are expanded into something superhuman.

When setting out to interpret a poem and answer multiple choice questions, authorial intention is a good starting point. What message was the author intending to convey with the piece? Read it through a few times, and pause to consider words or references you don't understand. Start with the easy solution, not every poem is a labyrinth of mysterious interpretations. Consider the fact that, in an enduring poem, nothing happens by accident. Each line, each word was selected very carefully by the poet for a specific effect. This will allow you to go deeper off of your original assessment of the poem, and to infer the meaning of unclear references and unusual devices.

Example Analysis

Let's try one. The following is one of the most revered poems in the English canon, "Ozymandias" by Percy Bysshe Shelley. Read it through, and see what your initial reactions are. Try reading it out loud as well. Some poems are better understand when heard.

I met a traveller from an antique land
Who said: "Two vast and trunkless legs of stone
Stand in the desert . . . Near them, on the sand,
Half sunk, a shattered visage lies, whose frown,
And wrinkled lip, and sneer of cold command,
Tell that its sculptor well those passions read
Which yet survive, stamped on these lifeless things,
The hand that mocked them, and the heart that fed:
And on the pedestal these words appear:
'My name is Ozymandias, king of kings:
Look on my works, ye Mighty, and despair!'
Nothing beside remains. Round the decay
Of that colossal wreck, boundless and bare
The lone and level sands stretch far away."

First, let's summarize the literal basics. What is the "story" of this poem? What is the "plot", the actual event being described? Our narrator is unnamed, and the story is told by him second hand, a tale he recalls from some traveler from an "antique land". The traveler describes a two pillars of stone he found in the endless desert, and next to them lay a shattered stone face, well-carved but slowly eroding away. Beside the face is a pedestal telling of some "king of kings", Ozymandias, who declares his "works" would cause even the mighty to despair. What "works" this describes is not clear to the traveler, for they seem to have crumbled to dust in the endless centuries, leaving only sand as far as the eye can see.

On a surface level, this is a simple tale of a stranger remembering a statue he found in the desert. Why is this important? Why did Shelley find this important to recount?

To answer this, we need to look past what is literally stated to find what is implied. We can infer that the pedestal once referred to some grander structure, a monument perhaps, or maybe a castle or city. The face and pillars, at the very least, likely towered above the desert sometime in the past, depicting their fearsome subject for all to see. Surely this Ozymandias must have been wealthy to erect such a large sculpture, and it is telling that he wished to be depicted with a commanding sneer. The face was carved by some sculptor who either feared or greatly revered his subject. Ozymandias fancied himself a conqueror, one who would inspire awe in all who see his monument.

But it did not last. The monument is crumbling, the desert around it is bare. Even this traveler from his "antique land" knows nothing of great Ozymandias except what he read on some plinth in the desert. Why did Ozymandias fade from memory? Who can say? Whatever great and terrible things Ozymandias accomplished, it was not enough to save him or his memory from the ravages of time.

The pedestal thus becomes sadly ironic – whereas once the mighty may have despaired upon seeing a fearsome monument that dwarfed them, today they will despair upon seeing that even the "king of kings", Ozymandias, has been forgotten for all time, his great accomplishments lost to the ages, never to be recalled. Shelley is trying to teach us that even the mightiest of conquerors can die and be forgotten. Time waits for no man.

What poetic devices are on display here? The poem is a sonnet, though not a typical one. There is a rhyme scheme but it is far less pronounced than in most sonnets – it makes frequent use of slant rhymes, such as "stone" and "frown" or "fear" and "despair", and the enjambment of the piece alters its flow, preventing "sing-song" rhymes from appearing. It contains no heroic couplet. The poem also features iambic pentameter, though it is less pronounced than in works such as Shakespeare's. Each line contains five iambs of two syllables each, with exactly one exception: line 10, "my name is Ozymandias", breaks the ten syllable pattern, offering eleven syllables instead. Perhaps this is Shelley's way of drawing attention to that line and to Ozymandias himself. Truly, Ozymandias was so great that even sonnet form could not contain him.

The poem also makes sparing using of alliteration, particularly in the last two lines with "boundless and bare" and "lone and level sands stretch". This seems to be Shelley's substitute for the heroic couplet. Rather than offering a two line rhyme to announce the poem's final thought, he builds more subtly with alliterative turns of phrase that offset the final words "far away". This is the note he leaves us on. There is nothing in the desert but sand, lone and level, boundless and bare. This is what history remembers and this is what he offers as his final word on the subject. It is also worth noting that the poem is told second hand – even the narrator is hearing about this from some nameless traveler from a nameless land. He's simply repeating what he heard. The great Ozymandias has been reduced to a half-remembered plaque in some forgotten desert that our raconteur thinks he remembered a stranger describe.

That's a heavy message for such a short poem, and it's Shelley's mastery of poetic forms that allow him to deliver it so forcefully. An AP English exam will likely require you to interpret a poem along a more specific guideline, such as how it might reflect the styles and forms of a specific movement of poetry. But if you can demonstrate a strong core knowledge of poetic style, you'll have little trouble passing the exam.

Strategy for Points: Poetry _____

1. Poetry is not about finding the "correct" answer. Many poems have multiple interpretations, while others are less obscure. Select the best answer of those offered, as sometimes more than one may appear right but there is always the right answer offered.

2. You must understand the names and functions of poetic devices. But don't just memorize them, as learning the different techniques will help you answer questions faster and correctly.

3. Many poems make references that are far out of the normal subjects to the modern reader. A good understanding of historical references is useful, but not essential. For instance, you need only infer that Ozymandias was a powerful ruler who faded from memory.

4. Understand that nothing in a poem happens by accident. Everything, even the most oblique stream-of-consciousness phrases, is selected for a specific effect.

5. It is also important to understand how poems fit into broader literary movements. Imagism, post-modernism, avant garde, classical, romantic, all offer unique takes on poetic styles and forms. Knowing generally when they were written may come in handy when answering multiple choice questions.

Section II: The Writing and Language Test Portion – Skills You Need To Succeed

Chapter 7: Grammar

Grammar is the proper usage of words and phrases. In multiple choice section of the CLEP exam, it is critical to demonstrate proper use of grammar to avoid errors in usage, spelling, diction, and rhetoric.

Multiple choice questions will test your knowledge of a variety of English grammar rules, such as: parts of speech, syntax, sentence types, sentence structure, sentence combining, phrases and clauses, modifiers, and capitalization. (If you choose to do the optional essay, the writing prompt will give you an opportunity to showcase your knowledge of these rules.) Recognition of sentence elements necessary to make a complete thought, proper use of independent and dependent clauses, and proper punctuation will correct such errors. Reviewing the following grammar points will assist in higher scores for both multiple choice and if you do the essay question.

Parts of Speech

There are eight parts of speech: nouns, verbs, adjectives, adverbs, pronouns, conjunctions, prepositions, and interjections.

Noun	A person, place or thing. (student, school, textbook)
Verb	An action word. (study, read, run)
Adjective	Describes an action word. (smart, beautiful, colorful)
Adverb	Describes a verb. (quickly, fast, intelligently)
Pronoun	Substitution for a noun. (he, she, it)
Conjunction	Joins two phrases. (because, but, so)
Preposition	Used before nouns to provide additional details. (before, after, on)
Interjection	Express emotion. (Ha!, Hello!, Stop!)

Although widely different in many aspects, written and spoken English share a common basic structure or syntax (subject, verb, and object) and the common purpose of fulfilling the need to communicate – but there, the similarities end.

Spoken English follows the basic word order mentioned above (subject, verb object) as does written English. We would write as we would speak: "I sang a song." It is usually only in poetry or music that that word order or syntax is altered: "Sang I a song."

Types of Sentences and Clauses

Sentence variety is a great way to demonstrate your knowledge of the various sentence types in the writing portions for the CLEP exam.

Sentence Types

Declarative	Makes a statement. *I bought a new textbook.*
Interrogative	Asks a question. *Where did you buy the textbook?*
Exclamatory	Expresses strong emotion. *I can't believe it's your birthday today!*
Imperative	Gives a command. *Put the birthday cake on the table.*

Clauses are connected word groups that are composed of at least one subject and one verb. (A subject is the doer of an action or the element that is being joined. A verb conveys either the action or the link.)

Students are waiting for the start of the assembly.
subject   verb

At the end of the play, students waited for the curtain to come down.
subject   verb

Clauses can be independent or dependent. **Independent clauses** can stand alone or can be joined to other clauses, either independent or dependent. Words that can be used to join clauses include the following:

> for
> and
> nor
> but
> or
> yet
> so

Dependent clauses, by definition, contain at least one subject and one verb. However, they cannot stand alone as a complete sentence. They are structurally dependent on an independent clause (the main clause of the sentence). There are two types of dependent clauses: (1) those with a subordinating conjunction and (2) those with a relative pronoun

Coordinating conjunctions include the following:

> although
> when
> if
> unless
> because

Example:

Unless a cure is discovered, many more people will die of the disease. (dependent clause with coordinating conjunction [unless] + independent clause)

Relative pronouns include the following:

> who
> whom
> which
> that

Example:

The White House has an official website, which contains press releases, news updates, and biographies of the president and vice president. (independent clause + relative pronoun [which] + relative dependent clause)

Sentence Structure

Recognize simple, compound, complex, and compound-complex sentences. Use dependent (subordinate) and independent clauses correctly to create these sentence structures.

Simple	Joyce wrote a letter.
Compound	Joyce wrote a letter and Dot drew a picture.
Complex	While Joyce wrote a letter, Dot drew a picture.

| Compound/ complex | When Mother asked the girls to demonstrate their newfound skills, Joyce wrote a letter and Dot drew a picture. |

Note: Do not confuse compound sentence elements with compound sentences.

Simple sentence with compound subject:

Joyce and Dot wrote letters.

The girl in row three and the boy next to her were passing notes across the aisle.

Simple sentence with compound predicate:

Joyce wrote letters and drew pictures.

The captain of the high school debate team graduated with honors and studied broadcast journalism in college.

Simple sentence with compound object of preposition:

Coleen graded the students' essays for style and mechanical accuracy.

Parallelism

Recognize parallel structures using phrases (prepositional, gerund, participial, and infinitive) and omissions from sentences that create the lack of parallelism.

Prepositional phrase/single modifier:

Incorrect: Coleen ate the ice cream with enthusiasm and hurriedly.

Correct: Coleen ate the ice cream with enthusiasm and in a hurry.

Correct: Coleen ate the ice cream enthusiastically and hurriedly.

Participial phrase/infinitive phrase:

Incorrect: After hiking for hours and to sweat profusely, Joe sat down to rest and drinking water.

Correct: After hiking for hours and sweating profusely, Joe sat down to rest and drink water.

Recognition of Misplaced and Dangling Modifiers

Dangling phrases are attached to sentence parts in such a way that they create ambiguity and incorrectness of meaning.

Participial phrase:

Incorrect: Hanging from her skirt, Dot tugged at a loose thread.

Correct: Dot tugged at a loose thread hanging from her skirt.

Infinitive phrase:

Incorrect: To improve his behavior, the dean warned Fred.

Correct: The dean warned Fred to improve his behavior.

Prepositional phrase:

Incorrect: On the floor, Father saw the dog eating table scraps.

Correct: Father saw the dog eating table scraps on the floor.

Particular phrases that are not placed near the word they modify often result in misplaced modifiers. Particular phrases that do not relate to the subject being modified result in dangling modifiers.

Error: Weighing the options carefully, a decision was made regarding the punishment of the convicted murderer.

Problem: Who is weighing the options? No one capable of weighing is named in the sentence; thus, the participle phrase weighing the options carefully dangles. This problem can be corrected by adding a subject of the sentence who is capable of doing the action.

Correction: Weighing the options carefully, the judge made a decision regarding the punishment of the convicted murderer.

Error: Returning to my favorite watering hole brought back many fond memories.

Problem: The person who returned is never indicated, and the participle phrase dangles. This problem can be corrected by creating a dependent clause from the modifying phrase.

Correction: When I returned to my favorite watering hole, many fond memories came back to me.

Error: One damaged house stood only to remind townspeople of the hurricane.

Problem: The placement of the modifier only suggests that the sole reason the house remained was to serve as a reminder. The faulty modifier creates ambiguity.

Correction: Only one damaged house stood, reminding townspeople of the hurricane.

Recognition of Syntactical Redundancy or Omission

These errors occur when superfluous words have been added to a sentence or key words have been omitted from a sentence.

Redundancy

Incorrect:: Joyce made sure that when her plane arrived that she retrieved all of her luggage.

Correct: Joyce made sure that when her plane arrived she retrieved all of her luggage.

Incorrect: He was a mere skeleton of his former self.

Correct: He was a skeleton of his former self.

Omission

Incorrect: Dot opened her book, recited her textbook, and answered the teacher's subsequent question.

Correct: Dot opened her book, recited from the textbook, and answered the teacher's subsequent question.

Avoidance of Double Negatives

This error occurs from positioning two negatives that cancel each other out (create a positive statement).

Incorrect: Dot didn't have no double negatives in her paper.

Correct: Dot didn't have any double negatives in her paper.

Spelling

Because spelling rules based on phonics, rules of letter doubling, and exceptions to rules are so complex, even adults who have a good command of written English benefit from using a dictionary. Because spelling mastery is also difficult for adolescents, they will also benefit from learning how to use a dictionary and thesaurus.

Most plurals of nouns that end in hard consonants or hard consonant sounds followed by a silent *e* are made by adding *s*. Some nouns ending in vowels only add *s*.

fingers

numerals

banks

bugs

riots

homes

gates

radios

bananas

Nouns that end in the soft consonant sounds *s, j, x, z, ch,* and *sh* add *es.* Some nouns ending in *o* add *es.*

dresses

waxes

churches

brushes

tomatoes

potatoes

Nouns ending in y preceded by a vowel just add *s.*

boys

alleys

Nouns ending in y preceded by a consonant change the *y* to *i* and add *es.*

babies

corollaries,

frugalities

poppies

Some noun plurals are formed irregularly or are the same as the singular.

sheep

deer

children

leaves

oxen

Some nouns derived from foreign words, especially Latin, may make their plurals in two different ways, one of them anglicized. Sometimes, the meanings are the same; other times, the two plurals are used in slightly different contexts. It is always wise to consult the dictionary.

appendices, appendixes

criterion, criteria

indexes, indices

crisis, crises

Make the plurals of closed (solid) compound words in the usual way except for words ending in -ful, which make their plurals on the root word.

> timelines
>
> hairpins
>
> cupsful

Make the plurals of open or hyphenated compounds by adding the change in inflection to the word that changes in number.

> fathers-in-law
>
> courts-martial
>
> masters of art
>
> doctors of medicine

Make the plurals of letters, numbers, and abbreviations by adding *s*.

> fives and tens
>
> IBMs
>
> 1990s
>
> *p*s and *q*s (Note that letters are italicized.)

Capitalization

Capitalize all proper names of persons (including specific organizations or agencies of government); places (countries, states, cities, parks, and specific geographical areas); things (political parties, structures, historical and cultural terms, and calendar and time designations); and religious terms (any deity, revered person or group, or sacred writing).

Percy Bysshe Shelley	Argentina	Mount Rainier National Park
Grand Canyon	League of Nations	the Sears Tower
Birmingham,	Lyric Theater	Americans
Midwesterners	Democrats	Renaissance
God	Easter	Boy Scouts of America
Bible	Dead Sea Scrolls	Koran

Capitalize proper adjectives and titles used with proper names.

> California Gold Rush
>
> President John Adams
>
> Senator John Glenn

Note: Some words that represent titles and offices are not capitalized unless used with a proper name.

Capitalized	Not Capitalized
Congressman McKay	the congressman from Florida
Commander Alger	commander of the Pacific Fleet
Queen Elizabeth	the queen of England
President George Washington	the president

Strategy for Points: Avoid Common Grammatical Errors:

1. Allocate you time wisely and don't rush through the multiple choice. That's how grammar mistakes are best caught – by taking your time and reading all of the possible answer choices.

2. Be mindful of the sentence types that you are reviewing, as different types may appear incorrect though are actually punctuated correctly.

3. Pay close attention to the use of commas. It may seem natural to insert a comma whenever you pause in reading the example question; this can lead to misuse and overuse of commas.

4. Review the parts of speech from the start of this chapter and write out several examples that will help you differentiate during the exam.

5. Be careful while incorporating words that are often misused. (You're-your; their-they're-there). This is a typical area the test creators try to catch in this section.

Chapter 8: Punctuation

Punctuation can have a big impact on the overall message that you're trying to convey, and it's almost guaranteed that points will be deducted if punctuation is used incorrectly or omitted within your essay questions. Using improper punctuation in your writing will create incorrect grammar and will confuse the reader. That's why the College Board tries to test this in the CLEP Analyzing and Interpreting Literature.

While working through multiple choice questions, be mindful of common punctuation mistakes and keep an eye out for catchy scenarios. Embedded in this chapter, there are opportunities to check your understanding for the punctuation points that you have just reviewed. This practice will help you zero in on areas that you may need to review before moving on to the sample tests and keep in mind if you take the optional essay portion of the CLEP exam.

Using commas

Commas indicate a brief pause. They are used to set off dependent clauses and long introductory word groups and they can also separate words in a series. Commas are used to set off unimportant material that interrupts the flow of the sentence, and they separate independent clauses joined by conjunctions.

Separate two or more coordinate adjectives modifying the same word and three or more nouns, phrases, or clauses in a list.

Maggie's hair was dull, dirty, and lice-ridden.

Dickens portrayed the Artful Dodger as skillful pickpocket, loyal follower of Fagin, and defender of Oliver Twist.

Ellen daydreamed about getting out of the rain, taking a shower, and eating a hot dinner.

In Elizabethan England, Ben Johnson wrote comedy, Christopher Marlowe wrote tragedies, and William Shakespeare composed both.

Use commas to separate antithetical or complimentary expressions from the rest of the sentence.

The veterinarian, not his assistant, would perform the delicate surgery.

The more he knew about her, the less he wished he had known.

Randy hopes to, and probably will, get an appointment to the United States Naval Academy.

His thorough, though esoteric, scientific research could not be easily understood by high school students.

Test your knowledge on the following errors:

1. *Error:* After I finish my master's thesis I plan to work in Chicago.
   Problem: A comma is needed after an introductory dependent word-group containing a subject and verb.
   Correction: After I finish my master's thesis, I plan to work in Chicago.

2. *Error:* I washed waxed and vacuumed my car today.
   Problem: Words in a series should be separated by commas. Although the word and is sometimes considered optional, it is often necessary to clarify the meaning.
   Correction: I washed, waxed, and vacuumed my car today.

3. *Error:* She was a talented dancer but she is mostly remembered for her singing ability.
   Problem: A comma is needed before a conjunction that joins two independent clauses (complete sentences).
   Correction: She was a talented dancer but she is mostly remembered for her singing ability.

Using Apostrophes

Apostrophes are used to show either contractions or possession. Contractions show the omission of a letter (wouldn't = would + not. The apostrophe takes the place of the o.) and possession represents ownership (Sam's new car. The apostrophe lets the reader know the new car belongs to Sam).

Test your knowledge on the following errors:

1. *Error:* She shouldnt be permitted to smoke cigarettes in the building.
   Problem: An apostrophe is needed in a contraction in place of the missing letter.
   Correction: She shouldn't be permitted to smoke cigarettes in the building.

2. *Error:* The childrens new kindergarten teacher was also a singer.

Problem: An apostrophe is needed to show possession.

Correction: The childrens' new kindergarten teacher was also a singer.

Note: The apostrophe after the s indicates that there are multiple children.

Using terminal punctuation in relation to quotation marks

In a quoted statement that is either declarative or imperative, place the period inside the closing quotation marks.

"The airplane crashed on the runway during takeoff."

If the quotation is followed by other words in the sentence, place a comma inside the closing quotations marks and a period at the end of the sentence.

"The airplane crashed on the runway during takeoff," said the announcer.

In most instances in which a quoted title or expression occurs at the end of a sentence, the period is placed before either the single or double quotation marks.

"The middle school readers were unprepared to understand Bryant's poem 'Thanatopsis.'"

Early book-length adventure stories like Don Quixote and The Three Musketeers were known as "picaresque novels."

There is an instance in which the final quotation mark would precede the period: if the content of the sentence were about a speech or quote so that the understanding of the meaning would be confused by the placement of the period.

The first thing out of his mouth was "Hi, I'm home."

but

The first line of his speech began "I arrived home to an empty house".

In sentences that are interrogatory or exclamatory, the question mark or exclamation point should be positioned outside the closing quotation marks if the quote itself is a statement, a command, or a cited title.

Who decided to lead us in the recitation of the "Pledge of Allegiance"?

Why was Tillie shaking as she began her recitation, "Once upon a midnight dreary…"?

In sentences that are declarative but in which the quotation is a question or an exclamation, place the question mark or exclamation point inside the quotation marks.

The hall monitor yelled, "Fire! Fire!"

The hall monitor asked, "Where's the fire?"

Test your knowledge on the following error:

1. *Error:* As the man fell to the ground, his daughter yelled, "Someone call 911"!

   Problem: Punctuation should always be placed inside quotation marks when it represents a quoted exclamation.

   Correction: As the man fell to the ground, his daughter yelled, "Someone call 911!"

Using periods with parentheses or brackets —————

Place the period inside the parentheses or brackets if they enclose a complete sentence independent of the other sentences around it.

Stephen Crane was a confirmed alcohol and drug addict. (He admitted as much to other journalists in Cuba.)

If the parenthetical expression is a statement inserted within another statement, the period in the enclosure is omitted.

Mark Twain used the character Indian Joe (he also appeared in The Adventures of Tom Sawyer) as a foil for Jim in The Adventures of Huckleberry Finn.

When enclosed matter comes at the end of a sentence requiring quotation marks, place the period outside the parentheses or brackets.

"The secretary of state consulted with the ambassador [Albright]."

Test your knowledge on the following error:

1. *Error:* Musician Kurt Cobain died of a drug overdose (making him a part of the 27 club.) in 1994.

   Problem: Statements within statements do not receive punctuation. The period within the parentheses is unnecessary.

   Correction: Musician Kurt Cobain died of a drug overdose (making him a part of the 27 club.) in 1994.

And now we'll add some items that are used rarely, but when you use them, you need to use them appropriately.

Rare Marks

Using double quotation marks with other punctuation

Quotations – whether words, phrases, or clauses – should be punctuated according to the rules of the grammatical function they serve in the sentence.

> The works of Shakespeare, "the bard of Avon," have been contested as originating with other authors.

> "You'll get my money," the old man warned, "when hell freezes over."

> Sheila cited the passage that began "Four score and seven years ago...." (Note the ellipsis followed by an enclosed period.)

> "Old Ironsides" inspired the preservation of the U.S.S. Constitution.

Use quotation marks to enclose the titles of shorter works: songs, short poems, short stories, essays, and chapters of books. (For title of longer works, see "Using italics," below.)

> "The Tell-Tale Heart" "Casey at the Bat" "America the Beautiful"

Test your knowledge on the following errors:

1. *Error:* Franklin Roosevelt once said, There is nothing to fear but fear itself.
   Problem: Double quotation marks are needed to set off the quotation.
   Correction: Franklin Roosevelt once said, "There is nothing to fear but fear itself".

2. *Error:* In his best-selling novel The Firm, published in 1991,author John Grisham probed the sinister doings in a Memphis law firm.
   Problem: Double quotation marks are needed to set off the title of an article.
   Correction: In his best-selling novel, "The Firm", published in 1991,author John Grisham probed the sinister doings in a Memphis law firm.

Using semicolons

Semicolons are needed to divide two or more closely related independent sentences. They are also needed to separate items in a series containing commas.

Use semicolons to separate independent clauses when the second clause is introduced by a transitional adverb. (These clauses may also be written as separate sentences, preferably by placing the adverb within the second sentence.)

The Elizabethans modified the rhyme scheme of the sonnet; thus, it was called the English sonnet.

or

The Elizabethans modified the rhyme scheme of the sonnet. It thus was called the English sonnet.

Use semicolons to separate items in a series that are long and complex or have internal punctuation.

The Italian Renaissance produced masters in the fine arts: Dante Alighieri, author of the Divine Comedy; Leonardo da Vinci, painter of The Last Supper; and Donatello, sculptor of the Quattro Santi Coronati, the Four Crowned Saints.

The leading scorers in the WNBA were Haizhou Zheng, averaging 23.9 points per game; Lisa Leslie, 22; and Cynthia Cooper, 19.5.

Test your knowledge on the following errors:

1. *Error:* I climbed to the top of the mountain, it took me three hours.
   Problem: A comma alone cannot separate two independent clauses. Instead a semicolon is needed to separate two related sentences.
   Correction: I climbed to the top of the mountain; it took me three hours.
2. *Error:* In the movie, asteroids destroyed Dallas, Texas, Kansas City, Missouri, and Boston, Massachusetts.
   Problem: Semicolons are needed to separate items in a series that already contains commas.
   Correction: In the movie, asteroids destroyed Dallas, Texas; Kansas City, Missouri; and Boston, Massachusetts.

Using colons

Colons are used to introduce lists and to emphasize what follows.

Place a colon at the beginning of a list of items. (Note its use in the sentence about Renaissance Italians under "Using semicolons," above.)

> The teacher directed us to compare Faulkner's three symbolic novels: *Absalom, Absalom!; As I Lay Dying,* and *Light in August.*

Do not use a colon if the list is preceded by a verb.

> Three of Faulkner's symbolic novels are *Absalom, Absalom!; As I Lay Dying,* and *Light in August.*

Test your knowledge on the following error:

1. *Error:* Essays will receive the following grades, A for excellent, B for good, C for average, and D for unsatisfactory.

   Problem: A colon is needed to emphasize the information or a list that follows.

   Correction: Essays will receive the following grades: A for excellent, B for good, C for average, and D for unsatisfactory.

Using dashes

Place "en" dashes (short dashes) to denote sudden breaks in thought.

> Some periods in literature – the Romantic Age, for example – spanned different time periods in different countries.

Use "em" dashes (long dashes) instead of commas if commas are used elsewhere in the sentence for amplification or explanation.

> The Fireside Poets included three Brahmans—James Russell Lowell, Henry Wadsworth Longfellow, Oliver Wendell Holmes—and John Greenleaf Whittier.

Test your knowledge on the following error:

1. *Error:* There are many works of art that combine historical and structural elements – Frida Kahlo's Blue House, for example.

   Problem: En dashes should be used for sudden breaks of thought. This break in thought should be placed in the center of the sentence instead of at the end. Placing it at the end makes it an afterthought.

   Correction: There are many works of art – Frida Kahlo's Blue House, for example – that combine historical and structural elements.

Using italics

Use italics to style the titles of long works of literature, names of periodical publications, musical scores, works of art, movies, and television and radio programs.

Idylls of the King
Hiawatha
The Sound and the Fury
Mary Poppins
Newsweek
Nutcracker Suite

Note: When unable to write in italics, you should underline where italics would be appropriate.

Test your knowledge on the following error:

1. *Error:* The historically non-profit National Geographic Magazine was sold to 21st Century Fox for $725 million dollars.

   Problem: The title of the magazine should be italicized, which is *National Geographic*. The word magazine is not a proper noun or part of the title, so it shouldn't be capitalized or italicized.

   Correction: The historically non-profit *National Geographic* magazine was sold to 21st Century Fox for $725 million dollars.

Strategy for Points: Identify and Avoid Punctuation Errors

1. Pace yourself with slow reading to catch grammatical mistakes.
2. Be mindful of the punctuation being used. It's better to avoid taking risks and ensure your punctuation has been used accurately.
3. Pay close attention to the use of apostrophes. For example, the word may have simply needed to be pluralized (automobiles) vs. made possessive (automobile's).
4. Review the proper uses for quotation marks from the start of this chapter and write out several examples that will help you differentiate during the exam.
5. Be careful when reviewing famous works of literature. You'll want to ensure they are spelled correctly and written out correctly (for example, italicized) so that points are not deducted for improper format.

Section III: Review of Effective Reading and Writing

Chapter 9: Analysis

While you are very well read at this point a variety of literary genres and authors, over the past four years you may have considered the volume of materials you've read as more important than what you were reading – or why you were reading it. When you are reading for comprehension, there are generally three types of ways to approach material in a test setting: problem solving, comprehension, or critical reasoning.

While each of these are related, it's not so much why you are being asked a question, but what is the goal of the question. It's likely that you are familiar with at least some of the passages used in the multiple choice section of the exam if you have read a lot of literature over the past four years, but your applied cognitive skills – how well you use what you know – as well as testing what you actually know, is just as important as having done your homework before getting to this exam.

For the practice exams and on the actual test day, you need to employ strategic reading tactics and critical reading to get the highest score; speed alone will lower your points. Critical reading involves dissecting the text to see the structure of the information presented and classify how things are said – if you were using critical thinking, as you would when completing classwork, you would be trying to validate or repudiate what the author says. Here, in Section I, you need to just take what the author says as true for multiple choice. You may not like it, but it's how you get more points in multiple choice – you get to use all the critical thinking you want for the optional free-response essays!

Modes of Each Text (or Passage)

The various pieces that you are asked to read do three things – the text states something, the text describes something, and the text means something. You need to use the various components of this guide and your lessons in English to determine what an author means by looking at the words chosen, the tone used, and any bias the author may readily present. When you break down all the words to what you need for a thorough analysis, you can handle all the reading passages and multiple choice questions very well. Analysis is what to look for in the passages for the multiple choice selections – remember, it's not about finding the deeper meaning of the literary passage. This test doesn't have time to get into all of that!

Types of Passages

It's fairly easy to spot **problem solving** selections, as they literally solve a problem. You could be given a passage that explains how a science project was conducted, or the techniques used to file through samples from an archeological site. There is usually a chronological progress to these passages, and you need to pay attention to the order in which information is presented in addition to what facts or numerical descriptions apply to which steps in a process. These passages tend to lure people towards thinking they can rapidly answer the questions following the selection, but will focus on descriptive words to get you to "just pick" and not think.

Reading comprehension passages typically have several complex paragraphs, especially in the CLEP Analyzing and Interpreting Literature. Just by looking at the passage, without any additional investigation, you should be able to determine that it is about comprehension. This means that while the testers do not intend to trick you, they likely will try to pick something that deals with a character's state of mind or an interaction between people that has an "unknown" aspect that isn't covered in much detail so that all students taking the test are being judged on comprehension – NOT what they memorized through class work.

When given **critical reasoning** options, these are typically shorter passages that will use persuasive arguments to reach an unstated conclusion. Most often, one of the questions will include "what was the author trying to convey" type of selection. In critical reasoning, you need to determine what the author is trying to state or prove, and it helps to figure out what assumption is made during the passage.

Types of Questions

Regardless of the type of passage provided, there are several kinds of questions to evaluate your reading skills when under time constraints.

The first kind of question is **inference** – by the passage suggesting ideas or presenting information that perhaps can be linked to a "position" or a belief held by a character or author, you need to determine what the author was trying to persuade you to believe. These multiple choice questions nearly always have an absolute wrong answer – a closely-worded option to the best answer, but uses words opposite of the structure in the passage or by throwing in an "absolute" – never, always, not, et cetera. It could also have an option that is way off topic from the main idea in the passage. You can go back to the paragraph in the passage to select the right answer, but read carefully so you don't pick the absolute wrong one.

The second way they test materials presented and your **knowledge** of what was presented in the passage. By giving details and facts in a passage, perhaps a very descriptive passage of the organization of a room from a character's viewpoint, the test coordinators can overwhelm you with lots of different kinds of information. This frequently happens in passages with a lot of numbers or many items of the same kind in a passage, and the multiple choice answer options will give numbers that are close to each other – and again, there will be at least one option that is the opposite of what you should answer and like one that is totally contrived, not to be found anywhere in the passage at all. These do not only deal with numbers, but those are the simplest to identify as they look to see if you can decipher the content of the passage.

Also, questions may be written to test your ability to induce or reason through an **assumption** begun by an author. This includes **cause-and-effect** scenarios, where the question asks "if" and The correct answer options present "then" finishing options based on the facts presented in the passage. Another way to look at this is making a **prediction** based on what the author presented. A possible question could ask what is likely to happen next between two characters – and you need to select the best answer based on the information given in the passage. You will have to use reasoning to answer the assumption sort of questions and ensure you follow the path established by the author of the passage, not just what you think would be the correct way to solve a problem.

Similar to assumption and inference is **sequential analysis** – but the difference here, and it is a slight difference but one you should be able to recognize – is when a set of instructions is given, results are posted yet the question reviews a slightly different set of information following the same set of instructions. You need to be able to follow through ordered steps to get to the right answer. This could be dance steps described in Victorian era, a servant's daily chores, or any number of options in literary examples. The point is that you need to follow the instructions of the author and not select The correct answer that you think sounds best or makes the most sense according to what you are accustomed to doing.

There are also some seemingly simpler questions on the exam in the multiple choice section that may cause you to miss points because they seem so easy that you don't really pay attention to them. These **story line** questions make you slow down and answer what you actually read, not what your mind thinks you read. You will be in a hurry on the exam, but remember you really do have enough time to answer all the questions thoughtfully. When faced with story detail questions, go back and find the exact point in question – the multiple choice answers will have four options that read very similar to one another and then the one odd-ball that is not like anything you read previously.

Other Important Aspects of Analysis

Knowing the ways passages are constructed as well as how questions are written are not the only things tested on the multiple choice section in this CLEP exam. The other areas of this guide have incorporated literary periods, vocabulary, details on various genres – and these will all be tested throughout the various multiple choice questions of the exam.

Strategy for Points: Analysis

1. Every multiple choice question includes one "trap" – you can determine which kind of trap depending on the style of the question.
2. You cannot answer questions in multiple choice based on your previous classwork or what you think you know – your experience can hurt you in multiple choice. You must answer passages based only on what's presented in front of you. All of the questions can be answered by the information presented.
3. Story line questions are frequently thought by test-takers to be the easiest and these are questions usually missed because they rely on memory instead of taking a few extra – and well rewarded – seconds to check the story facts and select the right answer.
4. Bias from an author can provoke an emotional response from you, but don't let it distract you from your goal of answering the questions accurately.

5. Some instructors recommend "test taking approaches" such as read the passage's questions (not The correct answer options) before you actually read the passage, so you can pre-sort the information as you read it according to the questions that will follow. This may allow you to erase or eliminate the trap answer choices because if you know the question first, you can be specific about your attention as you read the passage. However, you need to know whatever is the best work method for you – now is not the time to change your good habits just because you think your score will improve. In all likelihood, making a change close to a test will add stress and possibly even bring down your score.

Chapter 10: Organization in Your Essays

When you are writing, you are trying to convey a message to the reader and persuade them to see your point of view. The CLEP essays are most often designed for you to write a persuasive supportive-style argument, where you lead off with your idea of how to answer the question and support it. There are certain points you need to ensure are understood, and there is a proper order to help the delivery of your information. All the facts or quotes that you can muster – even when they are true and correctly used – cannot help you make your points if they aren't well organized.

Throughout the middle section of this CLEP study guide, you have seen individual chapters review many important topics that must be utilized throughout a good essay – correct punctuation, appropriate grammar, sophisticated vocabulary and solid syntax. There is no "right time" to apply these tools – they must be used all of the time. If any of these topics are weak and reveal your efforts as wrought with mistakes, your score automatically is lowered.

However, the contents of your essay also are a significant portion of how you are graded. It is important to use the conventional structure to receive the highest grade – and these high scores are only granted to essays that make the most sense. There is a pattern that should be followed, and this is NOT the time to attempt to highlight your uniqueness by venturing off in another pattern. Rather than fight the organizational structure, use your content within your essay and the standard structure to illustrate your brilliant points using strong critical thinking and good organization.

Make an Outline – Your Map for the Essay_____

As you begin to develop the message that you want the reader to understand, it's best to form an outline (or "mind map", if that's a more comfortable term for you). Any time there is a limited timeframe to finish writing, the few minutes spent organizing your thoughts are very beneficial because it saves time as you translate thoughts to full sentences. Most people need to write an outline (or type it out) and not rely on what they can track in their head (that makes it too easy for errors, and the hard copy allows you to check off when you complete that discussion area in your essay).

To create an outline, brainstorm things about the book, author or subject matter first. These are the three areas that CLEP essays are usually going to ask you to consider. You may ask yourself 'what questions does this raise for me?' and write The correct answers down in a list. Perhaps there are obvious messages conveyed in the text, and you should put those on the list. Don't forget to include any large topics or themes of the book, such as gender issues, good versus evil, or the individual versus society – again, these are all favorites on exams.

Essentially, this is all you need to do for the short time you have for an CLEP essay. You have created a list of important topics, questions, and likely can just use symbols or lines to connect the related items. As you write the essay on the paper, you may list these out first on a page that is not to be scored, then draw lines or symbols to get related ideas next to one another and place them in appropriate order. Finally, don't forget to look back at your outline. This now serves as a checklist to help you maintain "integrity" of the essay – meaning, the topics you need to cover and the order you need to do it, so it helps readers understand (especially when they are reading and grading hundreds of essays).

With the time constrictions of the CLEP essay, it is strongly recommended that you create an outline and map your important points in order to make sure a) they support your main idea, b) you can create a clear paragraph around that thought and c) your ideas don't drift (meaning your paper has a different main idea than the one you first thought you had). Short sentence fragments allow you to organize what you know and then write out complete thoughtful sentences – rather than spending lots of time rewriting at the end when you are pressed for time.

This process is the strongest way to form a persuasive argument. When you have taken a few minutes to draft the outline, when you reach the concluding portion, it is fairly easy to determine if you have indeed identified the correct thesis or you should change it – much simpler to do before you get deep into writing. Use the following to help you organize your composition.

Short Well-Organized Essays _____

The structure of an essay, regardless of length, is fairly consistent and expected by readers – it is critical in an CLEP essay. Beginning with a thesis paragraph, you relay the main idea of your essay and introduce what you will be discussing. The next several paragraphs of your essay support your main idea, using examples from various books that give credence to your main idea. However, sometimes if you have a very strong thesis statement, you may use the compare-and-contrast organizational style that gives "counterpoints" at the end of your supporting paragraphs to show you recognize the opposite argument, though can show how it is not correct. Lastly, you need to share a concluding statement in the last paragraph (which does not mean you just restate the first paragraph a little), and bring the ideas for the reader together and give resolution to your analysis.

Introduction and Main Idea or "Thesis" of your Essay

The traditional essays – and the ones that score the highest – begin with the main idea early in the first paragraph. It is this topic paragraph that answers a question or expresses the writer's position, lays an argument, and presents brief highlights of how the writer plans on support for that argument. This first paragraph makes a claim (statement) and shows how your composition will support it. Typically, this paragraph should only be five or six sentences long – so from the very beginning, you must be well-organized.

The most common introduction sentences (usually two at the beginning of this paragraph) begin to set the tone and topic for a reader. When you begin outlining what you want to say, typically one of the first things you put into your notes is this main idea. "Frankenstein was not a monster, but rather a representation of the ills in society" is an example of a strong main idea that could be supported by passages in Mary Shelley's book as well as other writings of that time. It clearly and plainly states what the reader will learn in the paper.

As you continue listing thoughts in your outline regarding your thesis, additional components for the essay start to shine. You can pull together a few themes that are clear, strongly supported with quotes or examples, and show the reader specifically how you are justified in making your main claim of the essay. These ideas support the thesis, and are the next three sentences in your introduction paragraph.

Using the idea that Frankenstein was a representation of societal ills, your next three sentences would be generalizations of how you intend to support your thesis. During the outline, you may see you have five, six or even seven points you want to make – which is an appropriate volume for the timeframe of the CLEP essay – it's not about how much you write, but how well you write it. Bundle these points into three categories, and generalize them for the introductory paragraph. In this illustration with Frankenstein, you may coordinate supporting ideas using boundaries, grotesqueness and secrecy/shame as the main ways you can show society's problems reflected in the novel.

The best introductory paragraphs avoid three mistakes. First, they don't restate the question either directly or paraphrased. You need to consider the question and formulate your answer in a manner that simply answers the question, as incorporation of the AP essay statement (or the college professor's assignment or your boss' question) will show you haven't given much thought to the assignment, even if that's untrue. Next, don't write about how you thought about the assignment or how you came to decide what you would write. That's all background that feeds the paper, but is NOT the paper. For the final 'mistake' to avoid, don't start your paper with what someone else has said – including the author, a dictionary, a character in the book, et cetera. This is about what you have considered and present, so it should start with your own main idea in your own words.

Remember, if you haven't captured the reader's attention in this first paragraph (or "hooked" them, as teachers like to say), they will not want to read further and that yields a lower grade for an CLEP essay. In your first five sentences, be certain you have presented an interesting idea, provoked the reader to think about your main idea in a new manner. You could also highlight support for a less appealing idea as these tactics will get them to read your content and score your essay higher than a boring paper.

Body - Persuasive Supportive-Style

It would not be surprising to know a high percentage of successful essays are constructed in the Persuasive Supportive-Style framework. This is a relatively easy method by which to make a point in a limited period of time. People are accustomed to reading lists of three. When considering that studies have shown repeatedly that it takes a person six times to hear a message in order to believe it, this three-fold format makes sense. Each of the three support ideas has two sub-supporting prongs that uphold or illustrate the supporting idea – that makes six points to support your main idea.

And again, this is where the outline is so important. When listing the ways you could prove your main idea, you should make sure you have six or seven specific examples to support the idea. As previously mentioned, you then generalize this list of examples to three categories, placing two into each "bundle" of support. This gives you three paragraphs in order to support your introductory thesis paragraph and each of these support paragraphs has two examples to support the topic of each paragraph as listed in your outline. Each paragraph should go back to your thesis and "question the question" you are answering, to ensure you are presenting arguments that support your main idea (and not just restating it).

Notice that this body of the paper will not include is a summary of what you've read, what the book has said, or what critics have stated about the topic. The reader – in this case, the CLEP grader (who is almost always a teacher or professor) – has likely read the book more than once, and won't need you to restate it. In fact, when you include summaries during a CLEP exam, you are reducing the time you have for thoughtful analysis. If you don't have time to incorporate solid commentary, your grade will drop. So stick with the outline, and you'll see another way it helps keep you on task during a timed writing event.

When reviewing your notes on each generalized item and the two examples that support each of the three ideas, you should feel that one of the generalizations is your strongest argument (that you can be the most certain, that it is the most logical, that it gives your essay a bang) – this strongest generalization with the best points should be your third in the series of three.

In music, composers build the momentum of a piece of music to a crescendo just before a finale. This is how you should consider yourself and your writing – the composer (the writer, you) uses phrases and parts to support a melody (your main idea) to a crescendo (the best of the three generalizations with the strongest examples) that nails your point just before your finale (conclusion and finish).

We will continue to use the Frankenstein example, where our generalization of societal ills incorporated the supportive categories of boundaries, grotesqueness and secrecy/shame. Under each of these, you would list the two points that helped you create these categories:

Point 1   Boundaries
                Subpoint A: isolation or alienation from society
                Subpoint B: perspectives alter viewpoint(s)' interpretation
Point 2   Grotesqueness
                Subpoint C: delusions of personal grandeur and lack of self-reflexion
                Subpoint D: personal assumptions based on appearance
Point 3   Secrecy/shame
                Subpoint E: shame of rejection, which leads to revenge
                Subpoint F: madness compels Victor to create his own reality

Use your knowledge of the book and the subpoints to determine the strongest one (the one you can write about the most easily and with the most confidence). You should shift the order of the list so that this identified strong point now is the last grouping. You may even reorder the subpoints within the point, to help ensure the final subpoint in each paragraph is the strongest. While your list may appear differently, your list may now appear as follows:

Point 1   Grotesqueness
                Subpoint A: delusions of personal grandeur and lack of self-reflexion
                Subpoint B: personal assumptions based on appearance
Point 2   Boundaries
                Subpoint C: perspectives alter viewpoint(s)' interpretation
                Subpoint D: isolation or alienation from society
Point 3   Secrecy/shame
                Subpoint E: madness compels Victor to create his own reality
                Subpoint F: shame of rejection, which leads to revenge

If this Persuasive Support is the style that you've chosen (and most students should use this style for the essays), you can then go to the outline for creating the conclusion paragraph before you being to write. However, if the question posed would be better addressed by showing how the phrase is not true, then the next style may be appropriate (but use it sparingly for CLEP responses).

Body - Persuasive Compare-And-Contrast Style

A Compare-And-Contrast argument is an alternative that, in rare instances for the CLEP essays, allows you to provide the alternative point of view, shows a reduction in potential bias, and when it is done property, builds to support the original thesis assertion. However, it is really not suggested for the essay unless absolutely necessary since more time is generally needed to construct and have a solid composition in this style. But, so you know how it works should you need to employ this tactic, we are including it for you here.

This structure can be written in point/counterpoint fashion or all pro then all con (block all of one side of the argument and then block all of the other side of the argument) – ensuring that the strongest arguments, just as before, are incorporated at the end of the composition. This means that another decision must be made before you can start writing – and it all comes from reviewing the ideas you "mapped" earlier for your outline.

If you find that you are comparing two people and how they performed their jobs – authors, politicians, characters or whomever – the block method is probably best suited for that persuasion. You take the points for each, but list Author A with all of her qualities on the topics (remember, it's best to stick to three) and then provide Author B with all of his qualities on the *same points*. In this way, you block the points one, two and three for each of the persons and your transitions explain the differences in the second person's outline by using such phrases as "compared to Author A, Author B said…" or "unlike Author A, Author B thought it important to focus on…" to related the blocks to each other.

When you are very organized and knowledgeable on a topic, you may decide to use the point/counterpoint method. Taking your six subpoints and again arranging them in order that builds toward your strongest argument, you then review them and pair two sides of the argument to develop these discussions. This involves you taking both sides without showing blatant favor to one side or the other. The way you show your "favoritism" is how you are going to make a supportive decision is by presenting one "side" stronger, and that's the side with which you finish the six points. That point leads directly into your conclusion when you link it to your final statements.

Persuasive arguments always engage a reader to follow your train of thought to reach a conclusion, but these two methods take much more energy, focus and commitment on your part as the author. The Block method in this particular style results in a composition that appears "A, A and A whereas B, B and B yield to conclusion that [A or B] was…" and the effort must be focused on showing the differences on these pieces and how or why one is preferred or the other option. The Point/Counterpoint method needs you to keep the reader engaged and wanting to read further as the "argument ball" goes back and forth between support, and the final "shot" is the one that cinches support for your main idea. Once your support pieces are completed, then you move to the final step of the essay.

Conclusion Section (Just One Paragraph)

The final piece of a story is always the most memorable – for good or bad. You want to make sure that your conclusion is NOT a mirror image with only a few word changes. Rather, you want to state your thesis slightly modified, building upon your facts and subpoints used. It's strongest when you are able to state your thesis in another manner, summarizing quickly and giving the reader something positive to consider for the future.

To restate the main idea of our Frankenstein paragraph, we can adjust the main idea to reflect the generalized supportive points. For example, we may wrap the conclusion around the main sentence for this paragraph as "The monster was a manifestation of personal flaws – shame, alienation, outrageous ego – and Shelley compelled the reader to reflect on how environment/nature shapes the development of a person and society's acceptance of things that are different."

This statement takes the reader back to what was included in the body, but in a different phrasing and actually gives the action item of how to read the story without asking a question. (It is considered very informal and should not be done in most any academic writing – you are answering a question inherently in the essay so don't dummy-it-down by stating it.) A strong conclusion practically begs the reader to ask himself or herself if he/she was smart enough to think of it in this light, which you just presented.

Score more points when you answer tough questions and by giving great supportive excerpts of examples during the body. You are leading the reader to a conclusion not only about the topic you've chosen, but also leading the reader to ask if he or she has ever considered it like this before reading your essay. It should be a graceful closure to a well-organized and considerate presentation of your evidence that supported your main idea.

As you write the critical finishing review of the body of your essay, you need to make sure the whole paragraph (because in this CLEP essay, it will be only one paragraph – later in college or professional writing, it will likely be more) clearly makes the reader feel like the discussion or presentation of your argument is completed. You can't have a dangling idea at the end of a great argument and expect to earn the highest score.

The conclusion is what the readers – graders – will remember. It is the last thing they see before giving you a score. Make it count – restate in a different way why your argument was oriented the way you chose, wrap up the ideas and complete the ending thought that clearly shows the reader that you had enough time to finish saying everything. That's another way the CLEP exam may catch you off guard – people drop off effort in the conclusion, so it counts for a significant weight of points (because they can tell if you rushed through it).

Special Notes About Organization of Supporting Information

There will be times when a question to which you are required to write a response is presented and the organization of your response may have unique needs. You will be able to determine this from the phrasing of the question or statement you need to address. All of these possibilities still need the strong foundation (punctuation, grammar, vocabulary and syntax) and thoughtful clear discussion around your thesis response to the question. But, how you provide the supporting ideas may vary.

For instance, if you need to provide instructions, there is a chronological order that needs to be followed. You cannot ice a cake before you bake it; nor can you easily or successfully discuss the Boston Tea Party without revealing aspects of the origin or impetus for the fighting. Rarely in a sophisticated essay should the support paragraphs be presented in a stepwise manner (as in literally "first, second and third") to give the reader baby-steps in understanding your points.

Similarly, and this is used in fiction quite frequently, there may be events that indeed happened in a certain order because there is a pinnacle event

– one that culminates the reader's experience in a grand climatic moment. Murder mysteries typically are written in chronological order, but give special consideration to the actual event that is the reason for the book. This may be incorporated into the Persuasive Support style, but must fall under the persuasive points listed previously and then used to order the separate points.

Conversely, popular criminal investigation television shows do not order by timelines – they have to piece together the mystery backwards after they stumble upon the crime. But this is actually a third way, through historical analysis, that is almost a reverse chronology to present the supporting facts of the main idea (such as the 'title' of that episode or the type of crime being investigated). Timing of events are still important, but review of data and information has to be researched in order to determine the correct order of events.

These three styles are not necessarily appropriate for CLEP essays. They take more time to develop than you will be given in the writing section of the exam. These methods may be used on college papers or if you write prose, so you should be aware that while the organization mechanism remains intact, there are various styles for supporting the main idea that may be more appropriate in other situations.

Similarly inappropriate for CLEP essays are the times when building support for a position that isn't stated until the last paragraph. It is strongly recommended that you do not try to use this more formal and difficult style for CLEP essays or even college entrance essays. It takes much practice and a great deal of time to organize, research, phrase, and conclude using this style since the conclusion is actually the thesis and requires great finesse – and requires the reader to have the energy and patience to realize by sentence five that you intend to change the typical format.

Keep your chances highest for the best score – practice using the formats that have proven success for years, and be successful in this exam.

The Two Essay "Prompts"

Should you select to do the optional essays that pair with the CLEP Analyzing and Interpreting Literature exam, you will need to answer each of them; you cannot pick to complete only one. The organization listed in this chapter should be used for all prompts, though you can vary the style slightly because the prompts are different.

The two prompts – poetry and prose "free response" – use vocabulary skills to build sophisticated and clear replies to the prompts. Every essay needs to incorporate grammar, punctuation, syntax and more for the highest store. Poetry focuses on technique and the meaning of a poem (or phrase in a poem). In Prose Free Response, you will use your own selection of a play or novel to explain how a literary concept or other community issue is handled by an author.

As mentioned previously, do not summarize the story or poem because the essays are intended to highlight your ability to analyze the technique or message. It's also not appropriate to use the personal pronoun "I" to state what you think or feel (you are writing it; it's obviously "I"). Using conflicts between characters, lines in a poem, the treatment of language in a work of prose are all ways you can reference the plot without giving a belabored "book review". Make sure you address the main point of each prompt in the time allotted – this is also about making sure you have good time management skills (90 minutes for two questions) as well as excellent writing ability.

Strategy for Points: Writing Essays _____

1. Just because it's true doesn't mean it has to go into your essay. More "stuff" doesn't give you a higher grade – only clear and direct support for your main idea will raise your grade.
2. Organizing in the traditional format for this AP exam may seem "boring" or "safe" – but consider your target audience: graders of hundreds of essays. If you help them fly through your essay with standard organization points, it will raise your grade.
3. Fancy writing doesn't elevate your grade. Solid sentences with flawless foundation (punctuation, grammar, vocabulary and syntax) are the best ways to get the top score.
4. Make sure you transition between thoughts and paragraphs smoothly, so your ideas flow from one another (instead of bouncing) for the highest possible score.
5. As you read each paragraph, continue asking yourself "so what" or "how does this support my thesis" to make sure everything relates to your main point, so you can earn the top score.

Chapter 11: Editing Your Own Writing

Far too often, English courses focus on generating content and not on refining it. Too many aspiring writers have become obsessed with making a deadline rather than crafting a piece that convinces and enthralls. The AP English exams are intended to measure one's affinity for the English language and the thinkers who have helped shape it. The test itself will not require an editing portion, but understanding how to redraft, review, and critique one's own work will serve you well when you are presented with an essay question or a piece of literature you must analyze. Remember, other eyes will read your piece come grading time. It behooves you to know how they will look at it.

Most writing teachers insist that editing your work as you write it is a poor habit. First drafts, even of pieces that go on to become great works of literature, are often shockingly sloppy. Existing early drafts of the works of Kafka, Hemingway, and Shakespeare are nearly blacked out by jagged corrective lines and exes. This is a natural part of the writing process. Some teachers even insist that considerations like grammar and spelling should be set aside while you churn out your first copy. Don't be afraid to be "wrong" with your first draft. It's called a "rough draft" for a reason.

So, once you've gotten it all on the page, it's time to, as the saying goes, "murder your darlings". Every writer becomes deeply attached to their prose. Chopping it to bits with a red pen just feels wrong. Unfortunately, if it has to go, it has to go. Be brutal. Cut out everything that does not serve the piece, no matter how pretty.

But how to know what to cut? One reliable method of identifying wooden phrasing and unrefined points is to read it out loud. Information entering through the ears passes through a different part of the brain than information that enters solely through the eyes. You're literally discovering the piece from a new perspective. So practice your public speaking. Go line by line through the piece, or at least the sections you're not sure of, and talk it out. For bonus efficacy, consider printing out the piece and holding the physical copy in your hand while you do this. Seeing it as a manuscript instead of glowing letters on a screen gives you some emotional distance from the thing. Ask yourself, what parts sound best out loud? What parts do you stumble over? Oftentimes, this will reveal awkward sections that your eyes thought were just fine.

This is also a good place to do some basic copyediting. Underline misspelled words, cross out superfluous passages, and feel free to scribble arrows and notes to your heart's content. The page will not look pretty when you're done. This is a good sign.

Here are a few less obvious issues you should trim out in the editing phase.

Redundancy and Superfluous Detail

Redundancy is the hallmark of mediocre writing. Good writing exists on the edge of discovery, always pushing through new details, new arguments. To repeat oneself is to insult the audience's attention span and cause the piece to drag as a result. Repetition can be a useful rhetorical device, but always be conscious of using it.

Superfluous detail is a similar issue. Authors are chronic over-explainers, eager to paint each scene with microscopic description. Come editing time, any section or phrase that repeats information we've already been told must go. Even embellishing descriptive words must be removed if they're communicating repetitive detail. For instance:

"John ran quickly down the hall."

There's no need for "quickly" in that sentence. "Ran" already implies "quickly". Is it possible for John to "run slowly" down a hall? "John ran down the hall" flows much better.

This strikes at another calling card of immature writing: the adverb. Far too much writing is cluttered by unnecessary modifiers like "shouted loudly" or "shone brightly". The odd adverb will not ruin your piece, but any word ending in -ly should be among the first on the chopping block when you're in editing mode. Be sparing.

Passive Voice

Passive voice dogs persuasive writing. As a writer, your job is to convince. Whether you're arguing why hot dogs are better than burgers or describing a character's beautiful hair, you must always speak with the authority of one who knows.

Passive voice ruins this. Too many authors couch their arguments in passive voice, burying attractive direct statements in layers of conjunctions and general pronouns. Case in point:

"The committee will be meeting at 4:30."

This sounds wishy-washy. If the committee is meeting at 4:30, then say so. "The committee will meet at 4:30" is leaner and quicker to the point.

Similarly, there is no need to pepper your work with prevarications like "I believe" or "in my opinion" or "seems to be" or "it appears as if". If we're reading your work, we know this is your opinion. That's the reason we're here. Be emphatic and the audience will respond.

Excessive Punctuation

This is an issue that goes beyond incorrect grammar. Plenty of punctuation is used correctly from a technical standpoint while still hampering the piece's readability. Commas are the worst offender. Older works are replete with commas, partially because authors used to get paid by the word and thus they took their time explaining everything in great detail to maximize a paycheck. Today, we favor slimmer writing. For example:

"This machine could, in theory, break down heavy plastics, and thus, reuse the base particles in creating newer, stronger kinds of materials."

Not only is this sentence loaded with passive voice, but the commas make it crawl. We can purge "in theory" from the sentence entirely, or insert it at the front with only one comma to separate it instead of two. "In theory, this machine could break down heavy plastics..." is already much better.

The comma after "plastics" is more justified as it separates two clauses in the sentence, but the one after "thus" isn't needed. If we remove that one, then suddenly the comma after "newer" reads better. Our complete sentence becomes "In theory, this machine could break down heavy plastics, and thus reuse the base particles in creating newer, stronger kinds of materials." Both sentences are grammatically correct, but the second one is a much better read.

A final note about commas – the **serial comma** (or Oxford comma) remains controversial amongst editors and writers, with no clear consensus on its usefulness or aesthetic appeal. Most American style guides, such as *Strunk & White* or *The MLA Style Manual,* suggest using a serial comma whenever possible. To them, "carrots, peas, and grapes" (with the serial comma before "and") is superior to "carrots, peas and grapes" (with no serial comma). Canadian or British style guides often recommend against using the serial comma, and thus confusion abounds. What IS certain is that you must be consistent. If you're using a serial comma, stick with it through the whole piece.

Here are a few more notes on common punctuation flaws:

- Ellipses require only three dots ("..."). No more are required, even if you're indicating a longer pause.
- One exclamation point is plenty. Those writing dialogue sometimes get away with two ("I'm so mad right now!!"), but there's rarely any need for it.
- The same applies for question marks. More than one is unnecessary.
- Semicolons are tricky to master, and many authors simply do without. Kurt Vonnegut famously quipped that even after decades of writing bestsellers, he still couldn't understand the value of a semicolon over a comma or a period.
- Quotation marks denote something that has been said, word for word. You should not put paraphrased statements in quotation marks. Be careful with this. Newspapers have been sued for adding a single word to a direct quotation.

And lastly, remember that there's only so much any author can do on their own. There's a reason we pay editors all that cash. Editing is a time-consuming process, far from an exact science. Errors of grammar and spelling can be removed with the push of a button, but creating a piece that entertains and informs requires a human touch. Give the piece your full attention for as long as you can, but understand, at some point you simply must put new eyes to it. There's no point in writing if no one gets to read it.

Strategy for Points: Proofreading Essays_____

1. Put it all on the page for your first draft. Considerations like grammar, spelling, and punctuation can come later, during the editing phase.
2. Avoid over-explaining. Trust the audience to follow what you're trying to say.

3. Always write with authority. Argue your point, describe what you see. Saying "in my opinion" only hinders your argument and patronizes your audience.

4. Consider printing out a physical copy and making changes on the page. This lets you see what you've altered.

5. Be spare. If a word, paragraph, or punctuation mark doesn't serve your needs, it has to be removed, no matter how pretty it might be.

Sample Test One

Instructions _____

This exam gives passages from known writings (fiction, poems, non-fiction/history, biographies, drama and more) over the past five hundred years. While the student taking the exam is not expected to have read the material or have familiarity with the passage prior to the exam, the test taker is expected to have the knowledge of an undergraduate English and writing class.

TIP: As the writing changes and the time periods change, it's important for a student to note the author and time period as that may assist in answering questions by either eliminating unlikely answers or allow the student to recall items about the author.

At the end of the test passages and answers, there is an answer key and a "rationale" key for each question. Take the test without referencing these guides. For questions that you guess The correct answers or get wrong, the rationale is provided to help you see how test makers frame answers to questions or explain pieces of information with which you are unfamiliar.

There are 80 questions on this particular practice test, and the CLEP also uses around 80 for the credit exam. As with the CLEP exam, the passages are taken primarily from American and British Literature - though at least once question, just as in the actual exam, is taken from another area of literature. Within the questions of the CLEP, the mixture of genre types falls typically almost 80-90% between poetry and prose (both fiction and non-fiction within the prose selections) and the remaining on drama. The entire test is balanced between three main eras – Renaissance/17th Century, 18th/19th Century, as well as 10th/21st Century; in the past, there is a slightly heavier emphasis on 18th/19th work, and usually there is one passage from the Classical/pre-Renaissance period.

The CLEP allows 98 minutes to take the exam of approximately 80 questions. Time yourself during the exam, but as you practice, focus more attention on accurately answering questions as the total number of correct answers impacts your score, not how many you skip or get wrong. If you skip any questions, make sure that you also skip that line on The correct answer sheet - or you may spend a lot of time erasing and redoing your answer key.

These passages do not actually appear on the CLEP exam, but are meant to show how the exam is written and the various range of questions, answers, and key knowledge points required in order to pass the CLEP exam. Read each question carefully and provide the best answer choice. Good luck.

Passage 1

(Prose fiction, American, 21st century)

Mornings, he likes to sit in his new leather chair by his new living room window, looking out across the rooftops and chimney pots, the clotheslines and telegraph lines and office towers. It's the first time Manhattan, from high above, hasn't crushed him with desire. On the contrary the view makes him feel smug. All those people down there, striving, hustling, pushing, shoving, busting to get what Willie's already got. In spades. He lights a cigarette, blows a jet of smoke against the window. Suckers.

– *J.R. Moehriger, 2012 p120*

1.) **The subject in this passage is:**

   (A) a character, and seems to be the lead of the story

   (B) a supporting character

   (C) someone with an attitude of a criminal

   (D) female

   (E) has been poor his whole life

2.) **What kind of description is the author providing of this scene?**

   (A) Backstory of the character

   (B) A characterization of what the character is like

   (C) A narrative, with the end of the selection giving thoughts in the first person

   (D) The unreliable narrative about a character

   (E) The author is using a persuasive argument

3. What types of words are "striving, hustling, pushing, shoving, bustling"?

(A) Adjectives

(B) Adverbs

(C) Nouns

(D) Gerunds

(E) Verbs

4. If you had to explain the phrase "crushed him" in the paragraph above and context of the paragraph, what would be the best appropriate explanation?

(A) The city sustained him with all the opportunity available.

(B) The city called to him to be part of its life.

(C) The city complimented him for everything he has achieved.

(D) The city had energized him to get what he felt he deserved.

(E) The city smothered him with all its offerings.

5. The author portrays the attitude of the character toward the people on the street below as:

(A) condescending

(B) sarcastic

(C) affectionate

(D) tolerant

(E) encouraged

Passage 2

(Poetry, American, 19th century)

, BOAT

There is no frigate like a book
To take us lands away,
Nor any coursers like a page
Of prancing poetry;
This traverse may the poorest take
Without oppress of toll;
How frugal is the chariot
That bears the human soul!
— *Emily Dickinson (1830-1886)*

6. **Authors use particular literary structures for descriptions. What best explains the one that Emily Dickinson employs in this poem?**

   (A) A literary allegory

   (B) Personification

   (C) Idioms

   (D) Similes

   (E) Flashbacks

7. **How many types of transport types does the author incorporate?**

   (A) Two

   (B) Three

   (C) Four

   (D) Five

   (E) None

8. If the words 'frigate, coursers, and chariot' were replaced with synonyms, what would the best choice of the following options include?

(A) Train, car, carriage

(B) Train, horse, carriage

(C) Ship, car, carriage °

(D) Ship, car, train

(E) Ship, horse, carriage °

9. Which of the following descriptions more closely describes the author's intended meaning of poem?

(A) Difficulties at work

(B) The importance of books

(C) Confessions for the soul

(D) Poverty makes things difficult

(E) Describing modes of transportation

10. There are very descriptive and strong feelings conveyed by the poet. Which of the following is not a feeling that this poem expresses?

(A) Enjoyment of reading

(B) Excitement of where reading can take you

(C) Encouragement to get others to read

(D) Fascination with topics in books

(E) Discouragement for new readers

11. What is a good paraphrase of "To take us lands away" that Ms. Dickinson writes in this poem?

(A) War makes it unsafe to travel, so we can just read about places. ∂

(B) Poems will drive us to save our souls.

✓ (C) Books can engage us to see new things.

(D) Authors can show us how to go on vacation. ○

(E) It shows poems are short and fun.

Passage 3
(Poetry, British, 17th century)

Since brass, nor stone, nor earth, nor boundless sea,
But sad mortality o'ersways their power,
How with this rage shall beauty hold a plea,
Whose action is no stronger than a flower? (line 4)
O how shall summer's honey breath hold out
Against the wrackful siege of batt'ring days,
When rocks impregnable are not so stout,
Nor gates of steel so strong, but Time decays? (line 8)
O fearful meditation! where, alack,
Shall Time's best jewel from Time's chest lie hid?
Or what strong hand can hold his swift foot back?
Or who his spoil of beauty can forbid? (line 12)
O none, unless this miracle have might,
That in black ink my love may still shine bright.
– *William Shakespeare, 1609*

12. In line four, what is the strength of a flower describing?

(A) Beauty (beauty line above)

(B) Time

(C) Summer's honey breath

(D) Strong hand

(E) Meditation

13. The first line of the poem tries to explain _____.

(A) that there are a lot of things discussed in the poem.

(B) that the strongest natural things are no match for beauty.

(C) where you can find love.

(D) what the author went through to write this poem.

(E) that prayer can solve any problems.

14. "Black ink" references what in the last line?

(A) Written poems

(B) Street signs

(C) Black diamonds

(D) Summer flowers dying

(E) Graffiti

15. The main idea of this poem is describing all of the following EXCEPT:

(A) hope

(B) time, aging and death overthrow beauty

(C) marriage

(D) things that time cannot destroy

(E) the author's victory

16. Shakespeare creates emotions in this poem, and expresses all of the following EXCEPT:

(A) rage

(B) defeat

(C) love

(D) devotion

(E) mortality

Passage 4

(Prose non-fiction, American, 20th century)

When rays of light pass through a prism, they undergo a change of direction: they are always deflected away from the refractive edge. It is possible to conceive an assembly of prisms whose refractive surfaces progressively become more nearly parallel to each other towards the middle: light rays passing through the outer prisms will undergo the greatest amount of refraction, with consequent deflection of their path towards the center, whereas the middle prism with its two parallel surfaces causes no deflection at all. When a beam of parallel rays passes through these prisms, the rays are all deflected towards the axis and converge at one point. Rays emerging from a point are also deflected by the prisms that they converge. A lens can be conceived as consisting of a large number of such prisms placed close up against one another, so that their surfaces merge into a continuous spherical surface. A lens of this kind, which collects the rays and concentrates them at one point, is called a convergent lens. Since it is thicker in the middle than at the edge, it is known as a convex lens.

In the case of a concave lens, which is thinner in the middle than at the edge, similar considerations show that all rays diverge from the center. Hence such a lens is called a divergent lens. After undergoing refraction, parallel rays appear to come from one point, while rays remerging from a point will, after passing through the lens, appear to emerge from another point. Lenses have surfaces in the same direction but having a different radii of curvature, these are known as meniscus lenses and are used more particularly in spectacles.
– *The Way Things Work*, ©1963

17. **According to the passage above, light rays hit convex mirror and:**

   (A) the rays pass straight through

   (B) the rays bounce only straight back to the light source

   (C) bend together to cross at a single point on the other side

   (D) are refracted to open outward on the other side

   ✓ (E) are reflected outward at angles back toward the light source

Sample Test One

18. **Light rays hit a concave surface. As the passage explains, light:**

(A) travels through the prism's surface, angling together to a point

(B) moves in the same direction but has a different radii of curvature

(C) the light merges to a point on the continuous spherical surface

(D) is always reflected away from the refractive edge

(E) experiences no deflection

19. **Spectacles use meniscus lenses, which are explained by the author that these lenses are:**

(A) flat

(B) concave lenses

(C) convex lenses

(D) round on both sides of the lens, meaning they have double refraction

(E) always convergent lenses

Passage 5
(Prose fiction, British, 18th century)

There is likewise another diversion, which is only shown before the Emperor and Empress, and first minister, upon particular occasions. The Emperor lays on a table three fine silken threads of six inches long. One is blue, the other red, and the third green. These threads are proposed as prizes for those persons whom the Emperor hath a mind to distinguish by a peculiar mark of his favor. The ceremony is performed in his Majesty's great chamber of state; where the candidates are to undergo a trial of dexterity very different from the former, and such as I have not observed the least resemblance of in any other country of the old or the new world. The Emperor holds a stick in his hands, both ends parallel to the horizon, while the candidates, advancing one by one, sometimes leap over the stick, sometimes creep under it backwards and forwards several times, according as the stick is advanced or depressed. Sometimes the Emperor holds one end of the stick, and his first minister holds the other; sometimes the minister has it entirely to himself. Whoever performs his part with most agility, and holds out the longest in leaping and creeping, is rewarded with the blue-colored silk; the red is given to the next, and the green is given to the third, which they all wear girt twice round the middle; and you see few great persons about this court who are not adorned with one of these girdles.

— Jonathan Swift, 1704

20. **The stick game described by the author in this passage is an allusion to what?**

(A) Jumping to the tune of the Emperor's (his boss') direction

(B) Baseball

(C) War games

(D) A circus

(E) Tennis

21. **Why are the silk threads highly valued?**

(A) Silk is a common material.

(B) Green is the Empress' favorite color.

(C) People don't give gifts very often.

(D) Silk was very expensive in the 1700s, when the story was written.

(E) All great persons wear silk.

22. **Using the information only in the passage, are the colors of the silk threads significant?**

(A) Yes, because they are royal colors.

(B) Yes, because they represent places of winners.

(C) No, because everyone has them.

(D) No, because hardly everyone has them.

(E) You cannot determine from the passage if the colors are important.

Passage 6

(Prose non-fiction, 20th century)

On the other hand, however, we have no intention whatever of maintaining such a foolish and doctrinaire thesis as that the spirit of capitalism could only have arisen as the result of certain effects of Reformation, or even that of capitalism as an economic system is a creation of the Reformation. In itself, the fact that certain important forms of capitalistic business organizations are known to be considerably older than the Reformation is a sufficient refutation of such a claim. On the contrary, we only wish to ascertain whether and to what extent religious forces have taken part in the qualitative formation and the quantitative expansion of that spirit over the world. Furthermore, what concrete aspects of our capitalistic culture can be traced to them. In the view of the tremendous confusion of interdependent influences between the material basis, the forms of social and political organization, and the ideas current in the time of Reformation, we can only proceed by investigating whether and at what points certain correlations between forms of religious belief and practical ethics can be worked out. At the same time, we shall as far as possible clarify the manner and the general direction which, by virtue of those relationships, the religious movements have influenced development of material culture. Only when this has been determined with reasonable accuracy can the attempt be made to estimate to what extent the historical development of modern culture can be attributed to those religious forces and to what extent others.

– *Max Weber, 1904*

23. **Capitalism is what type of system according to this passage?**

    (A) Democratic

  ✓ (B) Economic

    (C) Religious

    (D) Cultural

    (E) Expansionist

24. When the author compares capitalism to the Reformation, what were the main ideas of the Reformation?

(A) Democratic

(B) Economic

(C) Religious

(D) Cultural

(E) Expansionist

25. What word or phrase originating at least in part in the above passage best describes the goal or target of capitalism?

(A) Ethics based

(B) Culture driven

(C) Historical application

✓ (D) Material accumulation

(E) Force of nature

26. From the passage above, which of the following phrases best describes the author's attitude toward capitalism?

(A) The author approves of capitalism if it involves religion.

(B) The author approves of capitalism when it is driven by "qualification expansion of spirit".

(C) The author disapproves of capitalism when it involves modern culture.

(D) The author disapproves of capitalism when Reformation is involved. ○

✓ (E) The author disapproves of capitalism but wants to investigate why it is wrong. ○

I'd like to say here, that I wasn't the only important one. I was part of a family, just like all of my brothers and sisters. The whole community was important. We used to discuss many of the community's problems together, especially when someone was ill and we couldn't buy medicine, because we were getting poorer and poorer. We'd start discussing and heaping insults on the rich who'd made us suffer for so long. It was about then I began learning about politics. I tried to talk to people who could help me sort my ideas out. I wanted to know what the world was like on the other side. I knew the finca, I knew the Altiplano. But what I didn't know was about the other problems of the Indians in Guatemala. I didn't know the problems the other groups had to holding onto their land. I knew there were lots of other Indians in other parts of the country, because I'd been meeting them in the finca since I was a child, but though we all worked together, we didn't know any of the names of the towns they came from, or how they lived, or what they ate. We just imagined that they were like us.

– *Rigoberta Menchu, Nobel Peace Prize Winner 1992*

27. **From the context of the passage, what is a finca?**

(A) A farm

(B) A village or town

(C) A mountain range

(D) A house

(E) It cannot be determined

28. **The author is telling a story about her own life. What is this kind of document called?**

(A) Autobiography – *WHEN THEY WRITE ABOUT THEMSELVES.*

(B) Mystery

(C) Biography

(D) Narrative

(E) Romance

29. Given the information in the passage, the author most likely worked as:

    (A) a washer woman

    (B) a seamstress

✓ (C) a farmer

    (D) a teacher

    (E) it cannot be determined from the passage

30. The author describes who is the most important. She defines it as:

    (A) herself

    (B) her family

    (C) her community

    (D) the rich people that employed them

    (E) the finca

Passage 8
(Poetry, British, 18th century)

Tyger! Tyger! burning bright
In the forests of the night,
What immortal hand or eye
Could frame thy fearful symmetry?

In what distant deeps or skies
Burnt the fire of thine eyes?
On what wings dare he aspire?
What the hand dare seize the flame?

And what shoulder, & what art,
Could twist the sinews of they heart?
And when thy heart began to beat,
What dread hand? & what dread feet?
– *Excerpt, William Blake, 1794*

31. **Which of the topics below is this best description of the poem's main idea?**

    (A) Strength, as sinews of the heart are strong.

    (B) Creationism, and the author asks what immortal being created the tiger.

    (C) Flying, because it talks about wings.

    (D) Fire, with references to flames and burning forests.

    (E) Love, describing the heart and how it beats.

32. **Sinews, in the third stanza, can be best compared to:**

    (A) thread

    (B) a cage

    (C) rope

    (D) heart strings or emotions

    (E) burnt fire, from the second stanza

33. **Another phrase for "deeps or skies" that would fit in this poem could be:**

    (A) caves or planes

    (B) trees or forests   ?

    (C) seas or air

    (D) waves or wind

    (E) oceans or lakes

34. **What is personified in the poem?**

    (A) A lion

    (B) Birds

    (C) Candle

    (D) A tiger

    (E) The sky

35. In line 7 of this poem, what word below most nearly means "aspire"?

(A) Soar

(B) Plunge

(C) Scheme

(D) Travel

(E) Admire

36. The poet, William Blake, uses all of the following literary tools to convey his message, EXCEPT:

(A) metaphors

(B) rhymed couplets

(C) personification

(D) symbols

(E) lyrics

Passage 9
(Prose fiction, British, 19th century)

"Without their visits you cannot hope to shun the path I tread. Expect the first tomorrow night, when the bell tolls One. Expect the second on the next night at the same hour. The third, upon the next night, when the last stroke of Twelve has ceased to vibrate Look to see me no more; and look that, for your own sake, you remember what has passed between us!"

It walked backward from him; and at every step it took, the window raised itself a little, so that, when the apparition reached it, it was wide open.

Scrooge closed the window, and examined the door by which the Ghost had entered. It was double-locked, as he had locked it with his own hands, and the bolts were undisturbed. Scrooge tried to say "Humbug!" but stopped at the first syllable. And being, from the emotion he had undergone, or the fatigues

of the day, or his glimpse of the invisible world, or the dull conversation of the Ghost, or the lateness of the hour, much in need of repose, he went straight to bed, without undressing, and fell asleep on the instant.
– *Charles Dickens, 1843*

37. What quality of the Ghost is the most likely trait that Scrooge dislikes the most?

(A) The Ghost's old fashioned speech bothers Scrooge the most.

(B) The authoritative nature the Ghost takes with Scrooge is the quality disliked the most.

(C) The fact that the Ghost could break into his house is the trait that Scrooge dislikes.

(D) The Ghost is taller than Scrooge, and that bothers him.

(E) Scrooge dislikes that his bedtime was later than usual.

38. The way Scrooge's reaction to the Ghost is portrayed could mean that according to this passage that Scrooge is:

(A) tired

(B) angry

(C) looking for excuses

(D) forgetful

(E) planning to ignore the Ghost

39. The Ghost's remarks listed in the passage can most likely be inferred as:

(A) a warning to Scrooge

(B) the Ghost is talking to the wrong person

(C) Scrooge is hallucinating

(D) a friend was playing a joke on Scrooge

(E) no inference can be made

40. Scrooge's reaction to the Ghost in this passage leads a reader to conclude:

(A) that Scrooge was just conducting a normal nighttime house-check

(B) when the Ghost comes back for him, Scrooge will go along willingly

(C) even wealthy people like Scrooge lock their houses

(D) that Scrooge does not believe in the supernatural

(E) Scrooge is likely overcome with exhaustion

41. The tone of the passage is intended to:

(A) serve as a warning to Scrooge about things he will be shown

(B) serve as a reminder that Scrooge has forgotten appointments

(C) describe how disconcerted Scrooge felt after the warning was given by the Ghost

(D) provide backstory

(E) explain why Scrooge is so stingy

Passage 10
(Prose, non-fiction, American, 20th century)

Using the Constitution to protect the minorities, James Madison's system of government is largely an attempt to divide and frustrate the majority. Madison envisioned a political system with the broadest possible power base. For example, he rejected the common belief that a democracy could work only in a very small area, arguing that it could succeed in a large country like the United States. A large population spread over a huge area would make it very difficult to force a permanent majority. Such a society would probably divide into varied and fluctuating minorities, making a long lasting majority unlikely. Instead, majorities would be created out of combinations of competing minorities. Thus, any majority would be temporary, and new ones would be elusive. This system, political scientists now term pluralism.
— *Leon Baradat, 1973*

42. **According to the passage, what is pluralism?**

   (A) Majorities created out of combinations of competing minorities

   (B) A new division of political science

   (C) A political system with the smallest possible power base

   (D) A new name for a permanent majority

   (E) The system for democracy to work in a very small area

43. **The Constitution mentioned in the first line, in context to this passage, is:**

   (A) James Madison's document to create a permanent majority

   (B) the document creating the United States

   (C) the personality of James Madison

   (D) the health of the majority

   (E) instructions on how to create combinations of competing minorities

44. **The passage talks about democracy. Another phrase for a democracy is:**

   (A) the rule of a few over the many

   (B) the welfare state

   (C) a laissez-faire economy

   (D) an elected government system

   (E) an appointed government by a monarch

Passage 11
(Prose non-fiction, British, 21st century)

American black music was going along like an express train. But white cats, after Buddy Holly died and Eddie Cochran died, and Elvis was in the army gone wonky, white American music when I arrived was the Beach Boys and Bobby Vee. They were still stuck in the past. The past was six months ago; it wasn't a long time. But things changed. The Beatles were the milestone. And then they got stuck inside their own cage. "The Fab Four." Hence, eventually, you got the Monkees, all this ersatz stuff. But I think there was a vacuum somewhere in white American music at the time.

When we first got to America and to LA, there was a lot of Beach Boys on the radio, which was pretty funny to us - it was before Pet Sounds - it was hot rod songs and surfing songs, pretty lousily played, familiar Chuck Berry licks going on. "Round, round get around / I get around," I though that was brilliant. It was later on, but Brian Wilson had something. "In My Room," "Don't Worry Baby." I was more interested in their B-sides, the ones he slipped in. There was no particular correlation with what we were doing so I could just listen to it on another level. I thought these are very well-constructed songs. I took easily to the pop song idiom. I'd always listened to everything, and America opened it all out - we were hearing records there that were regional hits. We'd get to know local labels and local acts, which is how we came across "Time Is on My Side," in LA, sung by Irma Thomas. It was a B-side of a record on Imperial Records, a label we'd have been aware of because it was independent and successful and based on Sunset Strip.
– *Keith Richards, 2010*

45. How many unique singers versus unique bands, respectively, are named in the passage above?

(A) Seven and Four

(B) Six and Three

(C) Eight and Three

(D) Seven and Three

(E) Six and Four

46. How many songs are referenced in the passage above?

(A) Two

(B) Three

(C) Four

(D) Five

(E) Six

47. **In the context of the selection's first paragraph, how many white singers or groups are named by the author?**

   (A) Four

   (B) Five

   (C) Three

   (D) Seven

   (E) One

48. **Given what the author says about the B-side of a record, which of the following sentences is closest to the author's opinion?**

   (A) The B-side had more creativity and outlets for artists, making it unique.

   (B) It was called the B-side because the songs were generally not as good.

   (C) Only regional labels took the time to press B-sides.

   (D) The B-side was where all the surfing songs were recorded.

   (E) Labels were strict about the contents of the B-sides.

49. **When the author talks about the Beatles and says "they got stuck inside their own cage," the author most likely means:**

   (A) that the Beatles always had to hide in hotels because they were so famous

   (B) that successful musical groups could never enjoy the publicity

   (C) that the Beatles were trapped on planes all the time

   (D) that the Beatles couldn't perform with anyone outside of their four members

   (E) the Beatles outgrew the standard previously set for successful musicians, and were trapped in their own famous sensation

50. Given the descriptions in the passage, the author's profession is likely:

(A) a roadie

(B) a writer

(C) a singer

(D) a photographer

(E) a teacher

Passage 12
(Prose fiction, British, pre-Ren/Classic)

A marvelous case is it to hear, either the warnings of that he should have voided, or the tokens of that he could not void. For the self night next before his death, the lord Stanley sent a trusty secret messenger unto him at midnight in all the haste, requiring him to rise and ride away with him, for he was disposed utterly no longer to bide; he had so fearful a dream, in which him thought that a boar with his tusks so raced them both by the heads, that the blood ran about both their shoulders. And forasmuch as the protector gave the boar for his cognizance, this dream made so fearful an impression in his heart, that he was thoroughly determined no longer to tarry, but had his horse ready, if the lord Hastings would go with him to ride so far yet the same night, that they should be out of danger ere day. Ay, good lord, quoth the lord Hastings to this messenger, leaneth my lord thy master so much to such trifles, and hath such faith in dreams, which either his own fear fantasieth or do rise in the night's rest by reason of his day thoughts? Tell him it is plain witchcraft to believe in such dreams; which if they were tokens of things to come, why thinketh he not that we might be as likely to make them true by our going if we were caught and brought back (as friends fail fleers), for then had the boar a cause likely to race us with his tusks, as folk that fled for some falsehood, wherefore either is there no peril (nor none there is indeed), or if any be, it is rather in going than biding. And if we should, needs cost, fall in peril one way or other, yet had I livelier that men should see it were by other men's falsehood, than think it were either our own fault or faint heart. And therefore go to thy master, man, and commend me to him, and pray him be merry and have no fear: for I ensure him I am as sure of the man that he wotteth of, as I am of my own hand. God send grace, sir, quoth the messenger, and went his way.

– *Sir Thomas More, 1513*

51. The beginning of the passage is describing what?

(A) An injury sustained by the main character

(B) A rider that is trying to escape injury

(C) The main character's dream

(D) A witch's story

(E) The boar that the character will grill for dinner

52. What is the cautionary message that the rider gets when he reaches his destination?

(A) Dreams are witchcraft if you believe in them.

(B) Dreams can come true if you believe in them.

(C) God sends His grace.

(D) Those faint of heart do not have dreams.

(E) Men cannot fall for other men's falsehoods.

53. Did the main character in this passage believe he could out run bad visions?

(A) No, the passage makes it clear you always get what's coming in a dream.

(B) No, dreams mean nothing, so the main character didn't pay any attention to it.

(C) Yes, it was possible to escape bad visions on horseback.

(D) Yes, the main character thought dancing would rid himself of bad dreams.

(E) There is nothing in the passage that assists in answering this question.

Passage 13

(Prose fiction, British, 19th century)

To go into solitude, a man needs to retire as much from his chamber as from society. I am not solitary whilst I read and write, though nobody is with me. But if a man would be alone, let him look at the stars. The rays that come from those heavenly worlds, will separate between him and what he touches. One might think the atmosphere was made transparent with this design, to give man, in the heavenly bodies, the perpetual presence of the sublime. Seen in the streets of cities, how great they are! If the stars should appear one night in a thousand years, how would men believe and adore; and preserve for many generations the remembrance of the city of God which had been shown! But every night come out these envoys of beauty, and light the universe with their admonishing smile.

– *Ralph Waldo Emerson, 1836*

54. **The first two lines of this passage imply what?**

   (A) A man is never alone.

   (B) A man is always alone.

   (C) A man can be alone if he turns his back on people.

   (D) A man can be alone if he makes his mind focus.

   (E) A man who is lonely is considered alone.

55. **Given the whole passage, which of the following is the best match for the author's opinion about nature?**

   (A) The author prefers to seek to retire in his chamber.

   (B) The author sees wonder in the sky and beauty at night.

   (C) The author does not like trees.

   (D) The author can only see stars one night in a thousand years.

   (E) You cannot tell the author's opinion from this passage.

56. The phrase "light the universe with their admonishing smile" is an example of:

(A) personification

(B) a simile

(C) a metaphor

(D) irony

(E) satire

Passage 14

(Poetry, American, 20th century)

Two roads diverged in a yellow wood,
And sorry I could not travel both
And be one traveler, long I stood
And looked down one as far as I could
To where it bent in the undergrowth;

Then took the other, as just as fair,
And having perhaps the better claim,
Because it was grassy and wanted wear;
Though as for that the passing there
Had worn them really about the same,

And both that morning equally lay
In leaves no step had trodden black.
Oh, I kept the first for another day!
Yet knowing how way leads on to way,
I doubted if I should ever come back.

I shall be telling this with a sigh
Somewhere ages and ages hence:
Two roads diverged in a wood, and I—
I took the one less traveled by,
And that has made all the difference.
– *Robert Frost, 1920*

57. **When the author uses the phrase "wanted wear" in the third stanza, what does that mean?**

   (A) It looked just as fair as the other path.

   (B) It was not as inviting.

   (C) The path didn't go the same way as the other one.

   (D) The path was less traveled than the other one.

   (E) You cannot determine what the author means.

58. **The author says that he "took the one less traveled by"; what does that mean?**

   (A) The other path looked like it was used more.

   (B) He did the right thing when others chose the wrong one.

   (C) He took the one on the left.

   (D) He took the one on the right.

   (E) It cannot be determined what the author meant by this short selection.

59. **What is another way the author states his path was the "one less traveled by"?**

   (A) "both that morning equally lay"

   (B) "no step had trodden black"

   (C) "Somewhere ages and ages hence"

   (D) "bent in the undergrowth"

   (E) "having perhaps the better claim"

60. What does the author imply since he took the path less traveled?

(A) He has run into fewer people that try to bully him into doing what they want.

(B) Life is tougher getting to see the light.

(C) He was sorry he didn't chose to go the more well-trod path.

(D) He didn't make as much money as the people that took the other path.

(E) His life is better for choosing to go his own path.

Passage 15
(Prose fiction, American, 20th century)

His memories of the Boston Society Contralto were nebulous and musical. She was a lady who sang, sang, sang in the music room on their house on Washington Square - sometimes with guests all about her, the men with their arms folded, balanced breathlessly on the edges of sofas, the women with their hands in their laps, occasionally making little whispers to the men and always clapping very briskly and uttering cooing cries after each song - and she often sang to Anthony alone, in Italian or French or in a strange and terrible dialect...

Oblivious to the social system, he lived for a while alone and unsought in a high room in Beck Hall - a slim dark boy of medium height with a shy sensitive mouth. His allowance was more than liberal. He laid the foundations for a library by purchasing from a wandering bibliophile first editions of Swinburne, Meredith, and Hardy, and a yellowed illegible autograph letter of Keats', finding later he had been amazingly overcharged. He became an exquisite dandy, amassed a rather pathetic collection of silk pajamas, brocaded dressing-gowns, and neckties too flamboyant to wear; in this secret finery he would parade before a mirror in his room or lie stretched in satin along the window-seat looking down on the yard and realizing this clamor, breathless and immediate, in which it seemed he was to never have a part.
– *F. Scott Fitzgerald, 1922*

61. **Based on the information in the passage, what is a "contralto"?**

(A) A Boston slang term for a high class man

(B) A female singer

(C) A female dancer

(D) A writer

(E) A bibliophile

62. **Based on the information in the passage, an "exquisite dandy" refers to:**

(A) the first editions of the books listed in the passage

(B) anyone who wears silk pajamas

(C) a gentleman who has money to spend extravagantly on fancy things

(D) someone who likes to parade before a mirror

(E) someone who likes candy

63. **Why would the social system be important in this reading selection?**

(A) Richer classes don't have dandies, so the main character can't be dandy.

(B) A rich man with no female friends is called a dandy, and it helps explain the story.

(C) The character seems ostracized and that can't happen in certain social classes.

(D) If the main character was of a lower class, he could not live the life described.

(E) No one lives the luxurious life described in the passage.

Passage 16

(Prose fiction, American, 20th century)

These are morning matters, pictures you dream as the final wave heaves you up on the sand in the bright light and drying air. You remember pressure, and a curved sleep you rested against, soft, like a scallop in its shell. But the air hardens your skin; you stand; you leave the lighted shore to explore some dim headland, and soon you're lost in the leafy interior, intent, remembering nothing.

I still think of that old tomcat, mornings, when I wake. Things are tamer now; I sleep with the window shut. The cats and our rites are gone and my life is changed, but the memory remains of something powerful playing over me. I wake expectant, hoping to see a new thing. If I'm lucky I might be jogged awake by a strange bird call. I dress in a hurry, imagining the yard flapping with auks, or flamingos. This morning it was a wood duck, down at the creek. It flew away.

– *Annie Dillard, 1975 Pulitzer Prize*

64. The tone of the selection is:

(A) reflective

(B) indulgent

(C) indifferent

(D) dishonest

(E) ironic

65. The author uses _____ to describe the setting.

(A) personification

(B) ambivalence

(C) satire

(D) allusion

(E) clichés

66. The phrase, "like a scallop in its shell" is an example of:

(A) irony

(B) a simile

(C) a metaphor

(D) personification

(E) euphemism

67. The author describes many of her feelings and situations by focusing the conversation on animals. Based on the information in the passage, one reason could be:

(A) animals are comforting and relax the reader

(B) birds are flighty and the center of her story

(C) the setting of this story is a farm

(D) the lead character doesn't have many human friends

(E) it is the backstory of how animals and nature are always present in the character's life

68. The phrase "the air hardens your skin" within the context of the passage most likely refers to what?

(A) The morning air woke the character up from dreaming.

(B) The scallop shell bed the character sleeps in has opened.

(C) The air dries out the character's skin.

(D) The coldness of the room turns off the brain of the character.

(E) The air turns the character's skin cold when the cat leaves the bed.

Passage 17

(Drama, British, 16th century/classical)

Bernardo: Welcome, Horatio: welcome, good Marcellus.
Marcellus: What, has this thing appear'd again to-night?
Bernardo: I have seen nothing.
Marcellus: Horatio says 'tis but our fantasy,
And will not let belief take hold of him
Touching this dreaded sight, twice seen of us:
Therefore I have entreated him along
With us to watch the minutes of this night;
That if again this apparition come,
He may approve our eyes and speak to it.
Horatio: Tush, tush, 'twill not appear.
Bernardo: Sit down awhile;
And let us once again assail your ears,
That are so fortified against our story
What we have two nights seen.
– *William Shakespeare, 1599-1602*

69. The three men in the play can be said, in this passage:

(A) to disagree about a ghost that was seen

(B) to disagree that two days ago they saw people meeting "twice seen of us"

(C) that Horatio and Bernardo are trying to persuade Marcellus they saw something

(D) that Horatio and Marcellus are trying to persuade Bernardo they saw something

(E) to meet for a drink for "fortification"

70. When Marcellus speaks of "approving our eyes", what is he saying?

(A) Marcellus and Bernardo need glasses.

(B) Bernardo didn't believe what Marcellus saw.

(C) Horatio believes what Marcellus saw.

(D) Horatio should see what Bernardo and Marcellus saw.

(E) Marcellus should believe what Bernardo saw.

71. When Bernardo says "once again assail your ears", what does he mean?

(A) He wants to repeat himself to Marcellus to make him believe him.

(B) He wants to repeat himself to Horatio to make him believe him.

(C) He wants to repeat himself to help all three of them believe the story.

(D) He wants Marcellus and Horatio to poke holes in the story.

(E) None of these are the meaning of that phrase in the passage.

72. In the context of the passage, entreated means:

(A) invited

(B) engaged

(C) demanded

(D) refused

(E) ignored

Passage 18

(Drama, American, 20th century)

Edmund: That's foolishness. You know it's only a bad cold.

Mary: Yes, of course, I know that!

Edmund: But listen, Mama. I want you to promise me that even if it turns out to be something worse, you'll know I'll soon be alright again, anyway, and don't worry yourself sick, and you'll keep on taking care of yourself -

Mary: I won't listen when you talk so silly! There's absolutely no reason to talk as if you expect something dreadful! Of course, I promise you I give you my sacred word of honor! But I suppose you're remembering I've promised before on my word of honor.

Edmund: No!

Mary: I'm not blaming you, dear. How can you help it? How can any one of us forget? That's what makes it so hard - for all of us. We can't forget.

Edmund: Mama! Stop it!

Mary: All right, dear. I didn't beam to be so gloomy. Don't mind me. Here. Let me feel your head. Why, it's nice and cool. You certainly don't have any fever now.

— Eugene O'Neill, 1955

73. It can be said that this passage of the drama:

   (A) puts American dream against American nightmare

   (B) describes the normal American family

   (C) portrays Americans in a very resilient fashion

   (D) was likely written during a war so obviously has negative overtones

   (E) has the mother remembering the death of another child

74. Mary changes the direction of the conversation by:

   (A) stopping Edmund from talking by taking his temperature

   (B) making Edmund feel badly about the death of his brother

   (C) walking out of the room

   (D) tucking the covers up to his chin

   (E) ignoring him

75. This portion of the play is a:

(A) monologue

(B) dialogue

(C) soliloquy

(D) entendre

(E) stichomythia

76. Mary talks about Edmund expecting something dreadful. What's a literary term for that action?

(A) Oxymoron

(B) Dissonance

(C) Foreshadowing

(D) Stream of consciousness

(E) Understatement

Passage 19

(Prose fiction, British, 18th century)

But though thus largely indebted to fortune, to nature she had yet greater obligation: her form was elegant, her heart was liberal. Her countenance announced the intelligence of her mind, her complexion varied with every emotion of her foul, and her eyes, the heralds of her speech, now beamed with understanding and now glistened with sensibility.

For the short period of her minority, the management of her fortune and the care of her person, had by the Dean been entrusted to three guardians, among whom her own choice was to settle to her residence: but her mind, saddened by the lots of all her natural friends, coveted to regain its serenity in the quietness of the country, and in the bosom of an aged and maternal counsellor, whom she loved as her mother, and to whom she had been known from her childhood.

– *Fanny Burney, 1782*

Sample Test One

77. **From the context of this passage, which of the following statements is the most likely to be true?**

(A) The main character is poor.

(B) The main character is an orphan.

(C) The setting of the story is in England.

(D) The main character is going to live with her aunt.

(E) The main character doesn't like to live in town.

78. **In the quote, "her heart was liberal", what is the author trying to express?**

(A) The author implies that the main character is of loose morals.

(B) The author implies that while ladylike, she has a wild streak.

(C) The author alludes that the woman is more open than her demeanor.

(D) The author makes it clear that she is alone.

(E) The author shows how she was older than her natural friends.

79. **What does the word "minority" mean in the context of the passage?**

(A) The woman in the passage is a Native American.

(B) The character is not yet an adult.

(C) The group of people in the story are members of the minority political party.

(D) The character has less money than her friends.

(E) None of the given options explain "minority" in this passage.

80. **What is another word for serenity in this passage?**

(A) Peacefulness

(B) Counsellor

(C) Bosom

(D) Rambunctiousness

(E) Prayerful

Sample Test One: Answer Key _____

Question Number	Correct Answer	Your Answer	Question Number	Correct Answer	Your Answer
1	A		31	B	
2	C		32	D	
3	E		33	C	
4	D		34	D	
5	A		35	A	
6	A		36	C	
7	B		37	B	
8	E		38	C	
9	B		39	A	
10	E		40	D	
11	C		41	C	
12	A		42	A	
13	B		43	B	
14	A		44	D	
15	C		45	D	
16	B		46	C	
17	E		47	D	
18	A		48	A	
19	B		49	E	
20	A		50	C	
21	D		51	C	
22	B		52	A	
23	B		53	C	
24	C		54	D	
25	D		55	B	
26	E		56	A	
27	B		57	D	
28	A		58	A	
29	C		59	B	
30	C		60	E	

Question Number	Correct Answer	Your Answer
61	B	
62	C	
63	D	
64	A	
65	D	
66	C	
67	E	
68	A	
69	A	
70	D	

Question Number	Correct Answer	Your Answer
71	B	
72	A	
73	E	
74	A	
75	B	
76	C	
77	B	
78	C	
79	B	
80	A	

Sample test One: Rationales _____

If there are words that are options for answers that you do not know, now is the time to look them up and prepare yourself for the CLEP exam! Many answer options includes words or phrases used in literary discussions, and some may not be familiar. It is possible they will be on the actual exam, so you should familiarize yourself with them now.

Passage 1
(Prose fiction, American, 21st century)

Mornings, he likes to sit in his new leather chair by his new living room window, looking out across the rooftops and chimney pots, the clotheslines and telegraph lines and office towers. It's the first time Manhattan, from high above, hasn't crushed him with desire. On the contrary the view makes him feel smug. All those people down there, striving, hustling, pushing, shoving, busting to get what Willie's already got. In spades. He lights a cigarette, blows a jet of smoke against the window. Suckers.
J.R. Moehringer, 2012 p120

1. **The subject in this passage is:**

    (A) a character, and seems to be the lead of the story

    (B) a supporting character

    (C) someone with an attitude of a criminal

    (D) female

    (E) has been poor his whole life

    The correct answer is A.
    The story being explained is about the main character. B is wrong because there are no other characters explained by the author, to have a main and a supporting character. You cannot tell if the person is a criminal or poor from this excerpt, so it is presumptuous to guess C or E could be The correct answers. D is also incorrect because the pronoun "he" is used so it is clearly wrong.

2. **What kind of description is the author providing of this scene?**

    (A) Backstory of the character

    (B) A characterization of what the character is like

    (C) A narrative, with the end of the selection giving thoughts in the first person

    (D) The unreliable narrative about a character

    (E) The author is using a persuasive argument

    The correct answer is C.
    The backstory of a character tells about some time in the past, and since this scene is of the present, that choice A is wrong. B is also incorrect as there is no descriptions about the main character, only the current scene he is observing. There is no basis to assume D is correct and in the option E, there is no argument for or against a topic. Therefore, the correct answer is C.

3. **What types of words are "striving, hustling, pushing, shoving, bustling"?**

    (A) Adjectives

    (B) Adverbs

    (C) Nouns

    (D) Gerunds

    (E) Verbs

    The correct answer is E.
    This is a simple definition of words. Verbs are listed for choice E.

4. **If you had to explain the phrase "crushed him" in the paragraph above and context of the paragraph, what would be the best appropriate explanation?**

(A) The city sustained him with all the opportunity available.

(B) The city called to him to be part of its life.

(C) The city complimented him for everything he has achieved.

(D) The city had energized him to get what he felt he deserved.

(E) The city smothered him with all its offerings.

The correct answer is D.

When looking at the context of the paragraph, there are no leading clues that the city has sustained the character, complimented him or smothered him. Of the options B and D, the better answer is D, as the city didn't call the character to join in the opportunity directly. D offers a description back to the excerpt - that he "deserved" what he has achieved.

5. **The author portrays the attitude of the character toward the people on the street below as:**

(A) condescending

(B) sarcastic

(C) affectionate

(D) tolerant

(E) encouraged

The correct answer is A.

Knowing what these words mean, the only choice that is close is A.

Passage 2

(Poetry, American, 19th century)

There is no frigate like a book
To take us lands away,
Nor any coursers like a page
Of prancing poetry;
This traverse may the poorest take
Without oppress of toll;
How frugal is the chariot
That bears the human soul!
– *Emily Dickinson (1830-1886)*

6. **Authors use particular literary structures for descriptions. What best explains the one that Emily Dickinson employs in this poem?**

    (A) A literary allegory

    (B) Personification

    (C) Idioms

    (D) Similes

    (E) Flashbacks

    The correct answer is A.

    This is another definition type of question, and the correct choice is A.

7. **How many types of transport types does the author incorporate?**

    (A) Two

    (B) Three

    (C) Four

    (D) Five

    (E) None

    The correct answer is B.

    This is a counting exercise - B, for three, as listed in the next question.

8. **If the words 'frigate, coursers, and chariot' were replaced with synonyms, what would the best choice of the following options include?**

(A) Train, car, carriage

(B) Train, horse, carriage

(C) Ship, car, carriage

(D) Ship, car, train

(E) Ship, horse, carriage

The correct answer is E.
Defining frigate (ship), coursers (horses) and chariots (similar to a carriage drawn by a horse), the best choice is E.

9. **Which of the following descriptions more closely describes the author's intended meaning of poem?**

(A) Difficulties at work

(B) The importance of books

(C) Confessions for the soul

(D) Poverty makes things difficult

(E) Describing modes of transportation

The correct answer is B.
This poem is about the journeys available through stories and books. From the first sentence, the author lays forth the meaning of the poem is B.

10. **There are very descriptive and strong feelings conveyed by the poet. Which of the following is not a feeling that this poem expresses?**

(A) Enjoyment of reading

(B) Excitement of where reading can take you

(C) Encouragement to get others to read

(D) Fascination with topics in books

(E) Discouragement for new readers

The correct answer is E.

It is important to read the questions carefully. This is a reverse question, asking which is not something that is mentioned or implied in the poem. Therefore, the correct answer is E. If you don't know The correct answer, you can try to look at all five options to select the one that doesn't fit with the others.

11. **What is a good paraphrase of "To take us lands away" that Ms. Dickinson writes in this poem?**

    (A) War makes it unsafe to travel, so we can just read about places.

    (B) Poems will drive us to save our souls.

    (C) Books can engage us to see new things.

    (D) Authors can show us how to go on vacation.

    (E) It shows poems are short and fun.

The correct answer is C.

Option A is very abrupt and makes too many assumptions; Option E is not relevant to the subject of the poem - both of these are obviously out. Of the choices remaining, using the references with the different ways people traveled in her earlier lines, the best answer is C.

Passage 3

(Poetry, British, 17th century)

Since brass, nor stone, nor earth, nor boundless sea,
But sad mortality o'ersways their power,
How with this rage shall beauty hold a plea,
Whose action is no stronger than a flower? (line 4)
O how shall summer's honey breath hold out
Against the wrackful siege of batt'ring days,
When rocks impregnable are not so stout,
Nor gates of steel so strong, but Time decays? (line 8)
O fearful meditation! where, alack,
Shall Time's best jewel from Time's chest lie hid?
Or what strong hand can hold his swift foot back?
Or who his spoil of beauty can forbid? (line 12)
O none, unless this miracle have might,
That in black ink my love may still shine bright.
– *William Shakespeare, 1609*

12. In line four, what is the strength of a flower describing?

(A) Beauty (beauty line above)

(B) Time

(C) Summer's honey breath

(D) Strong hand

(E) Meditation

The correct answer is A.

This is a direct answer from line three – A.

13. The first line of the poem tries to explain _____.

(A) that there are a lot of things discussed in the poem.

(B) that the strongest natural things are no match for beauty.

(C) where you can find love.

(D) what the author went through to write this poem.

(E) that prayer can solve any problems.

The correct answer is B.

The author does not mention love, personal struggles, or prayer in this poem. Of the remaining answers, A is too general and B is the correct answer (using many of the lines about strength that cannot compare to beauty).

14. "Black ink" references what in the last line?

(A) Written poems

(B) Street signs

(C) Black diamonds

(D) Summer flowers dying

(E) Graffiti

The correct answer is A.

A is the best answer, as all others are not pertaining to the time period or not mentioned even indirectly with the poem.

15. The main idea of this poem is describing all of the following EXCEPT:

(A) hope

(B) time, aging and death overthrow beauty

(C) marriage

(D) things that time cannot destroy

(E) the author's victory

The correct answer is C.

This is another question where you must read carefully. All of the items are mentioned or alluded to with the exception of C; therefore, that is The correct answer that is NOT in the poem.

16. **Shakespeare creates emotions in this poem, and expresses all of the following EXCEPT:**

(A) rage

(B) defeat

(C) love

(D) devotion

(E) mortality

The correct answer is B.

Again, another question to make sure you are reading and not just going with the first answer that matches a word in the passage, making B the correct answer.

Passage 4

(Prose non-fiction, American, 20th century)

When rays of light pass through a prism, they undergo a change of direction: they are always deflected away from the refractive edge. It is possible to conceive an assembly of prisms whose refractive surfaces progressively become more nearly parallel to each other towards the middle: light rays passing through the outer prisms will undergo the greatest amount of refraction, with consequent deflection of their path towards the center, whereas the middle prism with its two parallel surfaces causes no deflection at all. When a beam of parallel rays passes through these prisms, the rays are all deflected towards the axis and converge at one point. Rays emerging from a point are also deflected by the prisms that they converge. A lens can be conceived as consisting of a large number of such prisms placed close up against one another, so that their surfaces merge into a continuous spherical surface. A lens of this kind, which collects the rays and concentrates them at one point, is called a convergent lens. Since it is thicker in the middle than at the edge, it is known as a convex lens.

In the case of a concave lens, which is thinner in the middle than at the edge, similar considerations show that all rays diverge from the center. Hence such a lens is called a divergent lens. After undergoing refraction, parallel rays appear to come from one point, while rays remerging from a point will, after passing through the lens, appear to emerge from another point. Lenses have surfaces in the same direction but having a different radii of curvature, these are known as meniscus lenses and are used more particularly in spectacles.
– *The Way Things Work,* ©1963

17. **According to the passage above, light rays hit convex mirror and:**

    (A) the rays pass straight through

    (B) the rays bounce only straight back to the light source

    (C) bend together to cross at a single point on the other side

    (D) are refracted to open outward on the other side

    (E) are reflected outward at angles back toward the light source

    The correct answer is E.

    The passage explains that a convex mirror "is thicker in the middle than at the edge" in the last line of the first paragraph. Thus, both A and B are wrong as the surface isn't flat (without curve). C describes a concave lens and D describes a lens not explained in the passage.

18. **Light rays hit a concave surface. As the passage explains, light:**

(A) travels through the prism's surface, angling together to a point

(B) moves in the same direction but has a different radii of curvature

(C) the light merges to a point on the continuous spherical surface

(D) is always reflected away from the refractive edge

(E) experiences no deflection

The correct answer is A.
Similar to 4.1, the definition is in the passage that matches A. The other four options are wrong or nonsensical as explained in the paragraphs.

19. **Spectacles use meniscus lenses, which are explained by the author that these lenses are:**

(A) flat

(B) concave lenses

(C) convex lenses

(D) round on both sides of the lens, meaning they have double refraction

(E) always convergent lenses

The correct answer is B.
Think about a pair of glasses. They aren't flat, so A is wrong. If they were D, round on both sides, then they wouldn't work. Within E, an extreme modifier is used - always - and when words are extreme - such as always, never, every - that is usually an indicator of a wrong answer (unless it's a quote). Thus, the correct choice is B.

Passage 5

(Prose fiction, British, 18th century)

There is likewise another diversion, which is only shown before the Emperor and Empress, and first minister, upon particular occasions. The Emperor lays on a table three fine silken threads of six inches long. One is blue, the other red, and the third green. These threads are proposed as prizes for those persons whom the Emperor hath a mind to distinguish by a peculiar mark of his favor. The ceremony is performed in his Majesty's great chamber of state; where the candidates are to undergo a trial of dexterity very different from the former, and such as I have not observed the least resemblance of in any other country of the old or the new world. The Emperor holds a stick in his hands, both ends parallel to the horizon, while the candidates, advancing one by one, sometimes leap over the stick, sometimes creep under it backwards and forwards several times, according as the stick is advanced or depressed. Sometimes the Emperor holds one end of the stick, and his first minister holds the other; sometimes the minister has it entirely to himself. Whoever performs his part with most agility, and holds out the longest in leaping and creeping, is rewarded with the blue-colored silk; the red is given to the next, and the green is given to the third, which they all wear girt twice round the middle; and you see few great persons about this court who are not adorned with one of these girdles.

– *Jonathan Swift, 1704*

20. The stick game described by the author in this passage is an allusion to what?

(A) Jumping to the tune of the Emperor's (his boss') direction

(B) Baseball

(C) War games

(D) A circus

(E) Tennis

The correct answer is A.

This is another passage where it makes sense to check the year the item was written. Baseball was not yet invented, and tennis as we know it today was not yet played - so both B and E are wrong. A circus doesn't have anything to do with a straight line, so D is also wrong. While A and C are both possible, only A is probable and directly connects to the passage.

21. Why are the silk threads highly valued?

(A) Silk is a common material.

(B) Green is the Empress' favorite color.

(C) People don't give gifts very often.

(D) Silk was very expensive in the 1700s, when the story was written.

(E) All great persons wear silk.

The correct answer is D.

A is not true, so it can be eliminated. B has no basis of support in the passage, so it is not true. E has some reference in the passage, but it uses one of those extreme words, so it can be eliminated. Between C and D, C has no mention in the passage whereas D references the time period of the story and is the best answer.

22. Using the information only in the passage, are the colors of the silk threads significant?

(A) Yes, because they are royal colors.

(B) Yes, because they represent places of winners.

(C) No, because everyone has them.

(D) No, because hardly everyone has them.

(E) You cannot determine from the passage if the colors are important.

The correct answer is B.

This question is straight from the passage and is explained in the third sentence.

Passage 6

(Prose non-fiction, 20th century)

On the other hand, however, we have no intention whatever of maintaining such a foolish and doctrinaire thesis as that the spirit of capitalism could only have arisen as the result of certain effects of Reformation, or even that of capitalism as an economic system is a creation of the Reformation. In itself, the fact that certain important forms of capitalistic business organizations are known to be considerably older than the Reformation is a sufficient refutation of such a claim. On the contrary, we only wish to ascertain whether and to what extent religious forces have taken part in the qualitative formation and the quantitative expansion of that spirit over the world. Furthermore, what concrete aspects of our capitalistic culture can be traced to them. In the view of the tremendous confusion of interdependent influences between the material basis, the forms of social and political organization, and the ideas current in the time of Reformation, we can only proceed by investigating whether and at what points certain correlations between forms of religious belief and practical ethics can be worked out. At the same time, we shall as far as possible clarify the manner and the general direction which, by virtue of those relationships, the religious movements have influenced development of material culture. Only when this has been determined with reasonable accuracy can the attempt be made to estimate to what extent the historical development of modern culture can be attributed to those religious forces and to what extent others.

– *Max Weber, 1904*

23. Capitalism is what type of system according to this passage?

(A) Democratic

(B) Economic

(C) Religious

(D) Cultural

(E) Expansionist

The correct answer is B.

This is a question where you have to understand that the passage discusses business organizations and actually refutes the religious forces interference. C is wrong, as per the passage. D is mentioned in capitalistic culture, but as you should not answer a question with a the same word as is being asked, the choice C is wrong. Democracy is a governmental system, so it does not define the capitalism. Expansionist is not relevant to the passage, therefore B is the correct answer.

24. **When the author compares capitalism to the Reformation, what were the main ideas of the Reformation?**

(A) Democratic

(B) Economic

(C) Religious

(D) Cultural

(E) Expansionist

The correct answer is C.

The passage describes the reformation as a religious movement.

25. **What word or phrase originating at least in part in the above passage best describes the goal or target of capitalism?**

(A) Ethics based

(B) Culture driven

(C) Historical application

(D) Material accumulation

(E) Force of nature

The correct answer is D.

Items A, B and C are talked about differently in the passage, and not about the goal of capitalism. D and E are the only possible remaining choices. There is nothing about nature in the paragraph, so D is the correct answer.

26. From the passage above, which of the following phrases best describes the author's attitude toward capitalism?

(A) The author approves of capitalism if it involves religion.

(B) The author approves of capitalism when it is driven by "qualification expansion of spirit".

(C) The author disapproves of capitalism when it involves modern culture.

(D) The author disapproves of capitalism when Reformation is involved.

(E) The author disapproves of capitalism but wants to investigate why it is wrong.

The correct answer is E.

The tone of the passage is disapproval, so A and B are automatically incorrect. D is also incorrect as the author does not describe the interaction with religion so this applies. Between C and E, culture is used to describe different components within the passage but not in this manner; therefore, E is the best answer.

Passage 7
(Prose non-fiction, 20th century)

I'd like to say here, that I wasn't the only important one. I was part of a family, just like all of my brothers and sisters. The whole community was important. We used to discuss many of the community's problems together, especially when someone was ill and we couldn't buy medicine, because we were getting poorer and poorer. We'd start discussing and heaping insults on the rich who'd made us suffer for so long. It was about then I began learning about politics. I tried to talk to people who could help me sort my ideas out. I wanted to know what the world was like on the other side. I knew the finca, I knew the Altiplano. But what I didn't know was about the other problems of the Indians in Guatemala. I didn't know the problems the other groups had to holding onto their land. I knew there were lots of other Indians in other parts of the country, because I'd been meeting them in the finca since I was a child, but though we all worked together, we didn't know any of the names of the towns they came from, or how they lived, or what they ate. We just imagined that they were like us.

— *Rigoberta Menchu, Nobel Peace Prize Winner 1992*

27. From the context of the passage, what is a finca?

(A) A farm

(B) A village or town

(C) A mountain range

(D) A house

(E) It cannot be determined

The correct answer is B.

In the passage, only two Spanish words are used. Since the author describes a group of unrelated people The correct answer is not D. When offered an option like E, typically that is not the correct choice in a reading comprehension exam. Of the three remaining choices, since it talks about a gathering at this location, C is not an appropriate choice. Either A or B could apply, but A is a workplace not a gathering place. Choose B as the best answer - note that it is also mentioned at the end of the paragraph about people living in towns, another clue that this is the best answer.

28. The author is telling a story about her own life. What is this kind of document called?

(A) Autobiography

(B) Mystery

(C) Biography

(D) Narrative

(E) Romance

The correct answer is A.

A is the type of story where someone talks about their own life. While narrative could be another possible answer, the best answer is A.

29. Given the information in the passage, the author most likely worked as:

(A) a washer woman

(B) a seamstress

(C) a farmer

(D) a teacher

(E) it cannot be determined from the passage

The correct answer is C.

There are no indications that the woman washed clothes, worked as a seamstress or a teacher. Thus, A, B and D are eliminated. Between choices C and E, you must decide. If you read the book in full, C is the correct answer. But because this is about this passage, you do not have enough information to decide and E is the best selection - a rare occurrence in this exam, but it does happen.

30. The author describes who is the most important. She defines it as:

(A) herself

(B) her family

(C) her community

(D) the rich people that employed them

(E) the finca

The correct answer is C.

It is clear that the author says the community is important. It is literally part of the passage. She denounces A (herself) and even to an extent her family (option B); she goes on to talk about the community together, so the best answer is C. D is opposite of the intent of the passage and E is incongruous, though the translation is town that is just a physical location. Community has stronger meaning and is the best answer.

Passage 8

(Poetry, British, 18th century)

Tyger! Tyger! burning bright
In the forests of the night,
What immortal hand or eye
Could frame thy fearful symmetry?   (line 4)

In what distant deeps or skies
Burnt the fire of thine eyes?
On what wings dare he aspire?
What the hand dare seize the flame?   (line 8)

And what shoulder, & what art,
Could twist the sinews of they heart?
And when thy heart began to beat,
What dread hand? & what dread feet?   (line 12)
– *Excerpt, William Blake, 1794*

31. **Which of the topics below is this best description of the poem's main idea?**

    (A) Strength, as sinews of the heart are strong.

    (B) Creationism, and the author asks what immortal being created the tiger.

    (C) Flying, because it talks about wings.

    (D) Fire, with references to flames and burning forests.

    (E) Love, describing the heart and how it beats.

    The correct answer is B.

    This passage references the first word of each answer, but only one explanation for the excerpt can be correct. Remember this is about the main idea, not just one idea of the passage. If all of these were right, you need to find the option that is the best choice of all the options - one that can be seen in all of the other options. B represents the best choice.

32. Sinews, in the third stanza, can be best compared to:

(A) thread

(B) a cage

(C) rope

(D) heart strings or emotions

(E) burnt fire, from the second stanza

The correct answer is D.

Sinews are like tendons. They are strong binding fibers. So, A is not correct, nor is E. The closest two options are C and D; however, since this is poetry, sinews are figurative and the meaning is emotions, choice D.

33. Another phrase for "deeps or skies" that would fit in this poem could be:

(A) caves or planes

(B) trees or forests

(C) seas or air

(D) waves or wind

(E) oceans or lakes

The correct answer is C.

In this selection, synonyms - or similar words - need to be used in the same order as the original passage. Knowing this, C is the best option. While D could be considered, the original words do not describe movement, so it is not the best selection.

34. What is personified in the poem?

(A) A lion

(B) Birds

(C) Candle

(D) A tiger

(E) The sky

The correct answer is D.

This should be a fairly straightforward question, with the correct answer being D.

35. In line 7 of this poem, what word below most nearly means "aspire"?

(A) Soar

(B) Plunge

(C) Scheme

(D) Travel

(E) Admire

The correct answer is A.

Again, look for synonym in the list. Plunge is an antonym. A is the right choice.

36. The poet, William Blake, uses all of the following literary tools to convey his message, EXCEPT:

(A) metaphors

(B) rhymed couplets

(C) personification

(D) symbols

(E) lyrics

The correct answer is C.

For this question, you need to know your literary terms. Look them up if there are any unfamiliar to you. C - personification - is the right answer... it was also hinted in question four for this passage.

Passage 9

(Prose fiction, British, 19th century)

"Without their visits you cannot hope to shun the path I tread. Expect the first tomorrow night, when the bell tolls One. Expect the second on the next night at the same hour. The third, upon the next night, when the last stroke of Twelve has ceased to vibrate Look to see me no more; and look that, for your own sake, you remember what has passed between us!"

It walked backward from him; and at every step it took, the window raised itself a little, so that, when the apparition reached it, it was wide open.

Scrooge closed the window, and examined the door by which the Ghost had entered. It was double-locked, as he had locked it with his own hands, and the bolts were undisturbed. Scrooge tried to say "Humbug!" but stopped at the first syllable. And being, from the emotion he had undergone, or the fatigues of the day, or his glimpse of the invisible world, or the dull conversation of the Ghost, or the lateness of the hour, much in need of repose, he went straight to bed, without undressing, and fell asleep on the instant.
– *Charles Dickens, 1843*

37. **What quality of the Ghost is the most likely trait that Scrooge dislikes the most?**

   (A) The Ghost's old fashioned speech bothers Scrooge the most.

   (B) The authoritative nature the Ghost takes with Scrooge is the quality disliked the most.

   (C) The fact that the Ghost could break into his house is the trait that Scrooge dislikes.

   (D) The Ghost is taller than Scrooge, and that bothers him.

   (E) Scrooge dislikes that his bedtime was later than usual.

The correct answer is B.
You should eliminate wrong answers. C is wrong because Scrooge checks his house and it is secure. D is wrong as there is no indication about a height difference. E is also not appropriate, though the passage notes he went straight to bed, it mentions no discomfort caused by the

ghost for this reason. Between choices A and B, either could be true but the stronger dislike would be B, so that makes it the correct answer.

38. The way Scrooge's reaction to the Ghost is portrayed could mean that according to this passage that Scrooge is:

(A) tired

(B) angry

(C) looking for excuses

(D) forgetful

(E) planning to ignore the Ghost

The correct answer is C.
Again, by eliminating the wrong choices, there is nothing that suggests Scrooge is forgetful so it isn't D. While any of the rest are possible, the fact that Scrooge checks around the house and looks for things that could be explanations leads to the most reasonable answer as C.

39. The Ghost's remarks listed in the passage can most likely be inferred as:

(A) a warning to Scrooge

(B) the Ghost is talking to the wrong person

(C) Scrooge is hallucinating

(D) a friend was playing a joke on Scrooge

(E) no inference can be made

The correct answer is A.
Of the five options, the middle choices - B, C and D - have no support in the passage. As E is not a typical choice for the exam, A is the correct answer.

40. Scrooge's reaction to the Ghost in this passage leads a reader to conclude:

(A) that Scrooge was just conducting a normal nighttime house-check

(B) when the Ghost comes back for him, Scrooge will go along willingly

(C) even wealthy people like Scrooge lock their houses

(D) that Scrooge does not believe in the supernatural

(E) Scrooge is likely overcome with exhaustion

The correct answer is D.

The first answer is not accurate, as it was not a normal nighttime house check with the ghost. Also, there is no indication that Scrooge will willingly go anywhere with the ghost, so B is wrong. The generalization about wealthy people doesn't apply to the whole passage making that assumption, so C is incorrect. While Scrooge is admittedly tired, the better answer is D, given the extent of reaction to the ghost's presence in his home.

41. The tone of the passage is intended to:

(A) serve as a warning to Scrooge about things he will be shown

(B) serve as a reminder that Scrooge has forgotten appointments

(C) describe how disconcerted Scrooge felt after the warning was given by the Ghost

(D) provide backstory

(E) explain why Scrooge is so stingy

The correct answer is C.

Since The correct answers must be given based on the passage, A is more in line with the full story. B is not what the ghost was saying. A backstory is something that happened to the character in the past, and the ghost talks about the future, so D is incorrect. Nothing explains why Scrooge is stingy, or even that he is (other than the meaning of his name), so C is the correct answer.

Passage 10

(Prose, non-fiction, American, 20th century)

Using the Constitution to protect the minorities, James Madison's system of government is largely an attempt to divide and frustrate the majority. Madison envisioned a political system with the broadest possible power base. For example, he rejected the common belief that a democracy could work only in a very small area, arguing that it could succeed in a large country like the United States. A large population spread over a huge area would make it very difficult to force a permanent majority. Such a society would probably divide into varied and fluctuating minorities, making a long lasting majority unlikely. Instead, majorities would be created out of combinations of competing minorities. Thus, any majority would be temporary, and new ones would be elusive. This system, political scientists now term pluralism.
— *Leon Baradat, 1973*

42. **According to the passage, what is pluralism?**

(A) Majorities created out of combinations of competing minorities

(B) A new division of political science

(C) A political system with the smallest possible power base

(D) A new name for a permanent majority

(E) The system for democracy to work in a very small area

The correct answer is A.

This is a simple reference to the passage.

43. **The Constitution mentioned in the first line, in context to this passage, is:**

(A) James Madison's document to create a permanent majority

(B) the document creating the United States

(C) the personality of James Madison

(D) the health of the majority

(E) instructions on how to create combinations of competing minorities

The correct answer is B.

This question discusses something that should be known outside of context, especially when referencing a President of the United States.

44. The passage talks about democracy. Another phrase for a democracy is:

(A) the rule of a few over the many

(B) the welfare state

(C) a laissez-faire economy

(D) an elected government system

(E) an appointed government by a monarch

The correct answer is D.

Using definitions of words, The correct answer should be obvious. A defines a monarchy or dictatorship; a welfare state could be socialist in B. A democracy doesn't describe economy, or an appointed government with monarchy, so the correct answer is D.

Passage 11

(Prose non-fiction, British, 21st century)

American black music was going along like an express train. But white cats, after Buddy Holly died and Eddie Cochran died, and Elvis was in the army gone wonky, white American music when I arrived was the Beach Boys and Bobby Vee. They were still stuck in the past. The past was six months ago; it wasn't a long time. But things changed. The Beatles were the milestone. And then they got stuck inside their own cage. "The Fab Four." Hence, eventually, you got the Monkees, all this ersatz stuff. But I think there was a vacuum somewhere in white American music at the time.

When we first got to America and to LA, there was a lot of Beach Boys on the radio, which was pretty funny to us - it was before Pet Sounds - it was hot rod songs and surfing songs, pretty lousily played, familiar Chuck Berry licks going on. "Round, round get around / I get around," I though that was brilliant. It was later on, but Brian Wilson had something. "In My Room," "Don't Worry Baby." I was more interested in their B-sides, the ones he slipped in. There was no particular correlation with what we were doing so I could just listen to it on another level. I thought these are very well-constructed songs. I took easily to the pop song idiom. I'd always listened to everything, and America opened it all out - we were hearing records there that were regional hits. We'd get to know local labels and local acts, which is how we came across "Time Is on My Side," in LA, sung by Irma Thomas. It was a B-side of a record on Imperial Records, a label we'd have been aware of because it was independent and successful and based on Sunset Strip.

– *Keith Richards, 2010*

45. How many unique singers versus unique bands, respectively, are named in the passage above?

(A) Seven and Four

(B) Six and Three

(C) Eight and Three

(D) Seven and Three

(E) Six and Four

The correct answer is D.
This is merely counting. There are Seven singers (Buddy Holly, Eddie Cochran, Elivs, Bobby Vee, Chuck Berry, Brian Wilson, Irma Thomas) and three bands (Beatles, Monkeys, Beach Boys). D The "Fab Four" is referring to the Beatles. (Note the author's group is not named in the passage, and neither is he.)

46. How many songs are referenced in the passage above?

(A) Two

(B) Three

(C) Four

(D) Five

(E) Six

The correct answer is C.
Count them - In My Room, Don't Worry Baby and Time Is On My Side. B (note "Round, round get around/I get around" are lyrics and not the name of a song.)

47. **In the context of the selection's first paragraph, how many white singers or groups are named by the author?**

   (A) Four

   (B) Five

   (C) Three

   (D) Seven

   (E) One

   The correct answer is D.

   The whole passage is about white male singers except Irma Thomas, but her name is in the second paragraph. This question is limited to the first paragraph. Seven singers or bands are named after the author's "white cats" comment.

48. **Given what the author says about the B-side of a record, which of the following sentences is closest to the author's opinion?**

   (A) The B-side had more creativity and outlets for artists, making it unique.

   (B) It was called the B-side because the songs were generally not as good.

   (C) Only regional labels took the time to press B-sides.

   (D) The B-side was where all the surfing songs were recorded.

   (E) Labels were strict about the contents of the B-sides.

   The correct answer is A.

   You need to read the passage to understand which is the most appropriate. A is the best answer. The others are wrong because B is opposite of what he expresses as his opinion, C is factually not what the author writes, D is the opposite of what he says about the Beach Boys, and E is also the opposite of what the author writes.

Sample Test One

49. **When the author talks about the Beatles and says "they got stuck inside their own cage," the author most likely means:**

    (A) that the Beatles always had to hide in hotels because they were so famous

    (B) that successful musical groups could never enjoy the publicity

    (C) that the Beatles were trapped on planes all the time

    (D) that the Beatles couldn't perform with anyone outside of their four members

    (E) the Beatles outgrew the standard previously set for successful musicians, and were trapped in their own famous sensation

    The correct answer is E.
    For this answer, you need to interpret the author's intention from the context of the passage. The first four options are not supported by the passage at all; E is the best interpretation of the author's phrase.

50. **Given the descriptions in the passage, the author's profession is likely:**

    (A) a roadie

    (B) a writer

    (C) a singer

    (D) a photographer

    (E) a teacher

    The correct answer is C.
    Understanding the author's voice is important. Even if you didn't know that author's name (though you could save time if you did), given the descriptions of what he writes, C is the best and right answer.

Passage 12
(Prose fiction, British, pre-Ren/Classic)

A marvelous case is it to hear, either the warnings of that he should have voided, or the tokens of that he could not void. For the self night next before his death, the lord Stanley sent a trusty secret messenger unto him at midnight in all the haste, requiring him to rise and ride away with him, for he was disposed utterly no longer to bide; he had so fearful a dream, in which him thought that a boar with his tusks so raced them both by the heads, that the blood ran about both their shoulders. And forasmuch as the protector gave the boar for his cognizance, this dream made so fearful an impression in his heart, that he was thoroughly determined no longer to tarry, but had his horse ready, if the lord Hastings would go with him to ride so far yet the same night, that they should be out of danger ere day. Ay, good lord, quoth the lord Hastings to this messenger, leaneth my lord thy master so much to such trifles, and hath such faith in dreams, which either his own fear fantasieth or do rise in the night's rest by reason of his day thoughts? Tell him it is plain witchcraft to believe in such dreams; which if they were tokens of things to come, why thinketh he not that we might be as likely to make them true by our going if we were caught and brought back (as friends fail fleers), for then had the boar a cause likely to race us with his tusks, as folk that fled for some falsehood, wherefore either is there no peril (nor none there is indeed), or if any be, it is rather in going than biding. And if we should, needs cost, fall in peril one way or other, yet had I livelier that men should see it were by other men's falsehood, than think it were either our own fault or faint heart. And therefore go to thy master, man, and commend me to him, and pray him be merry and have no fear: for I ensure him I am as sure of the man that he wotteth of, as I am of my own hand. God send grace, sir, quoth the messenger, and went his way.

– *Sir Thomas More, 1513*

51. The beginning of the passage is describing what?

(A) An injury sustained by the main character

(B) A rider that is trying to escape injury

(C) The main character's dream

(D) A witch's story

(E) The boar that the character will grill for dinner

The correct answer is C.

Discounting the incorrect description of what's in the passage (such as in option E and A as well as B), that leaves options C and D. There is no reference to a witch, so the best choice is C. He even states that it is a dream.

52. **What is the cautionary message that the rider gets when he reaches his destination?**

    (A) Dreams are witchcraft if you believe in them.

    (B) Dreams can come true if you believe in them.

    (C) God sends His grace.

    (D) Those faint of heart do not have dreams.

    (E) Men cannot fall for other men's falsehoods.

    The correct answer is A.
    The rider warns the statement included in A.

53. **Did the main character in this passage believe he could out run bad visions?**

    (A) No, the passage makes it clear you always get what's coming in a dream.

    (B) No, dreams mean nothing, so the main character didn't pay any attention to it.

    (C) Yes, it was possible to escape bad visions on horseback.

    (D) Yes, the main character thought dancing would rid himself of bad dreams.

    (E) There is nothing in the passage that assists in answering this question.

    The correct answer is C.
    Again, the main character gives indications that the correct answer is C. The other options of No are wrong, as is The correct answer given in E. Answer D can be discounted because dancing is not discussed in the passage.

Passage 13

(Prose fiction, British, 19th century)

To go into solitude, a man needs to retire as much from his chamber as from society. I am not solitary whilst I read and write, though nobody is with me. But if a man would be alone, let him look at the stars. The rays that come from those heavenly worlds, will separate between him and what he touches. One might think the atmosphere was made transparent with this design, to give man, in the heavenly bodies, the perpetual presence of the sublime. Seen in the streets of cities, how great they are! If the stars should appear one night in a thousand years, how would men believe and adore; and preserve for many generations the remembrance of the city of God which had been shown! But every night come out these envoys of beauty, and light the universe with their admonishing smile.

– *Ralph Waldo Emerson, 1836*

54. The first two lines of this passage imply what?

(A) A man is never alone.

(B) A man is always alone.

(C) A man can be alone if he turns his back on people.

(D) A man can be alone if he makes his mind focus.

(E) A man who is lonely is considered alone.

The correct answer is D.

Given this is fiction and nearly a poem, you need to interpret what the author intends. The first two options use those extreme words, so they are not the best choices. The literal description of turning a back on people is not discussed. The difference between lonely and being alone is not discussed, either. So, D is the correct answer you should choose.

55. **Given the whole passage, which of the following is the best match for the author's opinion about nature?**

(A) The author prefers to seek to retire in his chamber.

(B) The author sees wonder in the sky and beauty at night.

(C) The author does not like trees.

(D) The author can only see stars one night in a thousand years.

(E) You cannot tell the author's opinion from this passage.

The correct answer is B.

You should realize by now - especially when understanding poems - that it would be extremely rare to select option E as the right answer. Option D is a misstatement of a phrase in the passage. There is no mention of the author even hinting that he does not like trees, so C is incorrect. When considering A or B, A does not resound as strongly as B, which is the right answer.

56. **The phrase "light the universe with their admonishing smile" is an example of:**

(A) personification

(B) a simile

(C) a metaphor

(D) irony

(E) satire

The correct answer is A.

Remember, the definition of personification is to give an inanimate object the attributes of a human, so A is correct. If you are unfamiliar with the other options in this example, it would be a good idea to look them up and learn them, as at least one of these five will be included on the exam.

Passage 14

(Poetry, American, 20th century)

Two roads diverged in a yellow wood,
And sorry I could not travel both
And be one traveler, long I stood
And looked down one as far as I could
To where it bent in the undergrowth;

Then took the other, as just as fair,
And having perhaps the better claim,
Because it was grassy and wanted wear;
Though as for that the passing there
Had worn them really about the same,

And both that morning equally lay
In leaves no step had trodden black.
Oh, I kept the first for another day!
Yet knowing how way leads on to way,
I doubted if I should ever come back.

I shall be telling this with a sigh
Somewhere ages and ages hence:
Two roads diverged in a wood, and I—
I took the one less traveled by,
And that has made all the difference.
– *Robert Frost, 1920*

57. **When the author uses the phrase "wanted wear" in the third
    stanza, what does that mean?**

    (A) It looked just as fair as the other path.

    (B) It was not as inviting.

    (C) The path didn't go the same way as the other one.

    (D) The path was less traveled than the other one.

    (E) You cannot determine what the author means.

    The correct answer is D.

    There are two possible correct answers. Both B and D are viable options; however, you are looking for the best answer. In the context of the whole poem, the explanation of B does not ring as true since that is the one that the author actually selected. D is the best answer.

58. **The author says that he "took the one less traveled by"; what does that mean?**

    (A) The other path looked like it was used more.

    (B) He did the right thing when others chose the wrong one.

    (C) He took the one on the left.

    (D) He took the one on the right.

    (E) It cannot be determined what the author meant by this short selection.

    The correct answer is A.

    This is another example of how a question is phrased to make sure you read it accurately. There is no statement about right or left direction, so both C and D are wrong. E is also eliminated as least probable answer because comprehension very rarely provides no correct answer. While B may bear some truth, in particular for the author as given in the end of the poem, A is the best answer.

59. **What is another way the author states his path was the "one less traveled by"?**

    (A) "both that morning equally lay"

    (B) "no step had trodden black"

    (C) "Somewhere ages and ages hence"

    (D) "bent in the undergrowth"

    (E) "having perhaps the better claim"

    The correct answer is B.

    This is another way to look for a synonym, but using a whole phrase. You should be able to narrow it down to D and B; however, B describes what happens when you walk on leaves that haven't been disturbed in a while. It is a parallel description to the straightforward "less traveled" statement, in that it describes the actions and ensuing results. Therefore, B is correct.

60. What does the author imply since he took the path less traveled?

(A) He has run into fewer people that try to bully him into doing what they want.

(B) Life is tougher getting to see the light.

(C) He was sorry he didn't chose to go the more well-trod path.

(D) He didn't make as much money as the people that took the other path.

(E) His life is better for choosing to go his own path.

The correct answer is E.

Running through the list of options, there is no mention of the author having people force him to make a decision (so A is wrong). B is also not applicable to this passage. There is no expression of remorse as provided in option C anywhere in the passage, so C is not correct. Monetary considerations - making money - are not mentioned either (as in D), so the only option left, which is correct, is E.

Passage 15

(Prose fiction, American, 20th century)

His memories of the Boston Society Contralto were nebulous and musical. She was a lady who sang, sang, sang in the music room on their house on Washington Square - sometimes with guests all about her, the men with their arms folded, balanced breathlessly on the edges of sofas, the women with their hands in their laps, occasionally making little whispers to the men and always clapping very briskly and uttering cooing cries after each song - and she often sang to Anthony alone, in Italian or French or in a strange and terrible dialect...

Oblivious to the social system, he lived for a while alone and unsought in a high room in Beck Hall - a slim dark boy of medium height with a shy sensitive mouth. His allowance was more than liberal. He laid the foundations for a library by purchasing from a wandering bibliophile first editions of Swinburne, Meredith, and Hardy, and a yellowed illegible autograph letter of Keats', finding later he had been amazingly overcharged. He became an exquisite dandy, amassed a rather pathetic collection of silk pajamas, brocaded dressing-gowns, and neckties too flamboyant to wear; in this secret finery he would parade before a mirror in his room or lie stretched in satin along the window-seat looking down on the yard and realizing this clamor, breathless and immediate, in which it seemed he was to never have a part.

– F. Scott Fitzgerald, 1922

61. Based on the information in the passage, what is a "contralto"?

(A) A Boston slang term for a high class man

(B) A female singer

(C) A female dancer

(D) A writer

(E) A bibliophile

The correct answer B.

Using the pronouns in the passage, contralto is a female - so A is obviously wrong. While any of the remaining options may be true, in the passage it talks about the woman singing, so B is the correct choice.

62. Based on the information in the passage, an "exquisite dandy" refers to:

(A) the first editions of the books listed in the passage

(B) anyone who wears silk pajamas

(C) a gentleman who has money to spend extravagantly on fancy things

(D) someone who likes to parade before a mirror

(E) someone who likes candy

The correct answer is C.

The term "dandy" references a person, so A is out. E is also out because candy is not mentioned in the passage; it is merely a rhyme for dandy. B is mentioned in the passage that the man like to wear silk pajamas and so is D, when it talks about the mirror. However, you have to look at the whole passage and the thing the man does, so C is the best answer if you do not know what "dandy" means.

63. **Why would the social system be important in this reading selection?**

   (A) Richer classes don't have dandies, so the main character can't be dandy.

   (B) A rich man with no female friends is called a dandy, and it helps explain the story.

   (C) The character seems ostracized and that can't happen in certain social classes.

   (D) If the main character was of a lower class, he could not live the life described.

   (E) No one lives the luxurious life described in the passage.

The correct answer is D.

In this question, it helps to know the meaning of dandy, which you may use from the previous answer if you do not know it. Since the man described in the passage seems to have a lot of money, A cannot be the right answer. E also is not a choice because it uses an extreme phrase - "no one". D is not correct because anyone can be excluded from a group (it also has an extreme contraction of "can't"). Between B and D, there are two reasons why B isn't a good choice. First, no female friends could be read as an extreme description, using "no". Another tip that this may not be the right choice is that if you removed the part of the passage about dandy, the story still works. Therefore, if you don't know that dandies are rarely lower classes, you can reason your way that D is correct.

Passage 16

(Prose fiction, American, 20th century)

These are morning matters, pictures you dream as the final wave heaves you up on the sand in the bright light and drying air. You remember pressure, and a curved sleep you rested against, soft, like a scallop in its shell. But the air hardens your skin; you stand; you leave the lighted shore to explore some dim headland, and soon you're lost in the leafy interior, intent, remembering nothing.

I still think of that old tomcat, mornings, when I wake. Things are tamer now; I sleep with the window shut. The cats and our rites are gone and my life is changed, but the memory remains of something powerful playing over me. I wake expectant, hoping to see a new thing. If I'm lucky I might be jogged awake by a strange bird call. I dress in a hurry, imagining the yard flapping with auks, or flamingos. This morning it was a wood duck, down at the creek. It flew away.

— Annie Dillard, 1975 Pulitzer Prize

64. The tone of the selection is:

(A) reflective

(B) indulgent

(C) indifferent

(D) dishonest

(E) ironic

The correct answer is A.

This is knowing what the different words mean. A is the correct answer. Review the definitions of these words if you don't know them, to make sure they won't trip you up on the exam.

65. The author uses _____ to describe the setting.

(A) personification

(B) ambivalence

(C) satire

(D) allusion

(E) clichés

The correct answer is D.

Definitions are a large part of reading comprehension answer possibilities, as they like to know that you understand more than just what the passage says. D is the correct answer.

66. The phrase, "like a scallop in its shell" is an example of:

(A) irony

(B) a simile

(C) a metaphor

(D) personification

(E) euphemism

The correct answer is C.

Again, this is about definitions. When you use the word "like" in a comparison, which is one hint that the phrase is a metaphor.

67. The author describes many of her feelings and situations by focusing the conversation on animals. Based on the information in the passage, one reason could be:

(A) animals are comforting and relax the reader

(B) birds are flighty and the center of her story

(C) the setting of this story is a farm

(D) the lead character doesn't have many human friends

(E) it is the backstory of how animals and nature are always present in the character's life

The correct answer is E.

There are some weigh out options for these answers! A, B, C and D make great leaps if you were to make those conclusions. E is the correct option.

68. **The phrase "the air hardens your skin" within the context of the passage most likely refers to what?**

   (A) The morning air woke the character up from dreaming.

   (B) The scallop shell bed the character sleeps in has opened.

   (C) The air dries out the character's skin.

   (D) The coldness of the room turns off the brain of the character.

   (E) The air turns the character's skin cold when the cat leaves the bed.

The correct answer is A.

This question looks at ensuring you understand the suggestions made by the author. B is totally made up. D is a bit far-fetched, to turn off her brain (what does that have to do with skin?) E gives the impression cats are extremely warm and somehow leaving the bed is related with her description, slightly implausible. A and C remain; but in the context of fiction, A is the better choice.

Passage 17
(Drama, British, 16th century/classical)

Bernardo: Welcome, Horatio: welcome, good Marcellus.
Marcellus: What, has this thing appear'd again to-night?
Bernardo: I have seen nothing.
Marcellus: Horatio says 'tis but our fantasy,
And will not let belief take hold of him
Touching this dreaded sight, twice seen of us:
Therefore I have entreated him along
With us to watch the minutes of this night;
That if again this apparition come,
He may approve our eyes and speak to it.
Horatio: Tush, tush, 'twill not appear.
Bernardo: Sit down awhile;

And let us once again assail your ears,
That are so fortified against our story
What we have two nights seen.
– *William Shakespeare, 1599-1602*

69. The three men in the play can be said, in this passage:

(A) to disagree about a ghost that was seen

(B) to disagree that two days ago they saw people meeting "twice seen of us"

(C) that Horatio and Bernardo are trying to persuade Marcellus they
saw something

(D) that Horatio and Marcellus are trying to persuade Bernardo they
saw something

(E) to meet for a drink for "fortification"

The correct answer is A.

Drama selections need you to pay close attention to the characters and who says what. B is not true - the two men don't disagree about what they saw. C and D do not list the characters correctly about who sees what. E isn't correct at all, so A is the correct answer.

70. When Marcellus speaks of "approving our eyes", what is he saying?

(A) Marcellus and Bernardo need glasses.

(B) Bernardo didn't believe what Marcellus saw.

(C) Horatio believes what Marcellus saw.

(D) Horatio should see what Bernardo and Marcellus saw.

(E) Marcellus should believe what Bernardo saw.

The correct answer is D.

You need to review the members of the scene if you got this

inaccurate. The only correct choice about who saw what and who needs to see what they saw is D.

71. When Bernardo says "once again assail your ears", what does he mean?

(A) He wants to repeat himself to Marcellus to make him believe him.

(B) He wants to repeat himself to Horatio to make him believe him.

(C) He wants to repeat himself to help all three of them believe the story.

(D) He wants Marcellus and Horatio to poke holes in the story.

(E) None of these are the meaning of that phrase in the passage.

The correct answer is B.
Pay attention to the characters. That's how these answer choices can be confusing.

72. In the context of the passage, entreated means:

(A) invited

(B) engaged

(C) demanded

(D) refused

(E) ignored

The correct answer is A.
Picking the best synonym should get easier at the end of the exam.

Passage 18
(Drama, American, 20th century)

Edmund: That's foolishness. You know it's only a bad cold.
Mary: Yes, of course, I know that!
Edmund: But listen, Mama. I want you to promise me that even if it turns out to be something worse, you'll know I'll soon be alright again, anyway, and don't worry yourself sick, and you'll keep on taking care of yourself –

Mary: I won't listen when you talk so silly! There's absolutely no reason to talk as if you expect something dreadful! Of course, I promise you I give you my sacred word of honor! But I suppose you're remembering I've promised before on my word of honor.

Edmund: No!

Mary: I'm not blaming you, dear. How can you help it? How can any one of us forget? That's what makes it so hard – for all of us. We can't forget.

Edmund: Mama! Stop it!

Mary: All right, dear. I didn't beam to be so gloomy. Don't mind me. Here. Let me feel your head. Why, it's nice and cool. You certainly don't have any fever now.

– Eugene O'Neill, 1955

73. It can be said that this passage of the drama:

(A) puts American dream against American nightmare

(B) describes the normal American family

(C) portrays Americans in a very resilient fashion

(D) was likely written during a war so obviously has negative overtones

(E) has the mother remembering the death of another child

The correct answer is E.

You may have read this play, but you have to limit your answers to the passage; therefore, A is not correct. B invites the reader to make assumptions about normal, and that does not usually happen in the exam. There is not enough information in the passage to presume C is correct. The passage is not overly negative, so E is the best answer.

74. Mary changes the direction of the conversation by:

(A) stopping Edmund from talking by taking his temperature

(B) making Edmund feel badly about the death of his brother

(C) walking out of the room

(D) tucking the covers up to his chin

(E) ignoring him

The correct answer is A.

You need to read the scene to make sure to pick the right answer.

75. This portion of the play is a:

(A) monologue

(B) dialogue

(C) soliloquy

(D) entendre

(E) stichomythia

The correct answer is B.

By definition, since there are two people, A and C are incorrect. While D is possible, E is wrong; B is the best choice. Look up the words if you are unfamiliar with them.

76. Mary talks about Edmund expecting something dreadful. What's a literary term for that action?

(A) Oxymoron

(B) Dissonance

(C) Foreshadowing

(D) Stream of consciousness

(E) Understatement

The correct answer is C.

Definitions again! The correct choice is C and by now you should automatically look up any definitions for words that are unfamiliar to you.

Passage 19

(Prose fiction, British, 18th century)

But though thus largely indebted to fortune, to nature she had yet greater obligation: her form was elegant, her heart was liberal. Her countenance announced the intelligence of her mind, her complexion varied with every emotion of her foul, and her eyes, the heralds of her speech, now beamed with understanding and now glistened with sensibility.

For the short period of her minority, the management of her fortune and the care of her person, had by the Dean been entrusted to three guardians, among whom her own choice was to settle to her residence: but her mind, saddened by the lots of all her natural friends, coveted to regain its serenity in the quietness of the country, and in the bosom of an aged and maternal counsellor, whom she loved as her mother, and to to whom she had been known from her childhood.

– *Fanny Burney, 1782*

77. **From the context of this passage, which of the following statements is the most likely to be true?**

   (A) The main character is poor.

   (B) The main character is an orphan.

   (C) The setting of the story is in England.

   (D) The main character is going to live with her aunt.

   (E) The main character doesn't like to live in town.

The correct answer is B.

The female character seems to have inherited money, so A is not correct. There is no way to know in what country the setting takes place, and remember that all answers are dependent on the passage; so C is incorrect. D is also incorrect because the passage explicitly talks about her wanting to set up her own house. B is the right answer.

78. **In the quote, "her heart was liberal", what is the author trying to express?**

    (A) The author implies that the main character is of loose morals.

    (B) The author implies that while ladylike, she has a wild streak.

    (C) The author alludes that the woman is more open than her demeanor.

    (D) The author makes it clear that she is alone.

    (E) The author shows how she was older than her natural friends.

    The correct answer is C.
    While this one may seem difficult, if you take each statement apart, The correct answer comes quickly. A is wrong because nowhere does the author talk about morals being questionable. B implies an overly outward exuberance by the main character, and that is overstating what is written. D is simply not accurate, and while there seems to be a difference between her and her friends, nowhere does the passage indicate she is older. C is correct. Also, when the author describes her "heart", it can mean that her inward thoughts, and since her demeanor is so proper, the outward indications of her character, C again is shown to be the right answer.

79. **What does the word "minority" mean in the context of the passage?**

    (A) The woman in the passage is a Native American.

    (B) The character is not yet an adult.

    (C) The group of people in the story are members of the minority political party.

    (D) The character has less money than her friends.

    (E) None of the given options explain "minority" in this passage.

    The correct answer is B.
    This passage does not talk about race or ethnicity or religion; A is wrong. C talks about politics and that is not within the passage, so it, too, is wrong. D is the opposite of what is implied by the author about

the main character; and as you have learned, E is likely the wrong choice. Choose B.

80. What is another word for serenity in this passage?

(A) Peacefulness

(B) Counsellor

(C) Bosom

(D) Rambunctiousness

(E) Prayerful

The correct answer is A.

Another synonym choice - A is correct.

Sample Test Two

Instructions _____

This exam gives passages from known writings (fiction, poems, non-fiction/history, biographies, drama and more) over the past five hundred years. While the student taking the exam is not expected to have read the material or have familiarity with the passage prior to the exam, the test taker is expected to have the knowledge of an undergraduate English and writing class.

TIP: As the writing changes and the time periods change, it's important for a student to note the author and time period as that may assist in answering questions by either eliminating unlikely answers or allow the student to recall items about the author.

At the end of the test passages and answers, there is an answer key and a "rationale" key for each question. Take the test without referencing these guides. For questions that you guess The correct answers or get wrong, the rationale is provided to help you see how test makers frame answers to questions or explain pieces of information with which you are unfamiliar.

There are 80 questions on this particular sample test, and the CLEP also uses around 80 for the credit exam. As with the CLEP exam, the passages are taken primarily from American and British Literature - though at least once question, just as in the actual exam, is taken from another area of literature. Within the questions of the CLEP, the mixture of genre types falls typically almost 80-90% between poetry and prose (both fiction and non-fiction within the prose selections) and the remaining on drama. The entire test is balanced between three main eras – Renaissance/17th Century, 18th/19th Century, as well as 10th/21st Century; in the past, there is a slightly heavier emphasis on 18th/19th work, and usually there is one passage from the Classical/pre-Renaissance period.

The CLEP allows 98 minutes to take the exam of approximately 80 questions. Time yourself during the exam, but as you practice, focus more attention on accurately answering questions as the total number of correct answers impacts your score, not how many you skip or get wrong. If you skip any questions, make sure that you also skip that line on The correct answer sheet - or you may spend a lot of time erasing and redoing your answer key.

These passages do not actually appear on the CLEP exam, but are meant to show how the exam is written and the various range of questions, answers, and key knowledge points required in order to pass the CLEP exam. Read each question carefully and provide the best answer choice. Good luck.

Passage 1

William Wordsworth

"I Wandered Lonely As A Cloud"

I wandered lonely as a cloud
That floats on high o'er vales and hills,
When all at once I saw a crowd,
A host, of golden daffodils;
Beside the lake, beneath the trees,
Fluttering and dancing in the breeze.

Continuous as the stars that shine
And twinkle on the milky way,
They stretched in never-ending line
Along the margin of a bay:
Ten thousand saw I at a glance,
Tossing their heads in sprightly dance.

The waves beside them danced; but they
Out-did the sparkling waves in glee:
A poet could not but be gay,
In such a jocund company:
I gazed—and gazed—but little thought
What wealth the show to me had brought:

For oft, when on my couch I lie
In vacant or in pensive mood,
They flash upon that inward eye
Which is the bliss of solitude;
And then my heart with pleasure fills,
And dances with the daffodils.

1. **What type of passage is the above selection?**

   (A) Lyrical poem

   (B) Haiku poem

   (C) Acrostic poem

   (D) Limerick poem

   (E) Cinquain poem

2. **The permanence of stars as compared with flowers emphasizes**

   (A) the impermanence of life.

   (B) the permanence of memory for the poet.

   (C) the earlier comparison of the sky to the lake.

   (D) that stars are frozen above and daffodils dance below.

   (E) the similarity of the inward eye with the fleeting bliss of solitude.

3. **The scheme of the poem is**

   (A) ballad.

   (B) Scottish stanza.

   (C) Spenserian stanza.

   (D) quatrain-couplet.

   (E) sonnet.

4. **This poem uses the _____ metric pattern.**

   (A) dactylic tetrameter

   (B) trochaic pentameter

   (C) trochaic tetrameter

   (D) iambic pentameter

   (E) iambic tetrameter

5. **What is a literary device used in the last two lines of the first two stanzas?**

(A) Simile.

(B) Metaphor.

(C) Personification.

(D) Allegory.

(E) Paradox.

6. **In what literary period did this author write?**

(A) Edwardian Movement.

(B) Romanticism.

(C) Existentialism.

(D) Renaissance Literature.

(E) Victorian Movement.

7. **As used in this poem, the best choice for a synonym of jocund means**

(A) pleasant.

(B) vapid.

(C) lonely.

(D) jovial.

(E) sad.

8. **What literary device is used in Line 9, "They stretched in never-ending line."**

(A) hyperbole.

(B) onomatopoeia.

(C) epithet.

(D) irony.

(E) anecdote.

Passage 2

"I went to work the next day, turning, so to speak, my back on that station. In that way only it seemed to me I could keep my hold on the redeeming facts of life. Still, one must look about sometimes; and then I saw this station, these men strolling aimlessly about in the sunshine of the yard. I asked myself sometimes what it all meant. They wandered here and there with their absurd long staves in their hands, like a lot of faithless pilgrims bewitched inside a rotten fence. The word 'ivory' rang in the air, was whispered, was sighed. You would think they were praying to it. A taint of imbecile rapacity blew through it all, like a whiff from some corpse. By Jove! I've never seen anything so unreal in my life. And outside, the silent wilderness surrounding this cleared speck on the earth struck me as something great and invincible, like evil or truth, waiting patiently for the passing away of this fantastic invasion.

— *Heart of Darkness*

9. **Who wrote this novel?**

(A) Joseph Conrad

(B) James Joyce

(C) Jane Austen

(D) Charlotte Brontë

(E) Charles Dickens

10. **What does the following line represent?**

"I saw this station, these men strolling aimlessly about in the sunshine of the yard."

(A) Soldiers enjoying their day

(B) Men being unaware of the negativity that surrounds them

(C) Positivity is infectious

(D) The station is a happy place

(E) Embracing the weather before a storm hits

11. **What does the word staves mean?**

(A) Machete

(B) Axe

(C) Gun

(D) Bomb

(E) Wooden club

12. **What does the ivory represent?**

(A) Death

(B) Prosperity

(C) Jewelry

(D) Trade

(E) None of the above

13. **What literary device is used when describing the ivory?**

(A) Alliteration

(B) Allegory

(C) Simile

(D) Personification

(E) Repetition

14. **What does rapacity represent?**

(A) Greed

(B) Rapid movement

(C) Intelligent

(D) Affluent

(E) Generous

15. What literary device is used in this passage?

"And outside, the silent wilderness surrounding this cleared speck on the earth struck me as something great and invincible, like evil or truth, waiting patiently for the passing away of this fantastic invasion."

(A) Simile

(B) Metaphor

(C) Illusion

(D) Personification

(E) Onomatopoeia

16. Which style of writing is represented in this novel?

(A) Biographical

(B) Autobiographical

(C) Expository

(D) Persuasive

(E) None of the above

Passage 3

"Finished, it's finished, nearly finished, it must be nearly finished. Grain upon grain, one by one, and one day, suddenly, there's a heap, a little heap, the impossible heap. I can't be punished any more. I'll go now to my kitchen, ten feet by ten feet by ten feet, and wait for him to whistle me. Nice dimensions, nice proportions, I'll lean on the table, and look at the wall, and wait for him to whistle me."

– *Endgame*

17. Who wrote this play?

(A) Anton Chekov

(B) William Shakespeare

(C) Lillian Hellman

(D) Athol Fugard

(E) Samuel Beckett

Sample Test Two

18. What literary device is used throughout this passage?

(A) Simile

(B) Metaphor

(C) Euphemism

(D) Flashback

(E) Repetition

19. What does the impossible heap represent?

(A) Life's greatest hurdles

(B) A pile of grain so tall it cannot be moved

(C) Death

(D) A mountain

(E) Heaven

20. The whistle symbolizes _____.

(A) A referee

(B) The character's father

(C) Death

(D) An angel

(E) All of the above

21. What is an endgame?

(A) The final play in a game, such as chess

(B) The end of a negotiation

(C) A wish

(D) The final approval for a lease

(E) None of the above

22. What is the author trying to portray in this selection?

(A) An old man

(B) A prisoner

(C) A farmer

(D) A mill worker

(E) A plantation

23. What best describes this selection?

(A) Epic

(B) Foreshadowing

(C) Cliffhanger

(D) Flashback

(E) Irony

Passage 4

A Bird Came Down the Walk – Emily Dickinson

IN THE GARDEN

A bird came down the walk:
He did not know I saw;
He bit an angle-worm in halves
And ate the fellow, raw.

And then, he drank a dew
From a convenient grass,
And then hopped sidewise to the wall
To let a beetle pass.

He glanced with rapid eyes
That hurried all abroad,—
They looked like frightened beads, I thought;
He stirred his velvet head

Like one in danger; cautious,
I offered him a crumb,

Sample Test Two

And he unrolled his feathers
And rowed him softer home

Than oars divide the ocean,
Too silver for a seam,
Or butterflies, off banks of noon,
Leap, plashless, as they swim.

24. **What type of literary device is used in the author's phrase, "drank a dew"?**

(A) Allusion.

(B) Foreshadowing.

(C) Juxtaposition.

(D) Satire.

(E) Alliteration.

25. **The author describes action beginning in line 15 of the bird's flight. What type of literary device is used?**

(A) Simile.

(B) Metaphor.

(C) Irony.

(D) Satire.

(E) None of these are correct.

26. **The scheme of the poem (except the final three stanzas) is**

(A) XAXA or Ghazal.

(B) Scottish stanza.

(C) Spenserian stanza.

(D) quatrain-couplet.

(E) Petrarchan sonnet.

27. **This poem uses a particular metric pattern throughout the poem, except in the third line of each stanza. What is the main metric pattern?**

(A) dactylic tetrameter

(B) trochaic trimeter

(C) trochaic tetrameter

(D) iambic pentameter

(E) iambic trimeter

28. **What literary device is used when the bird's eyes are compared to frightened beads?**

(A) Reverse Personification.

(B) Metaphor.

(C) Simile.

(D) Allegory.

(E) Paradox.

29. **What does the dash at the end of line 12 represent?**

(A) A change in focus from the bird to the water.

(B) An abrupt change for the bird.

(C) An emotional shift from fear to fascination.

(D) It only shows the middle of the poem.

(E) None of these accurately describe the meaning of the dash.

Sample Test Two

30. What is the author's tone in this poem?

(A) She takes the perspective of the bird.

(B) The author's tone is harsh toward potential prey.

(C) The tone is factual, describing the actions of a bird.

(D) Ornithology fascinated the author and she uses flowery language to describe it.

(E) The author's tone is gentle and respectful demeanor regarding nature.

31. What is a potential meaning of the allegory used by the author?

(A) It could reveal the author's perceptions of God.

(B) The allegory could be looking at the author's view of marriage.

(C) The author could reveal the hierarchy between man and beast.

(D) Descriptions of the forces of nature could parallel emotions.

(E) There is no allegory used as a literary device in this poem.

Passage 5

These are morning matters, pictures you dream as the final wave heaves you up on the sand in the bright light and drying air. You remember pressure, and a curved sleep you rested against, soft, like a scallop in its shell. But the air hardens your skin; you stand; you leave the lighted shore to explore some dim headland, and soon you're lost in the leafy interior, intent, remembering nothing.

I still think of that old tomcat, mornings, when I wake. Things are tamer now; I sleep with the window shut. The cats and our rites are gone and my life is changed, but the memory remains of something powerful playing over me. I wake expectant, hoping to see a new thing. If I'm lucky I might be jogged awake by a strange bird call. I dress in a hurry, imagining the yard flapping with auks, or flamingos. This morning it was a wood duck, down at the creek. It flew away.

32. The tone of the selection is:

(A) reflective.

(B) indulgent.

(C) indifferent.

(D) dishonest.

(E) ironic.

33. The author uses _____ to describe the setting

(A) personification

(B) ambivalence

(C) satire

(D) allusion

(E) cliches

34. The phrase, "like a scallop in its shell" is an example of:

(A) an irony

(B) a smilie.

(C) a metaphor.

(D) personification.

(E) euphemism.

35. The literary style is:

(A) Expository

(B) Didactic

(C) Persuasive

(D) Descriptive

(E) Theatrical

36. **The author describes many of her feelings and situations by focusing the conversation on animals. Based on the information in the passage, one reason could be:**

(A) animals are comforting, and relax the reader.

(B) birds are flighty and the center of her story.

(C) the setting of this story is a farm.

(D) the lead character doesn't have many human friends.

(E) it is the backstory of how animals and nature are always present in the character's life.

37. **How is this passage narrated?**

(A) First person.

(B) Second person.

(C) Third person.

(D) Omniscient observer.

(E) None of these.

38. **The phrase "the air hardens your skin" within the context of the passage most likely refers to what?**

(A) The morning air woke the character up from dreaming.

(B) The scallop shell bed the character sleeps in has opened.

(C) The air dries out the character's skin.

(D) The coldness of the room turns off the brain of the character.

(E) The air turns the character's skin cold when the cat leaves the bed.

39. What is the significance of the author using cats and birds in the passage?

(A) The author has always had cats while growing up.

(B) She creates allusions to changes in which animals are predators and prey.

(C) There are more birds, or opportunities, available today.

(D) Cats are lower to the ground and she wants to be a bird in the sky.

(E) There is no significance in the choice of her animals.

Passage 6

Jason threw into the fire. It hissed, uncurled, turning black. Then it was gray. Then it was gone. Caddy and Father and Jason were in Mother's chair. Jason's eyes were puffed shut and his mouth moved, like tasting. Caddy's head was on Father's shoulder. Her hair was like fire, and little points of fire were in her eyes, and I went and Father lifted me into the chair too, and Caddy held me. She smelled like trees.

She smelled like trees. In the corner it was dark, but I could see the window. I squatted there, holding the slipper. I couldn't see it, but my hands saw it, and I could hear it getting night, and my hands saw the slipper but I couldn't see myself, but my hands could see the slipper, and I squatted there, hearing it getting dark.

Here you is, Luster said. Look what I got. He showed it to me. You know where I got it. Miss Quentin give it to me. I knowed they couldn't keep me out. What you doing, off in here. I thought you done slipped back out doors. Aint you done enough moaning and slobbering today, without hiding off in this here empty room, mumbling and taking on. Come on here to bed, so I can get up there before it starts. I cant fool with you all night tonight. Just let them horns toot the first toot and I done gone.

40. The subject in this passage is:

(A) is female.

(B) a supporting character.

(C) has an attitude of a criminal.

(D) a character, and seems to be the lead of the story.

(E) is well-educated.

41. What kind of description is the author providing of this scene?

(A) Backstory of the environment of one of the characters.

(B) A narrative in the first person.

(C) Information about a dream she had.

(D) An unreliable narrative about a character.

(E) The author is using a persuasive argument.

42. What are types of narration style is used in this passage?

(A) Defamiliarization.

(B) Audience surrogate, trying to convey the audience's confusion.

(C) A stream of consciousness of one character's opinion of another's situation.

(D) Unreliable narrator.

(E) Hamartia style.

43. One of the themes of the book is

(A) changes in family values away from chastity and sin strain families.

(B) that people are all the same, rich or poor.

(C) rivers of emotion run deep.

(D) religion can hold a family together.

(E) obstacles can be overcome with hard work.

44. The phrase, "Her hair was like fire," is what kind of literary device?

   (A) Simile.

   (B) Metaphor.

   (C) Reverse Personification.

   (D) Allusion.

   (E) Denotation.

45. The phrase, "little points of fire were in her eyes," is what kind of literary device?

   (A) Simile.

   (B) Metaphor.

   (C) Reverse Personification.

   (D) Allusion.

   (E) Denotation.

46. By using incorrect speech patterns, the author achieves what?

   (A) An optimistic tone for the passage.

   (B) Changing of the time in history for this character.

   (C) An indicator of internal thoughts, not "scrubbed" for other's hearing.

   (D) A and D.

   (E) None of these.

47. By repeating the phrase "She smelled like trees,", the author

   (A) uses anaphora.

   (B) uses pleonasm.

   (C) changes pace through repetition.

   (D) uses consonance.

   (E) uses the lacan technique.

Sample Test Two

Passage 7

"If people bring so much courage to this world the world has to kill them to break them, so of course it kills them. The world breaks every one and afterward many are strong at the broken places. But those that will not break it kills. It kills the very good and the very gentle and the very brave impartially. If you are none of these you can be sure it will kill you too but there will be no special hurry."

– *A Farewell to Arms*

48. Who wrote this novel?

(A) Henry David Thoreau

(B) Ernest Hemmingway

(C) F. Scott Fitzgerald

(D) Harper Lee

(E) J.R.R. Tolkien

49. What is the theme of this novel?

(A) Innocence

(B) War

(C) Love

(D) Death

(E) Grief

50. What does the title symbolize?

(A) An amputation caused during war

(B) Being discharged

(C) Saying goodbye to the arms of someone you love

(D) Saying goodbye to weaponry and warfare

(E) C & D

51. Which literary device is used to describe war?

(A) Personification

(B) Alliteration

(C) Simile

(D) Metaphor

(E) Idiom

52. Which of the following best represents this passage?

(A) Sarcasm

(B) Resentment

(C) Irony

(D) Sympathy

(E) Affectionate

53. What best describes the author's intention in the following line?

"It kills the very good and the very gentle and the very brave impartially."

(A) Everyone will die sooner or later

(B) Murderers target nice people

(C) The good, gentle and brave are easier to kill

(D) The good, gentle and brave die protecting others

(E) War kills everyone, it doesn't have a bias

54. How does the world break people?

(A) It creates challenging times

(B) It represents being shot and not dying

(C) It causes extreme wounds, mentally and physically

(D) People can have broken bones

(E) Physical objects and precious belongings can be broken

55. Which literary period is this from?

(A) Romanticism

(B) Renaissance

(C) The Enlightenment

(D) Existentialism

(E) Modernism

Passage 8
(Poetry, American, 19th century)

There is no frigate like a book
To take us lands away,
Nor any coursers like a page
Of prancing poetry;
This traverse may the poorest take
Without oppress of toll;
How frugal is the chariot
That bears the human soul!
– *Emily Dickinson (1830-1886)*

56. Authors use particular literary structures for descriptions. What best explains the type that Emily Dickinson employs in this poem?

(A) Connotative

(B) Argumentative

(C) Narrative

(D) Rhetoric

(E) Expository

57. **How many types of transport does the author incorporate?**

   (A) Two

   (B) Three

   (C) Four

   (D) Five

   (E) None

58. **If the words 'frigate, coursers, and chariot' were replaced with synonyms, what would the best choice of the following options include?**

   (A) Train, car, carriage

   (B) Train, horse, carriage

   (C) Ship, car, carriage

   (D) Ship, car, train

   (E) Ship, horse, carriage

59. **Which of the following descriptions more closely describes the author's intended meaning of poem?**

   (A) Difficulties at work

   (B) The importance of books

   (C) Confessions for the soul

   (D) Poverty makes things difficult

   (E) Describing modes of transportation

60. There are very descriptive and strong feelings conveyed by the poet. Which of the following is not the definition of what she shares?

(A) Overstatement

(B) Paradox

(C) Understatement

(D) Irony

(E) Sarcasm

61. What kind of poetry form is utilized by Ms. Dickinson in this poem?

(A) Alexandrine

(B) Didactic poetry

(C) Ballad stanza

(D) Epitaph

(E) Rondel

62. Who is the author of this poem?

(A) Emily Dickinson

(B) Emily Bronte

(C) Emily Mortimer

(D) Lord Byron

(E) William Blake

63. When the boat is compared to a book, that is an example of:

(A) a metaphor.

(B) personification.

(C) a simile.

(D) an extended metaphor.

(E) none of these.

Passage 9

Okonkwo and his fellow prisoners were set free as soon as the fine was paid. The District Commissioner spoke to them again about the great queen, and about peace and good government. But the men did not listen. They just sat and looked at him and at his interpreter. In the end they were given back their bags and sheathed machetes and told to go home. They rose and left the courthouse. They neither spoke to anyone nor among themselves.

The courthouse, like the church, was but a little way outside the village. The footpath that linked them was a very busy one because it also led to the stream, beyond the court. It was open and sandy. Footpaths were open and sandy in the dry season. But when the rains came the bush grew thick on either side and closed in on the path. It was now dry season.

As they made their way to the village the six men met women and children going to the stream with their waterpots. But them wore such heavy and fearsome looks to them, but edged out of the way to let them pass. In the village little groups of men joined them until they became a sizable company. They walked silently. As each of the six men got to his compound, he turned in, taking some of the crowd with him. The village was air in a silent, suppressed way.

Ezinma had prepared some food for her father as soon as news spread that the six men would be released. She took it to him in his obi. He ate absent-mindedly. He had no appetite, he only ate to please her. His male relations and friends had gathered in his obi, and Obierika was urging him to eat. Nobody else spoke, but they noticed the log stripes on Okonkwo's back where the warder's whip had cut into his flesh.

64. Who is the protagonist of this story?

(A) Obierika

(B) Ezinma

(C) Okonkwo

(D) The District Commissioner

(E) Okonkwo's wife

65. What is the name of this book?

(A) Obi

(B) Things Fall Apart

(C) Let the Circle Be Unbroken

(D) Ashes and Dust

(E) The Rainy Season

66. What category of literature does this book represent?

(A) Romantic.

(B) Victorian.

(C) Modernism.

(D) Transcendentalism.

(E) Post Colonial.

67. The main character of the book appears to have what occur throughout the book?

(A) He is a champion of his village.

(B) He shows that he is good provider for his family.

(C) He represents the disintegration of his society against the change.

(D) The village doesn't support him.

(E) The courthouse is targeting him to get rid of the village.

68. The narrative structure of this passage is:

(A) simple narrative.

(B) cause and effect.

(C) chronological.

(D) inductive.

(E) deductive.

69. The literary style of the book is:

(A) comedy.

(B) tragedy.

(C) drama.

(D) exploration.

(E) quest.

70. How is this passage narrated?

(A) First person.

(B) Second person.

(C) Third person.

(D) Omniscient observer.

(E) None of these.

71. What is the main idea of this passage?

(A) The village members continue to carry out the traditions of their ancestors.

(B) There is a drought affecting crops and village life.

(C) The interpreter was sharing with them a new way of life.

(D) The government and church were coming together for the people.

(E) People are resistant to change, and the village and protagonist illustrate it.

Passage 10

"Where, in Heaven's name, could anyone even be alone in Calcutta? What hanky-panky business, in my mother's words, could go on? Everyone knew the rules and the rules stated caste and community narrowed the range of intimate contact."

— *Desirable Daughters by Bharati Mukherjee*

Sample Test Two

72. Where is Calcutta?

(A) Indonesia

(B) China

(C) New Zealand

(D) Jamaica

(E) India

73. Why is it abnormal for someone to be alone in Calcutta?

(A) Everyone travels with their spouses

(B) It's a very busy city

(C) The city is very dangerous

(D) It's sarcastic because it's such a rural place

(E) None of the above

74. What is hanky-panky business?

(A) Dancing

(B) Illegal trade

(C) Corruption

(D) A romantic kiss

(E) Sexual activity

75. What does the word caste mean?

(A) Division of the classes

(B) Enclosed

(C) Oppression

(D) Sin

(E) Sexualized

76. **What form of speech is in heaven's name?**

    (A) Analogy

    (B) Definition

    (C) Idiom

    (D) Quotation

    (E) Allegory

77. **What is the author implying in this passage?**

    (A) Sexual abuse

    (B) Adultery

    (C) Secret lovers

    (D) Pregnancy

    (E) All of the above

78. **This novel represents _____.**

    (A) Feminism

    (B) Nature

    (C) Misogyny

    (D) City life

    (E) None of the above

79. **How could community narrow the range of intimate contact?**

    (A) Arranged marriage is common

    (B) Rural areas limit physical contact

    (C) People do not associate with others outside of their class

    (D) Communities are not tightknit

    (E) Men and women attend same-sex schools

80. What era of writing is this passage?

(A) Romantic.

(B) Victorian.

(C) Modernism.

(D) Transcendentalism.

(E) Edwardian.

Question Number	Correct Answer	Your Answer	Question Number	Correct Answer	Your Answer
1	A		31	A	
2	B		32	A	
3	D		33	D	
4	E		34	C	
5	C		35	D	
6	B		36	A	
7	D		37	D	
8	A		38	A	
9	A		39	B	
10	B		40	B	
11	E		41	A	
12	B		42	C	
13	B		43	A	
14	A		44	A	
15	A		45	B	
16	D		46	C	
17	E		47	A	
18	E		48	B	
19	C		49	B	
20	C		50	D	
21	A		51	A	
22	B		52	B	
23	B		53	E	
24	E		54	C	
25	B		55	E	
26	A		56	A	
27	E		57	B	
28	C		58	E	
29	B		59	B	
30	E		60	E	

Question Number	Correct Answer	Your Answer	Question Number	Correct Answer	Your Answer
61	C		71	E	
62	A		72	E	
63	C		73	B	
64	C		74	E	
65	B		75	A	
66	C		76	C	
67	C		77	A	
68	A		78	A	
69	B		79	C	
70	C		80	C	

Sample Test Two

Sample test Two: Rationales

Passage 1

William Wordsworth

"I Wandered Lonely As A Cloud"

I wandered lonely as a cloud
That floats on high o'er vales and hills,
When all at once I saw a crowd,
A host, of golden daffodils;
Beside the lake, beneath the trees,
Fluttering and dancing in the breeze.

Continuous as the stars that shine
And twinkle on the milky way,
They stretched in never-ending line
Along the margin of a bay:
Ten thousand saw I at a glance,
Tossing their heads in sprightly dance.

The waves beside them danced; but they
Out-did the sparkling waves in glee:
A poet could not but be gay,
In such a jocund company:
I gazed—and gazed—but little thought
What wealth the show to me had brought:

For oft, when on my couch I lie
In vacant or in pensive mood,
They flash upon that inward eye
Which is the bliss of solitude;
And then my heart with pleasure fills,
And dances with the daffodils.

1. **What type of passage is the above selection?**

   (A) Lyrical poem

   (B) Haiku poem

   (C) Acrostic poem

   (D) Limerick poem

   (E) Cinquain poem

   The correct answer is A.

   A lyrical poem expresses emotion by the author and a reader can imagine it being sung. A haiku is written in 17 syllables divided into 3 lines of 5, 7, and 5 syllables. Acrostic poetry has the first, last or other letters in a line spell out a particular word or phrase. Limerick poems have a humor theme and are written with a strict rhyme scheme (such as AABBA). A cinquain is only five lines long.

2. **The permanence of stars as compared with flowers emphasizes**

   (A) the impermanence of life.

   (B) the permanence of memory for the poet.

   (C) the earlier comparison of the sky to the lake.

   (D) that stars are frozen above and daffodils dance below.

   (E) the similarity of the inward eye with the fleeting bliss of solitude.

   The correct answer is B.

   A is wrong because it talks about impermanence. E is wrong because there is no parallelism presented. C is wrong because the sky and lake were not compared in the poem. Of the remaining choices, B and D, dancing does not relate to permanence so B is the correct choice.

3. **The scheme of the poem is**

   (A) ballad.

   (B) Scottish stanza.

   (C) Spenserian stanza.

   (D) quatrain-couplet.

   (E) sonnet.

The correct answer is D.
Even if you do not recognize any of these types, look at the words. Quatrain means four and couplet is two. Each verse is four lines of two. But if you didn't work through the words, you should know that a ballad is a short story in poem form (typically with no known author). A sonnet is fourteen lines long, all as one verse. Scottish stanzas were invented by Robert Burns, and is six lines in length and rhymes aaabab, with tetrameter a lines and dimeter b lines. Lastly, a Spenserian stanza is eight line total with a specific rhyme pattern (ababbcbcc).

4. **This poem uses the _____ metric pattern.**

   (A) dactylic tetrameter

   (B) trochaic pentameter

   (C) trochaic tetrameter

   (D) iambic pentameter

   (E) iambic tetrameter

The correct answer is E.
Iambic tetrameter refers to the syllables and the number of words in the phrase. Iambic is two syllables in the 'beat' and you should be able to recognize tetra, which means four - so there are four sets of the two-beat rhythm. Using the same rationale for other answers, only D is a possible other answer, but "pent" refers to five (like pentagram) and that is not correct, which you can tell by counting the words in each line.

5. **What is a literary device used in the last two lines of the first two stanzas?**

   (A) Simile.

   (B) Metaphor.

   (C) Personification.

   (D) Allegory.

   (E) Paradox.

The correct answer is C.
Definitions are important for the test. These all should be recognizable

to you, so you would know a paradox - something that leads to illogical or contradictory purposes - is the correct answer.

6. **In what literary period did this author write?**

   (A) Edwardian Movement.

   (B) Romanticism.

   (C) Existentialism.

   (D) Renaissance Literature.

   (E) Victorian Movement.

   The correct answer is B.
   Wordsworth wrote in the Romantic movement, which in Britain was from the eighteenth century to around 1870. The other movements listed were: Edwardian (with King Edward right after Queen Victoria, 1901-1910 or a little after), Existentialism (beginning in the 19th century, topic specific), Renaissance (right after the Dark Ages fourteenth to sixteenth century), Victorian (with Queen Victoria, 1830-1900).

7. **As used in this poem, the best choice for a synonym of jocund means**

   (A) pleasant.

   (B) vapid.

   (C) lonely.

   (D) jovial.

   (E) sad.

   The correct answer is D.
   Knowing the definition of words is important for this test. Reading more helps you improve your vocabulary. If you don't know jocund, you should know the other four words and by deduction, jovial is a synonym of jocund.

8. **What literary device is used in Line 9, "They stretched in never-ending line."**

(A) hyperbole.

(B) onomatopoeia.

(C) epithet.

(D) irony.

(E) anecdote.

The correct answer is A.

Again, you need to know literary terms for the test - and we provide many of them in this book for you. Review them and know them. A hyperbole is an exaggerated statement, and applies to the statement.

Passage 2

"I went to work the next day, turning, so to speak, my back on that station. In that way only it seemed to me I could keep my hold on the redeeming facts of life. Still, one must look about sometimes; and then I saw this station, these men strolling aimlessly about in the sunshine of the yard. I asked myself sometimes what it all meant. They wandered here and there with their absurd long staves in their hands, like a lot of faithless pilgrims bewitched inside a rotten fence. The word 'ivory' rang in the air, was whispered, was sighed. You would think they were praying to it. A taint of imbecile rapacity blew through it all, like a whiff from some corpse. By Jove! I've never seen anything so unreal in my life. And outside, the silent wilderness surrounding this cleared speck on the earth struck me as something great and invincible, like evil or truth, waiting patiently for the passing away of this fantastic invasion.
– *Heart of Darkness*

9. **Who wrote this novel?**

(A) Joseph Conrad

(B) James Joyce

(C) Jane Austen

(D) Charlotte Brontë

(E) Charles Dickens

The correct answer is A.

This is another question where you may have to eliminate answers to help you pick the right one. Charles Dickens and Charlotte Bronte could be eliminated as can Jane Austen - they do not write novels in this syntax and manner. Of the two remaining, James Joyce was an Irish poet and novelist, most famous for writing Ulysses and short stories if not poems. Joseph Conrad was a Polish author, writing in English, and this is one of his most famous works.

10. **What does the following line represent?**

"I saw this station, these men strolling aimlessly about in the sunshine of the yard."

(A) Soldiers enjoying their day

(B) Men being unaware of the negativity that surrounds them

(C) Positivity is infectious

(D) The station is a happy place

(E) Embracing the weather before a storm hits

The correct answer is B.

You should eliminate the obvious wrong answers, such as A (when the College Board asks questions, there is more meaning than this option is portraying) and C (as there is no lead in the sentence that brings you to this conclusion). Of the three remaining choices, D and E could be true, but the key phrase "strolling aimlessly" makes you believe that there is more meaning than just being in the sunshine.

11. **What does the word staves mean?**

(A) Machete

(B) Axe

(C) Gun

(D) Bomb

(E) Wooden club

The correct answer is E.

Using the context of the passage if you don't know the definition of

Sample Test Two

the word, the clues there are "long" and in their hands. That reduces the likelihood that either gun or bomb are appropriate choices. There is no indication that there are machetes or axes involved, but this is a question where better vocabulary increases the likelihood that you know the right synonym.

12. What does the ivory represent?

(A) Death

(B) Prosperity

(C) Jewelry

(D) Trade

(E) None of the above

The correct answer is B.

If an person possessed ivory, it was very expensive and represented wealth, which is another word for prosperity. There are no clues that would lead the other three options are appropriate in the passage. Hint: the College Board very rarely uses "none of these" or "all of these" as appropriate choices.

13. What literary device is used when describing the ivory?

(A) Alliteration

(B) Allegory

(C) Simile

(D) Personification

(E) Repetition

The correct answer is B.

From the list, you should be able to easily eliminate C, D and E. Between the first two, you need to know the definitions presented earlier, but if you forget, you should at least be able to make a 50-50 guess.

14. What does rapacity represent?

(A) Greed

(B) Rapid movement

(C) Intelligent

(D) Affluent

(E) Generous

The correct answer is A.

From the context of the passage (a taint that blew through), you should be able to eliminate C, D, and E. There is nothing else in the passage that implies rapid movement, so if you don't know what the word means, you should still be able to eliminate the wrong choices.

15. What literary device is used in this passage?

"And outside, the silent wilderness surrounding this cleared speck on the earth struck me as something great and invincible, like evil or truth, waiting patiently for the passing away of this fantastic invasion."

(A) Simile

(B) Metaphor

(C) Illusion

(D) Personification

(E) Onomatopoeia

The correct answer is A,

as simile means a figure of speech comparing two things, making a vivid description. You should know the other definitions - if you got this wrong, look up the other terms to refresh your memory.

16. Which style of writing is represented in this novel?

(A) Biographical

(B) Autobiographical

(C) Expository

(D) Persuasive

(E) None of the above

The correct answer is D.

You should know from middle school that biography is when you write about an actual person's life and the autobiography is when a person writes about his or her own life - so eliminate these. If you are unsure of the definition of persuasive, and don't remember that expository means "to explain something", you may have needed to guess between the two.

Passage 3

"Finished, it's finished, nearly finished, it must be nearly finished. Grain upon grain, one by one, and one day, suddenly, there's a heap, a little heap, the impossible heap. I can't be punished any more. I'll go now to my kitchen, ten feet by ten feet by ten feet, and wait for him to whistle me. Nice dimensions, nice proportions, I'll lean on the table, and look at the wall, and wait for him to whistle me."

– *Endgame*

17. Who wrote this play?

(A) Anton Chekov

(B) William Shakespeare

(C) Lillian Hellman

(D) Athol Fugard

(E) Samuel Beckett

The correct answer is E.

You should be able to eliminate A, B and C as options as soon as you read them. This story, Endgame, is one of the more famous books by Beckett; Athol Fugard is a South African writer mostly working on plays and or films.

Sample Test Two

18. What literary device is used throughout this passage?

(A) Simile

(B) Metaphor

(C) Euphemism

(D) Flashback

(E) Repetition

The correct answer is E.
Knowing the definitions would rule out A, B and C. But seeing the word finished many times should tip you to the correct answer.

19. What does the impossible heap represent?

(A) Life's greatest hurdles

(B) A pile of grain so tall it cannot be moved

(C) Death

(D) A mountain

(E) Heaven

The correct answer is C.
Both B and D would be a more literal meaning that wasn't present in context of the passage, so they should be eliminated. If it was asking about the whole series, then A would be accurate. The correct answer is C, the action not the destination (represented by Heaven in E).

20. The whistle symbolizes _____.

(A) A referee

(B) The character's father

(C) Death

(D) An angel

(E) All of the above

The correct answer is C.
The whistle would be a literal representation of a device used by a

referee but we have to consider context. That also eliminates B and C as the passage talks about the characters approach to death.

21. What is an endgame?

(A) The final play in a game, such as chess

(B) The end of a negotiation

(C) A wish

(D) The final approval for a lease

(E) None of the above

The correct answer is A.

The end of a negotiation is an end result, not endgame (which is the final or last move). C and D are also not appropriate answers and as previously explained, the "none of the above" answer is rarely right, if you are having to guess for a correct answer.

22. What is the author trying to portray in this selection?

(A) An old man

(B) A prisoner

(C) A farmer

(D) A mill worker

(E) A plantation

The correct answer is B.

E is not correct as that is a place and the description is for a person. Of the four remaining, and using other questions (such as the definition of an endgame), and knowing that death is coming for the person, the best answer is B.

23. What best describes this selection?

(A) Epic

(B) Foreshadowing

(C) Cliffhanger

(D) Flashback

(E) Irony

The correct answer is B.

From the selection, irony is not present, nor is a flashback or cliffhanger (a suspense scene). Of the two remaining selections, you should know what they both are - an epic is a story about a hero, and there are no indications that is who is being describe or is present in the passage.

Passage 4

A Bird Came Down the Walk – Emily Dickinson

IN THE GARDEN

A bird came down the walk:
He did not know I saw;
He bit an angle-worm in halves
And ate the fellow, raw.

And then, he drank a dew
From a convenient grass,
And then hopped sidewise to the wall
To let a beetle pass.

He glanced with rapid eyes
That hurried all abroad,—
They looked like frightened beads, I thought;
He stirred his velvet head

Like one in danger; cautious,
I offered him a crumb,
And he unrolled his feathers
And rowed him softer home

Than oars divide the ocean,
Too silver for a seam,
Or butterflies, off banks of noon,
Leap, plashless, as they swim.

24. **What type of literary device is used in the author's phrase, "drank a dew"?**

(A) Allusion.

(B) Foreshadowing.

(C) Juxtaposition.

(D) Satire.

(E) Alliteration.

The correct answer is E.
B is obviously incorrect, as is juxtaposition (C). A satire is a holistic picture, not a description of a phrase. Between A and E, an allusion describes something without explicitly stating it - and drinking is mentioned in the phrase, leaving E as the right answer if you didn't know alliteration was repeating the first letter to achieve an effect.

25. **The author describes action beginning in line 15 of the bird's flight. What type of literary device is used?**

(A) Simile.

(B) Metaphor.

(C) Irony.

(D) Satire.

(E) None of these are correct.

The correct answer is B.
All four words presented should be known for the test, so you should be able to pick the right answer.

26. The scheme of the poem (except the final three stanzas) is

(A) XAXA or Ghazal.

(B) Scottish stanza.

(C) Spenserian stanza.

(D) quatrain-couplet.

(E) Petrarchan sonnet.

The correct answer is A.

Definitions of B, C, and D were given earlier in the rationale. But if you didn't remember, the pattern of XAXA can be used with the poem (except the last three lines), so you should be able to easily pick the right answer.

27. This poem uses a particular metric pattern throughout the poem, except in the third line of each stanza. What is the main metric pattern?

(A) dactylic tetrameter

(B) trochaic trimeter

(C) trochaic tetrameter

(D) iambic pentameter

(E) iambic trimeter

The correct answer is E.

This tests your knowledge of poetic descriptions - these are things you can memorize. But there is a way to look at the five options and get a hint. Tetra is four; pent is five; tri is three. Knowing from looking at the poem and the pattern, B or E is correct. Iambic is two syllables; trochaic is four syllables and more rare than iambic verse. use these clues to guess if you don't remember the words.

28. **What literary device is used when the bird's eyes are compared to frightened beads?**

(A) Reverse Personification.

(B) Metaphor.

(C) Simile.

(D) Allegory.

(E) Paradox.

The correct answer is C.

These terms should be memorized so this should have been an easy guess, with the vivid description of the eyes making them more interesting.

29. **What does the dash at the end of line 12 represent?**

(A) A change in focus from the bird to the water.

(B) An abrupt change for the bird.

(C) An emotional shift from fear to fascination.

(D) It only shows the middle of the poem.

(E) None of these accurately describe the meaning of the dash.

The correct answer is B.

The poem is about the bird, so A is incorrect. C gives a reverse description from fear to fascination, so it is incorrect. D says it could be the middle of the poem, but it's not, sot hat's not right, either. If you are guessing, the best guess is B.

30. **What is the author's tone in this poem?**

(A) She takes the perspective of the bird.

(B) The author's tone is harsh toward potential prey.

(C) The tone is factual, describing the actions of a bird.

(D) Ornithology fascinated the author and she uses flowery language to describe it.

(E) The author's tone is gentle and respectful demeanor regarding nature.

The correct answer is E

The author wrote in the American Romantic movement, and answer E is a hallmark of that time period.

31. What is a potential meaning of the allegory used by the author?

(A) It could reveal the author's perceptions of God.

(B) The allegory could be looking at the author's view of marriage.

(C) The author could reveal the hierarchy between man and beast.

(D) Descriptions of the forces of nature could parallel emotions.

(E) There is no allegory used as a literary device in this poem.

The correct answer is A.

C is not correct because there isn't a hierarchy depicted; likewise, the forces of nature in this passage are not parallel so D is not correct. E is rarely The correct answer, with no allegory in the passage. Of the two remaining, it would be a stretch to review this as a perception of marriage; plus, the romantic movement reveals bonds with nature and thoughts of God, which would help lead to the right answer.

Passage 5

These are morning matters, pictures you dream as the final wave heaves you up on the sand in the bright light and drying air. You remember pressure, and a curved sleep you rested against, soft, like a scallop in its shell. But the air hardens your skin; you stand; you leave the lighted shore to explore some dim headland, and soon you're lost in the leafy interior, intent, remembering nothing.

I still think of that old tomcat, mornings, when I wake. Things are tamer now; I sleep with the window shut. The cats and our rites are gone and my life is changed, but the memory remains of something powerful playing over me. I wake expectant, hoping to see a new thing. If I'm lucky I might be jogged awake by a strange bird call. I dress in a hurry, imagining the yard flapping with auks, or flamingos. This morning it was a wood duck, down at the creek. It flew away.

32. The tone of the selection is:

(A) reflective.

(B) indulgent.

(C) indifferent.

(D) dishonest.

(E) ironic.

The correct answer is A.

The correct answer should be based on your vocabulary.

33. The author uses _____ to describe the setting.

(A) personification

(B) ambivalence

(C) satire

(D) allusion

(E) clichés

The correct answer is D.

These literary terms need to be recognizable by you for you to do well on the exam, so make sure you learn them.

34. The phrase, "like a scallop in its shell" is an example of:

(A) an irony

(B) a smilie.

(C) a metaphor.

(D) personification.

(E) euphemism.

The correct answer is C.

The phrase uses "like", which is a tip-off for metaphors. You need to know all of these definitions to score as high as possible on the exam.

35. The literary style is:

(A) Expository

(B) Didactic

(C) Persuasive

(D) Descriptive

(E) Theatrical

The correct answer is D.

These different writing styles should be apparent to you.

36. The author describes many of her feelings and situations by focusing the conversation on animals. Based on the information in the passage, one reason could be:

(A) animals are comforting, and relax the reader.

(B) birds are flighty and the center of her story.

(C) the setting of this story is a farm.

(D) the lead character doesn't have many human friends.

(E) it is the backstory of how animals and nature are always present in the character's life.

The correct answer is A.

The description of the author relaxing is translated to the reader as she describes the tomcat's moves. B is incorrect as a bird and descriptions of it is not the center of the passage. C and D would be making assumptions and are incorrect. E may also seem correct because it gives some backstory, but makes a huge leap that they are always present from this short passage in the novel, so it is not correct.

37. How is this passage narrated?

(A) First person.

(B) Second person.

(C) Third person.

(D) Omniscient observer.

(E) None of these.

The correct answer is D.

You need to know these types of narrations to do well on the test.

38. **The phrase "the air hardens your skin" within the context of the passage most likely refers to what?**

    (A) The morning air woke the character up from dreaming.

    (B) The scallop shell bed the character sleeps in has opened.

    (C) The air dries out the character's skin.

    (D) The coldness of the room turns off the brain of the character.

    (E) The air turns the character's skin cold when the cat leaves the bed.

    The correct answer is A

    Option B is not mentioned at all. C is too literal and uses none of the imagery from the passage. D takes it a step further than the author's description of her skin and there is no support for this. E may be right, but the phrase makes no reference to the cat.

39. **What is the significance of the author using cats and birds in the passage?**

    (A) The author has always had cats while growing up.

    (B) She creates allusions to changes in which animals are predators and prey.

    (C) There are more birds, or opportunities, available today.

    (D) Cats are lower to the ground and she wants to be a bird in the sky.

    (E) There is no significance in the choice of her animals.

    The correct answer is B.

    There is no information to support A or E. C and D take animals from the passage and make incongruent assumptions.

Sample Test Two

Passage 6

Jason threw into the fire. It hissed, uncurled, turning black. Then it was gray. Then it was gone. Caddy and Father and Jason were in Mother's chair. Jason's eyes were puffed shut and his mouth moved, like tasting. Caddy's head was on Father's shoulder. Her hair was like fire, and little points of fire were in her eyes, and I went and Father lifted me into the chair too, and Caddy held me. She smelled like trees.

She smelled like trees. In the corner it was dark, but I could see the window. I squatted there, holding the slipper. I couldn't see it, but my hands saw it, and I could hear it getting night, and my hands saw the slipper but I couldn't see myself, but my hands could see the slipper, and I squatted there, hearing it getting dark.

Here you is, Luster said. Look what I got. He showed it to me. You know where I got it. Miss Quentin give it to me. I knowed they couldn't keep me out. What you doing, off in here. I thought you done slipped back out doors. Aint you done enough moaning and slobbering today, without hiding off in this here empty room, mumbling and taking on. Come on here to bed, so I can get up there before it starts. I cant fool with you all night tonight. Just let them horns toot the first toot and I done gone.

40. The subject in this passage is:

    (A) is female.

    (B) a supporting character.

    (C) has an attitude of a criminal.

    (D) a character, and seems to be the lead of the story.

    (E) is well-educated.

The correct answer is B.
You cannot determine the gender of the character. The attitude of the character described shows no criminal intent, nor is there overwhelming evidence to show that the character is well-educated. Between B and C, you need to understand the context of the passage to pick the right answer.

41. What kind of description is the author providing of this scene?

(A) Backstory of the environment of one of the characters.

(B) A narrative in the first person.

(C) Information about a dream she had.

(D) An unreliable narrative about a character.

(E) The author is using a persuasive argument.

The correct answer is A.

as it provides backstory of a character. There is no evidence that any of the other options would be correct.

42. What are types of narration style is used in this passage?

(A) Defamiliarization.

(B) Audience surrogate, trying to convey the audience's confusion.

(C) A stream of consciousness of one character's opinion of another's situation.

(D) Unreliable narrator.

(E) Hamartia style.

The correct answer is C.

There is no attempt in the passage to confuse readers (A and B are similar answers in this respect) and there is no context to show the narrator is unreliable. If you don't know Hamartia, describing a fatal flaw, you can't eliminate this option, but you should be able to follow the passage that is like a stream of the character's thoughts.

43. One of the themes of the book is:

(A) changes in family values away from chastity and sin strain families.

(B) that people are all the same, rich or poor.

(C) rivers of emotion run deep.

(D) religion can hold a family together.

(E) obstacles can be overcome with hard work.

Sample Test Two

The correct answer is A

as the description shows changes away from family values. It may be true that B, C, and E are true, but remember you need to use clues from the book to pick the right answer.

44. **The phrase, "Her hair was like fire," is what kind of literary device?**

    (A) Simile.

    (B) Metaphor.

    (C) Reverse Personification.

    (D) Allusion.

    (E) Denotation.

    The correct answer is A.

    You need to know these definitions, and that describing an object like another is a simile.

45. **The phrase, "little points of fire were in her eyes," is what kind of literary device?**

    (A) Simile.

    (B) Metaphor.

    (C) Reverse Personification.

    (D) Allusion.

    (E) Denotation.

    The correct answer is B.

    Again, knowing the definitions will show you that metaphor is the correct choice as the eyes are being described like something for rhetorical effect using a common characteristic.

46. By using incorrect speech patterns, the author achieves what?

(A) An optimistic tone for the passage.

(B) Changing of the time in history for this character.

(C) An indicator of internal thoughts, not "scrubbed" for other's hearing.

(D) A and D.

(E) None of these.

The correct answer is C.

As this is a stream of consciousness, that also contributes to you picking the right answer on this one. Speech patterns wouldn't reflect time changes, and there is no overly optimistic tone of the passage.

47. By repeating the phrase "She smelled like trees,", the author

(A) uses anaphora.

(B) uses pleonasm.

(C) changes pace through repetition.

(D) uses consonance.

(E) uses the lacan technique.

The correct answer is A.

You can eliminate C as it uses reputation but not to change pace. Consonance is not appropriate here, the agreement between actions. Lecan deals with psychoanalysis, and doesn't apply here, either. Between A and B, B is incorrect as it uses too many words to convey meaning.

Passage 7

"If people bring so much courage to this world the world has to kill them to break them, so of course it kills them. The world breaks every one and afterward many are strong at the broken places. But those that will not break it kills. It kills the very good and the very gentle and the very brave impartially. If you are none of these you can be sure it will kill you too but there will be no special hurry."

— A Farewell to Arms

48. Who wrote this novel?

(A) Henry David Thoreau

(B) Ernest Hemingway

(C) F. Scott Fitzgerald

(D) Harper Lee

(E) J.R.R. Tolkien

The correct answer is B,
one of his most famous novels.

49. What is the theme of this novel?

(A) Innocence

(B) War

(C) Love

(D) Death

(E) Grief

The correct answer is B.
This is one of the books you should know; but the title also gives clues to the meaning. There are some authors, like those in question 48's options, that you should be able to recognize a few of the more famous works.

50. What does the title symbolize?

(A) An amputation caused during war

(B) Being discharged

(C) Saying goodbye to the arms of someone you love

(D) Saying goodbye to weaponry and warfare

(E) C & D

The correct answer is D.
Rarely in multiple choice questions like this are there two correct answers. If you recognize the title of the book and general theme, this will be easier to answer.

51. Which literary device is used to describe war?

(A) Personification

(B) Alliteration

(C) Simile

(D) Metaphor

(E) Idiom

The correct answer is A.

You should know all of these terms and be able to answer questions like this quickly and correctly. Review any terms that are unfamiliar.

52. Which of the following best represents this passage?

(A) Sarcasm

(B) Resentment

(C) Irony

(D) Sympathy

(E) Affectionate

The correct answer is B.

This is reading comprehension and interpreting the correct tone from the author's work.

53. What best describes the author's intention in the following line?

"It kills the very good and the very gentle and the very brave impartially."

(A) Everyone will die sooner or later

(B) Murderers target nice people

(C) The good, gentle and brave are easier to kill

(D) The good, gentle and brave die protecting others

(E) War kills everyone, it doesn't have a bias

The correct answer is E.

The key word is impartially, meaning without bias. E is the only possible answer.

54. How does the world break people?

(A) It creates challenging times

(B) It represents being shot and not dying

(C) It causes extreme wounds, mentally and physically

(D) People can have broken bones

(E) Physical objects and precious belongings can be broken

The correct answer is C.

This is not a physical action of breaking only, as there are other ways people are broken described in the passage; therefore, answers with only physical or only mental are not correct, leaving C as the only option.

55. Which literary period is this from?

(A) Romanticism

(B) Renaissance

(C) The Enlightenment

(D) Existentialism

(E) Modernism

The correct answer is E.

Knowing the dates of when movements happened will help you identify authors or movements, which appear frequently in the exams.

Passage 8
(Poetry, American, 19th century)

There is no frigate like a book
To take us lands away,
Nor any coursers like a page
Of prancing poetry;
This traverse may the poorest take
Without oppress of toll;
How frugal is the chariot
That bears the human soul!
– *Emily Dickinson (1830-1886)*

56. Authors use particular literary structures for descriptions. What best explains the type that Emily Dickinson employs in this poem?

(A) Connotative

(B) Argumentative

(C) Narrative

(D) Rhetoric

(E) Expository

The correct answer is A.

You need to know the definitions of literary terms.

57. How many types of transport does the author incorporate?

(A) Two

(B) Three

(C) Four

(D) Five

(E) None

The correct answer is B.

You can see the next question to identify the three options.

58. If the words 'frigate, coursers, and chariot' were replaced with synonyms, what would the best choice of the following options include?

(A) Train, car, carriage

(B) Train, horse, carriage

(C) Ship, car, carriage

(D) Ship, car, train

(E) Ship, horse, carriage

The correct answer is E.

Defining frigate (ship), coursers (horses) and chariots (similar to a carriage drawn by a horse), the best choice is E.

59. **Which of the following descriptions more closely describes the author's intended meaning of poem?**

(A) Difficulties at work

(B) The importance of books

(C) Confessions for the soul

(D) Poverty makes things difficult

(E) Describing modes of transportation

The correct answer is B.

The main idea of the poem is stated in the first line.

60. **There are very descriptive and strong feelings conveyed by the poet. Which of the following is not the definition of what she shares?**

(A) Overstatement

(B) Paradox

(C) Understatement

(D) Irony

(E) Sarcasm

The correct answer is E.

The other four selections are used at various times in the poem and you must read carefully as the question asks for the one that isn't used.

61. **What kind of poetry form is utilized by Ms. Dickinson in this poem?**

(A) Alexandrine

(B) Didactic poetry

(C) Ballad stanza

(D) Epitaph

(E) Rondel

The correct answer is C.

You should be able to eliminate B, D, and E immediately. Alexandrine is a French style that has twelve syllables. If you didn't know that, and you probably won't, a ballad stanza is four line verses - and that should be enough to get it right.

62. Who is the author of this poem?

(A) Emily Dickinson

(B) Emily Bronte

(C) Emily Mortimer

(D) Lord Byron

(E) William Blake

The correct answer is A.

Sometimes they give you The correct answer in another question or in the passage - it checks to see if you are actually reading!

63. When the boat is compared to a book, that is an example of:

(A) a metaphor.

(B) personification.

(C) a simile.

(D) an extended metaphor.

(E) none of these.

The correct answer is C.

You should know the definitions of these literary terms.

Passage 9

Okonkwo and his fellow prisoners were set free as soon as the fine was paid. The District Commissioner spoke to them again about the great queen, and about peace and good government. But the men did not listen. They just sat and looked at him and at his interpreter. In the end they were given back their bags and sheathed machetes and told to go home. They rose and left the courthouse. They neither spoke to anyone nor among themselves.

The courthouse, like the church, was but a little way outside the village. The footpath that linked them was a very busy one because it also led to the stream, beyond the court. It was open and sandy. Footpaths were open and sandy in the dry season. But when the rains came the bush grew thick on either side and closed in on the path. It was now dry season.

As they made their way to the village the six men met women and children going to the stream with their waterpots. But them wore such heavy and fearsome looks to them, but edged out of the way to let them pass. In the village little groups of men joined them until they became a sizable company. They walked silently. As each of the six men got to his compound, he turned in, taking some of the crowd with him. The village was air in a silent, suppressed way.

Ezinma had prepared some food for her father as soon as news spread that the six men would be released. She took it to him in his obi. He ate absent-mindedly. He had no appetite, he only ate to please her. His male relations and friends had gathered in his obi, and Obierika was urging him to eat. Nobody else spoke, but they noticed the log stripes on Okonkwo's back where the warder's whip had cut into his flesh.

64. Who is the protagonist of this story?

(A) Obierika

(B) Ezinma

(C) Okonkwo

(D) The District Commissioner

(E) Okonkwo's wife

The correct answer is C.
You need to know literary terms - such as protagonist. It is the lead character and you need to pick out the name from the story.

65. What is the name of this book?

(A) *Obi*

(B) *Things Fall Apart*

(C) *Let the Circle Be Unbroken*

(D) *Ashes and Dust*

(E) *The Rainy Season*

The correct answer is B.

This is one of the most frequently cited world literature pieces, and should be recognizable to you.

66. What category of literature does this book represent?

(A) Romantic.

(B) Victorian.

(C) Modernism.

(D) Transcendentalism.

(E) Post Colonial.

The correct answer is C.

You need to know the literary periods. While modernism may not seem the best choice, this is the first novel of modern African literature.

67. The main character of the book appears to have what occur throughout the book?

(A) He is a champion of his village.

(B) He shows that he is good provider for his family.

(C) He represents the disintegration of his society against the change.

(D) The village doesn't support him.

(E) The courthouse is targeting him to get rid of the village.

The correct answer is C.

In this passage and the book, it's bigger than the village or his family, which is why the book has been on reading lists for many years.

Sample Test Two

68. The narrative structure of this passage is:

(A) simple narrative.

(B) cause and effect.

(C) chronological.

(D) inductive.

(E) deductive.

The correct answer is A.

You need to be familiar with these literary terms.

69. The literary style of the book is:

(A) comedy.

(B) tragedy.

(C) drama.

(D) exploration.

(E) quest.

The correct answer is B.

You need to be familiar with these literary terms.

70. How is this passage narrated?

(A) First person.

(B) Second person.

(C) Third person.

(D) Omniscient observer.

(E) None of these.

The correct answer is C.

You need to be familiar with these narration options.

71. What is the main idea of this passage?

(A) The village members continue to carry out the traditions of their ancestors.

(B) There is a drought affecting crops and village life.

(C) The interpreter was sharing with them a new way of life.

(D) The government and church were coming together for the people.

(E) People are resistant to change, and the village and protagonist illustrate it.

The correct answer is E.

Using a word from an earlier question, protagonist, you should be able to check the passage and see this is the best answer.

Passage 10

"Where, in Heaven's name, could anyone even be alone in Calcutta? What hanky-panky business, in my mother's words, could go on? Everyone knew the rules and the rules stated caste and community narrowed the range of intimate contact."

– *Desirable Daughters by Bharati Mukherjee*

72. Where is Calcutta?

(A) Indonesia

(B) China

(C) New Zealand

(D) Jamaica

(E) India

The correct answer is E.

While it is a geography question, it is important for the understanding of the book.

Sample Test Two

73. Why is it abnormal for someone to be alone in Calcutta?

(A) Everyone travels with their spouses

(B) It's a very busy city

(C) The city is very dangerous

(D) It's sarcastic because it's such a rural place

(E) None of the above

The correct answer is B.

When the author asks how could anyone be alone there, it implies that it is a very busy place. You need to decipher implied information in these passages.

74. What is hanky-panky business?

(A) Dancing

(B) Illegal trade

(C) Corruption

(D) A romantic kiss

(E) Sexual activity

The correct answer is E.

You have likely heard this before, but when the character discusses this, you should be able to infer the meaning.

75. What does the word caste mean?

(A) Division of the classes

(B) Enclosed

(C) Oppression

(D) Sin

(E) Sexualized

The correct answer is A.

You likely have heard this discussed before, as a mechanism for dividing communities on income and race or ethnicity.

76. What form of speech is in heaven's name?

(A) Analogy

(B) Definition

(C) Idiom

(D) Quotation

(E) Allegory

The correct answer is C.

You need to be familiar with literary terms.

77. What is the author implying in this passage?

(A) Sexual abuse

(B) Adultery

(C) Secret lovers

(D) Pregnancy

(E) All of the above

The correct answer is A.

By referencing the hanky-panky business and difficulty in having any time alone, you need to infer this is the best answer.

78. This novel represents _____.

(A) Feminism

(B) Nature

(C) Misogyny

(D) City life

(E) None of the above

The correct answer is A.

You should be able to eliminate B and C as options. Also, E is rarely used as a correct answer when "none of the above" appears. Between A and D, since the passage doesn't describe only busy scenes or what you see in the city, the correct option is A.

Sample Test Two

79. How could community narrow the range of intimate contact?

(A) Arranged marriage is common

(B) Rural areas limit physical contact

(C) People do not associate with others outside of their class

(D) Communities are not tightknit

(E) Men and women attend same-sex schools

The correct answer is C.

This is part of the inherent definition in Caste. It's more than physical contact of B. While A is true and D is false, you cannot also make the conclusion listed in E.

80. What era of writing is this passage?

(A) Romantic.

(B) Victorian.

(C) Modernism.

(D) Transcendentalism.

(E) Edwardian.

The correct answer is C.

You need to be aware of the dates and some examples of the literary movements for the exam. Also, world literature is more often either very recent (such as this and Things Fall Apart) or ancient (such as The Iliad or other ancient texts)

Sample Test Three

Instructions _____

This exam gives passages from known writings (fiction, poems, non-fiction/history, biographies, drama and more) over the past five hundred years. While the student taking the exam is not expected to have read the material or have familiarity with the passage prior to the exam, the test taker is expected to have the knowledge of an undergraduate English and writing class.

TIP: As the writing changes and the time periods change, it's important for a student to note the author and time period as that may assist in answering questions by either eliminating unlikely answers or allow the student to recall items about the author.

At the end of the test passages and answers, there is an answer key and a "rationale" key for each question. Take the test without referencing these guides. For questions that you guess The correct answers or get wrong, the rationale is provided to help you see how test makers frame answers to questions or explain pieces of information with which you are unfamiliar.

There are 80 questions on this particular sample test, and the CLEP also uses around 80 for the credit exam. As with the CLEP exam, the passages are taken primarily from American and British Literature - though at least once question, just as in the actual exam, is taken from another area of literature. Within the questions of the CLEP, the mixture of genre types falls typically almost 80-90% between poetry and prose (both fiction and non-fiction within the prose selections) and the remaining on drama. The entire test is balanced between three main eras – Renaissance/17th Century, 18th/19th Century, as well as 10th/21st Century; in the past, there is a slightly heavier emphasis on 18th/19th work, and usually there is one passage from the Classical/pre-Renaissance period.

The CLEP allows 98 minutes to take the exam of approximately 80 questions. Time yourself during the exam, but as you practice, focus more attention on accurately answering questions as the total number of correct answers impacts your score, not how many you skip or get wrong. If you skip any questions, make sure that you also skip that line on The correct answer sheet - or you may spend a lot of time erasing and redoing your answer key.

These passages do not actually appear on the CLEP exam, but are meant to show how the exam is written and the various range of questions, answers, and key knowledge points required in order to pass the CLEP exam. Read each question carefully and provide the best answer choice. Good luck.

Passage 1

On the domestic front, life was not easy. England was not a wealthy country and its people endured relatively poor living standards. The landed classes – many of them enriched by the confiscated wealth of former monasteries – were determined in the interests of profile to convert their arable land into pasture for sheep, so as to produce the wool that supported the country's chief economic asset, the woolen cloth trade. But the enclosing of the land only added to the misery of the poor, many of whom, evicted and displaced, left their decaying villages and gravitated to the towns where they joined the growing army of beggars and vagabonds that would become such a feature of Elizabethan life. Once, the religious houses would have dispensed charity to the destitute, but Henry VIII had dissolved them all in the 1530s, and many former monks and nuns were now themselves beggars. Nor did the civic authorities help: they passed laws in an attempt to ban the poor from towns and cities, but to little avail. It was a common sight to see men and women lying in the dusty streets, often dying in the dirt like dogs or beasts, without human compassion being shown to them. 'Certainly, wrote a Spanish observer in 1558, 'the state of England lay now most afflicted.' And although people looked to the new Queen Elizabeth to put matters right, there were so many who doubted if she could overcome the seemingly insurmountable problems she faced, or even remain queen long enough to begin tacking them. Some, both at home and abroad, were the opinion that her title to the throne rested on very precarious foundations. Many regarded the daughter of Henry VIII and Anne Boleyn as a bastard from the time of her birth on 7 September 1533, although, ignoring such slurs on the validity of his second marriage, Henry had declared Elizabeth his heir.

1. **Why was land confiscated from the poor?**

    (A) The town wanted to build a new monastery.

    (B) To create pastures for sheep, ultimately increasing the export of wool.

    (C) The town wanted to create housing for monks and nuns.

    (D) Queen Elizabeth wanted to expand her property.

    (E) The poor did not pay their taxes.

2. **A vagabond is a _____.**

    (A) Wanderer

    (B) Prisoner

    (C) Poor person

    (D) Rich person

    (E) Fighter

3. **Why didn't the poor have shelter with the churches?**

    (A) They were already filled with beggars.

    (B) Religious houses have never offered shelter to the poor.

    (C) They were also being used to raise sheep.

    (D) Henry VIII had dissolved them all in the 1530s.

    (E) Queen Elizabeth dissolved them all in the 1530s.

4. **How were civic authorities unsuccessful?**

    (A) Poor people remained within city limits

    (B) Public service funds ran out

    (C) Public housing plans extended deadlines

    (D) Churches did not open their doors to the poor

    (E) The poor overthrew them to gain their land back

Sample Test Three

5. **What is a synonym for precarious?**

(A) Strong

(B) Careful

(C) Risky

(D) Determined

(E) Illegitimate

6. **What is the author's view towards Queen Elizabeth?**

(A) Doubtful

(B) Vengeful

(C) Resentful

(D) Supportive

(E) Confident

7. **How is the English culture portrayed in this passage?**

(A) Religious

(B) Elitist

(C) Racist

(D) Diverse

(E) Spiritual

8. **What is Elizabeth's relationship to Henry?**

(A) Wife

(B) Cousin

(C) Lover

(D) Daughter

(E) Niece

Passage 2

"Mother," said little Pearl, "the sunshine does not love you. It runs away and hides itself, because it is afraid of something on your bosom. . . . It will not flee from me, for I wear nothing on my bosom yet!"

"Nor ever will, my child, I hope," said Hester.

"And why not, mother?" asked Pearl, stopping short....

"Will it not come of its own accord, when I am a woman grown?"

– *The Scarlett Letter*

9. **Who is the author of this book?**

   (A) William Faulkner

   (B) Nathaniel Hawthorne

   (C) William Blake

   (D) William Shakespeare

   (E) Frederick Douglass

10. **What is the relationship between these two characters?**

    (A) Mother and daughter

    (B) Sisters

    (C) Aunt and niece

    (D) Cousins

    (E) Grandmother and grandchild

11. **What kind of description is the author providing of this scene?**

    (A) A symbolic, metaphorical description that provides a backstory of the main character

    (B) A characterization of what the character is like

    (C) A narrative, with the end of the selection giving thoughts in the first person

    (D) The unreliable narrative about a character

    (E) The author is using a persuasive argument

Sample Test Three

12. What does the "sunshine" represent?

(A) Light

(B) Hope

(C) Purity

(D) Heaven

(E) Good luck

13. Why doesn't Pearl have anything on her bosom?

(A) Only one person in the village wears the symbol at a time.

(B) The symbol is used to signify divorce, and Pearl is not yet married.

(C) It represents pregnancy and she is too young to be pregnant.

(D) She will inherit the symbol to wear when her mother dies.

(E) It's a symbol of womanhood, and Pearl is still considered a child.

14. The author portrays the attitude of the character Pearl as:

(A) condescending

(B) loving

(C) disrespectful

(D) innocent

(E) resentful

15. What is the author implying that Pearl is asking for?

"Will it not come of its own accord, when I am a woman grown?"

(A) If the scarlet letter will be handed down to her when she becomes a woman.

(B) If she will become pregnant when she becomes mature enough.

(C) Whether or not she will get divorced when she marries.

(D) If she will find true love when she grows up.

(E) If her mother will share this symbol with her when she is old enough.

16. Which of the following best describes the author's message?

(A) Little girls are oblivious to the world around them.

(B) Daughters always question things that their mothers do.

(C) Growing up means losing your innocence.

(D) The world will know when you have sinned.

(E) None of the above.

Passage 3

Death, be not Proud
Death, be not proud, though some have called thee
Mighty and dreadful, for thou art not so;
For those whom thou think'st thou dost overthrow
Die not, poor Death, nor yet canst thou kill me.
From rest and sleep, which but thy pictures be,
Much pleasure; then from thee much more must flow,
And soonest our best men with thee do go,
Rest of their bones, and soul's delivery.
Thou art slave to fate, chance, kings, and desperate men,
And dost with poison, war, and sickness dwell,
And poppy or charms can make us sleep as well
And better than thy stroke; why swell'st thou then?
One short sleep past, we wake eternally
And death shall be no more; Death, thou shalt die.

17. Who wrote this poem, titled "Death, be not Proud?

(A) John Donne

(B) William Shakespeare

(C) Emily Dickinson

(D) Edgar Allen Poe

(E) William Wordsworth

Sample Test Three

18. What type of poem is this?

(A) Ballad

(B) Epic

(C) Haiku

(D) Prose

(E) Sonnet

19. What is the rhyme scheme in the first stanza?

(A) ABBAABBA

(B) AABBABBA

(C) ABCABCBC

(D) AABBCCAA

(E) ABBBAAAB

20. What is the author implying in the following line?

"Die not, poor Death, nor yet canst thou kill me."

(A) He/She is invincible.

(B) His/Her soul will go to heaven; therefore, death does not end life.

(C) Death does not decide when he/she will die.

(D) Poor people do not decide when they will die.

(E) He/she will defend themselves against a murderer.

21. What does the following line represent?

"One short sleep past, we wake eternally"

(A) Being buried

(B) A coma

(C) Fighting off disease

(D) A dream

(E) Resurrection

22. The last line of the poem tries to explain _____.

(A) that heaven/the afterlife defeats death.

(B) that death dies when the human body dies.

(C) that death can be defeated with death.

(D) that death is only a threat to those that are alive.

(E) None of the above.

23. Why are poison, war, and sickness mentioned?

(A) To give examples of cowardly death scenarios.

(B) To show that you can be killed by others or in a passive way.

(C) To provoke memories from the reader.

(D) To personify death as a bully.

(E) None of the above.

24. The author speaks about death as if it's a/an _____.

(A) theory

(B) legacy

(C) person

(D) threat

(E) imaginary concept

Passage 4

"And if she thought anything, it was No. No. Nono. Nonono. Simple. She just flew. Collected every bit of life she had made, all the parts of her that were precious and fine and beautiful, and carried, pushed, dragged them through the veil, out, away, over there where no one could hurt them. Over there. Outside this place, where they would be safe."

—Beloved

25. Who wrote Beloved?

(A) Martin Luther King

(B) Frederick Douglass

(C) Maya Angelou

(D) Toni Morrison

(E) Zora Neal Hurston

26. What does "No. No. Nono. Nonono." represent?

(A) Children fighting with their parents

(B) Parents defending discipline

(C) Teachers arguing with parents

(D) Children being defiant

(E) Parents defending their children

27. What are "bits of life"?

(A) Children

(B) Belongings

(C) Crops

(D) Flowers

(E) Poems

28. What does the veil represent?

(A) A screen of oppression

(B) A funeral

(C) Birth

(D) Puberty

(E) None of the above

29. Where is "over there"?

(A) Africa

(B) The Underground Railroad

(C) The slaves quarters

(D) The afterlife

(E) The garden

30. Where would they be safe?

(A) Nowhere on this earth

(B) Off the plantation

(C) Back in Africa

(D) In school

(E) Up North

31. The author implies that the main character _____.

(A) would rather see her children die than watch them suffer.

(B) is trying to hide her children from the master.

(C) is planning on escaping on the Underground Railroad.

(D) would like to return to Africa.

(E) is hiding her belongings from fellow slaves.

32. What literary device is used in this passage?

(A) Alliteration

(B) Allegory

(C) Analogy

(D) Anecdote

(E) Anagram

Sample Test Three

Passage 5

"Then you must tell 'em dat love ain't somethin' lak uh grindstone dat's de same thing everywhere and do de same thing tuh everything it touch. Love is lak de sea. It's uh movin' thing, but still and all, it takes its shape from de shore it meets, and it's different with every shore."
– *Their Eyes Were Watching God*

33. **Who wrote this novel?**

    (A) Toni Morrison

    (B) Zora Neal Hurston

    (C) W.E.B. Dubois

    (D) Maya Angelou

    (E) Richard Wright

34. **What literary device is used to show the similarity between love and the sea?**

    (A) Simile

    (B) Metaphor

    (C) Euphemism

    (D) Flashback

    (E) Foreshadowing

35. **In what form is this written?**

    (A) Phonetic

    (B) Informal

    (C) With an accent

    (D) Vernacular

    (E) Stream of consciousness

36. _____ is used to describe the sea.

    (A) Imagery

    (B) Alliteration

    (C) Action

    (D) Personification

    (E) All of the above

37. How does the author portray love?

    (A) It's different for each relationship.

    (B) It's unobtainable.

    (C) It causes waves in your life.

    (D) It comes and goes like the tide.

    (E) None of the above.

38. What is a grindstone?

    (A) A stone made of sand

    (B) A workday

    (C) A square stone used to grind sediment

    (D) A round stone used to sharpen tools

    (E) A plantation

39. What best describes love in this passage?

    (A) Grindstone

    (B) Uh movin' thing

    (C) Still

    (D) Same thing

    (E) Everyone

Passage 6

"Oh, Jake," Brett said, "we could have had such a damned good time together."

Ahead was a mounted policeman in khaki directing traffic. He raised his baton. The car slowed suddenly pressing Brett against me.

"Yes," I said. "Isn't it pretty to think so?"

– *The Sun Also Rises*

40. Who wrote this novel?

(A) Henry David Thoreau

(B) Ernest Hemmingway

(C) F. Scott Fitzgerald

(D) Harper Lee

(E) J.R.R. Tolkien

41. What is the significance of the policeman waiting his baton?

(A) It symbolizes that it's time to move along

(B) Their love will never be legal

(C) If they get caught they will go to jail

(D) It shows their love stuck, as if in traffic

(E) All of the above

42. Which is true about Brett?

(A) She has always been in love with Jake.

(B) She refuses to go anywhere without Jake.

(C) She sees Jake in her future.

(D) She regrets the past.

(E) All of the above.

43. Which is true about Jake?

(A) He sees Brett in his future.

(B) He wants to marry Brett.

(C) He doesn't think their relationship would ever work out.

(D) He loves Brett as a friend.

(E) He thinks Brett is pretty.

44. Which literary device would be most appropriate before this dialogue?

(A) Flashforward

(B) Foreshadowing

(C) Backflash

(D) Metaphor

(E) Flashback

45. Which literary device would be most appropriate after this dialogue?

(A) Flashforward

(B) Foreshadowing

(C) Backflash

(D) Metaphor

(E) Flashback

46. Which is the best description of this dialogue and its placement in the story?

(A) Introduction

(B) Cliffhanger

(C) Frame story

(D) Backstory

(E) Setting

Sample Test Three

47. Why did the car slow down?

    (A) There was traffic.

    (B) The policeman waved his baton.

    (C) The driver needed directions.

    (D) The driver was picking up another passenger.

    (E) It was time to get out.

Passage 7

O for a Muse of fire, that would ascend
The brightest heaven of invention,
A kingdom for a stage, princes to act
And monarchs to behold the swelling scene!
Then should the warlike Harry, like himself,
Assume the port of Mars; and at his heels,
Leash'd in like hounds, should famine, sword and fire
Crouch for employment. But pardon, and gentles all,
The flat unraised spirits that have dared
On this unworthy scaffold to bring forth
So great an object: can this cockpit hold
The vasty fields of France? or may we cram
Within this wooden O the very casques
That did affright the air at Agincourt?
O, pardon! since a crooked figure may
Attest in little place a million;
And let us, ciphers to this great account,
On your imaginary forces work.
Suppose within the girdle of these walls
Are now confined two mighty monarchies,
Whose high upreared and abutting fronts
The perilous narrow ocean parts asunder:
Piece out our imperfections with your thoughts;
Into a thousand parts divide one man,
And make imaginary puissance;
Think when we talk of horses, that you see them

Printing their proud hoofs i' the receiving earth;
For 'tis your thoughts that now must deck our kings,
Carry them here and there; jumping o'er times,
Turning the accomplishment of many years
Into an hour-glass: for the which supply,
Admit me Chorus to this history;
Who prologue-like your humble patience pray,
Gently to hear, kindly to judge, our play.

48. The first four lines could best be described as...

(A) A warning of violence to come.

(B) A celebration of military victory.

(C) An exultation of creative vision.

(D) A lamentation of the inadequacy of mortals.

(E) A plea for patience from the audience.

49. What can the reader infer from lines 5-8?

(A) Harry was a man who inspired awe and fear.

(B) Harry was a god.

(C) Harry will soon rule over all people.

(D) Harry is the villain of the play.

(E) Harry was a sailor.

50. What is meant by the line "since a crooked figure may attest in little place a million"?

(A) Small men can enact great change if they fulfill their potential.

(B) One actor can play many parts.

(C) Trials can be overcome through perseverance.

(D) Some tests are insurmountable to any man.

(E) There are mysteries we cannot solve.

51. What does the narrator wish for the audience to do in lines 20-28?

(A) Draw upon their own experiences at the theater.

(B) Imagine the horror and glory of war.

(C) Pretend the physical aspects of the theater reflect things far greater than can be shown onstage.

(D) Appreciate history, both the good and bad aspects.

(E) Understand their own smallness in the face of this epic tale.

52. What is the narrator's attitude towards the audience?

(A) Egocentric disdain

(B) Haughty dismissal

(C) Meek terror

(D) Wide-eyed fascination

(E) Humble entreating

53. What is the "unworthy scaffold"?

(A) A run-down building

(B) A poorhouse

(C) The barracks

(D) The stage itself

(E) A church

54. The narrator wishes to

(A) Deceive the audience with propaganda.

(B) Relay a tale too great for the stage to contain.

(C) Repent for the sins committed by his people.

(D) Slander the memory of a great leader.

(E) Absolve himself of any guilt he may be feeling.

55. Who are the "ciphers to this great account"?

(A) Soldiers

(B) Actors

(C) Women

(D) Scholars

(E) Royalty

Passage 8

In a village of La Mancha, the name of which I have no desire to call to mind, there lived not long since one of those gentlemen that keep a lance in the lance-rack, an old buckler, a lean hack, and a greyhound for coursing. An olla of rather more beef than mutton, a salad on most nights, scraps on Saturdays, lentils on Fridays, and a pigeon or so extra on Sundays, made away with three-quarters of his income. The rest of it went in a doublet of fine cloth and velvet breeches and shoes to match for holidays, while on week-days he made a brave figure in his best homespun. He had in his house a housekeeper past forty, a niece under twenty, and a lad for the field and market-place, who used to saddle the hack as well as handle the bill-hook. The age of this gentleman of ours was bordering on fifty; he was of a hardy habit, spare, gaunt-featured, a very early riser and a great sportsman. They will have it his surname was Quixada or Quesada (for here there is some difference of opinion among the authors who write on the subject), although from reasonable conjectures it seems plain that he was called Quexana. This, however, is of but little importance to our tale; it will be enough not to stray a hair's breadth from the truth in the telling of it.

You must know, then, that the above-named gentleman whenever he was at leisure (which was mostly all the year round) gave himself up to reading books of chivalry with such ardour and avidity that he almost entirely neglected the pursuit of his field-sports, and even the management of his property; and to such a pitch did his eagerness and infatuation go that he sold many an acre of tillageland to buy books of chivalry to read, and brought home as many of them as he could get. But of all there were none he liked so well as those of the famous Feliciano de Silva's composition, for their lucidity of style and complicated conceits were as pearls in his sight, particularly when in his

Sample Test Three

reading he came upon courtships and cartels, where he often found passages like "the reason of the unreason with which my reason is afflicted so weakens my reason that with reason I murmur at your beauty;" or again, "the high heavens, that of your divinity divinely fortify you with the stars, render you deserving of the desert your greatness deserves." Over conceits of this sort the poor gentleman lost his wits, and used to lie awake striving to understand them and worm the meaning out of them; what Aristotle himself could not have made out or extracted had he come to life again for that special purpose. He was not at all easy about the wounds which Don Belianis gave and took, because it seemed to him that, great as were the surgeons who had cured him, he must have had his face and body covered all over with seams and scars. He commended, however, the author's way of ending his book with the promise of that interminable adventure, and many a time was he tempted to take up his pen and finish it properly as is there proposed, which no doubt he would have done, and made a successful piece of work of it too, had not greater and more absorbing thoughts prevented him.

56. The author's tone in this piece can best be described as...

(A) Heroic

(B) Comedic

(C) Florid

(D) Epic

(E) Mysterious

57. The line "were as pearls to his site" is an example of a...

(A) Metaphor

(B) Analogy

(C) Simile

(D) Allegory

(E) Conceit

58. **Our main character's attitude towards reading can best be described as…**

(A) Lackadaisical

(B) Unusual

(C) Illiterate

(D) Obsessive

(E) Joyous

59. **The passage "the high heavens, that of your divinity divinely fortify you with the stars, render you deserving of the desert your greatness deserves" contains several examples what poetic device?**

(A) Alliteration

(B) Onomatopoeia

(C) Diction

(D) Resonance

(E) Enjambment

60. **According to the text, who is Count Belianis?**

(A) A historical champion

(B) A fictional character

(C) A competing nobleman

(D) A romantic rival

(E) A dead family member

Sample Test Three

61. The passage "it will be enough not to stray a hair's breadth from the truth in the telling of it" characterizes the previous passage as...

(A) Essential

(B) Metaphorical

(C) Unimportant

(D) Esoteric

(E) Bland

62. What are the two defining traits of the main character described above?

(A) Laziness and obsessiveness

(B) Ignorance and piousness

(C) Diligence and valor

(D) Prideful and vain

(E) Curious and kindhearted

63. The final sentence of this excerpt is an example of...

(A) Satire

(B) Foreshadowing

(C) Interstitial

(D) Subtext

(E) Premonition

Passage 9

O wild West Wind, thou breath of Autumn's being,

Thou, from whose unseen presence the leaves dead
Are driven, like ghosts from an enchanter fleeing,

Yellow, and black, and pale, and hectic red,
Pestilence-stricken multitudes: O thou,
Who chariotest to their dark wintry bed

The winged seeds, where they lie cold and low,
Each like a corpse within its grave, until
Thine azure sister of the Spring shall blow

Her clarion o'er the dreaming earth, and fill
(Driving sweet buds like flocks to feed in air)
With living hues and odors plain and hill:

Wild Spirit, which art moving everywhere;
Destroyer and preserver; hear, oh, hear!

Thou on whose stream, 'mid the steep sky's commotion,
Loose clouds like earth's decaying leaves are shed,
Shook from the tangled boughs of Heaven and Ocean,

Angels of rain and lightning: there are spread
On the blue surface of thine aery surge,
Like the bright hair uplifted from the head

Of some fierce Maenad, even from the dim verge
Of the horizon to the zenith's height,
The locks of the approaching storm. Thou dirge

Of the dying year, to which this closing night
Will be the dome of a vast sepulchre,
Vaulted with all thy congregated might

Of vapors, from whose solid atmosphere
Black rain, and fire, and hail will burst: oh, hear!

64. The first line of this poem exhibits what poetic devices?

I. Alliteration
II. Personification
III. Onomatopoeia

(A) Only I

(B) Only II

(C) Only III

(D) I and II

(E) I, II, and III

Sample Test Three

65. What best describes the final stanza of this selection?

(A) Slant rhyme

(B) Heroic couplet

(C) Hyperbole

(D) Irony

(E) Blank verse

66. "Wild Spirit, which art moving everywhere;

Destroyer and preserver; hear, oh, hear!"
This passage displays a...

(A) Enjambment

(B) Slant rhyme

(C) Simile

(D) Iamb

(E) Allegory

67. This poem is written in what style?

(A) Vers libre

(B) Heroic couplet

(C) Epic saga

(D) Imagist soliloquy

(E) Iambic pentameter

68. What in the poem is compared to "Angels of rain and lightning"?

(A) The wind

(B) Maenads

(C) Clouds

(D) Human souls

(E) Autumn

69. **"Of the dying year, to which this closing night/ Will be the dome of a vast sepulchre, / Vaulted with all thy congregated might"**

    This passage exhibits…

    (A) A metaphor

    (B) An allegory

    (C) A comparison

    (D) A consonance

    (E) An allusion

70. **How many stanzas does this poem contain?**

    (A) Four

    (B) Five

    (C) Eight

    (D) Ten

    (E) Twelve

Passage 10

When it was first perceived, in early times, that no middle course for America remained between unlimited submission to a foreign legislature and a total independence of its claims, men of reflection were less apprehensive of danger from the formidable power of fleets and armies they must determine to resist than from those contests and dissensions which would certainly arise concerning the forms of government to be instituted over the whole and over the parts of this extensive country. Relying, however, on the purity of their intentions, the justice of their cause, and the integrity and intelligence of the people, under an overruling Providence which had so signally protected this country from the first, the representatives of this nation, then consisting of little more than half its present number, not only broke to pieces the chains which were forging and the rod of iron that was lifted up, but frankly cut asunder the ties which had bound them, and launched into an ocean of uncertainty.

Sample Test Three

The zeal and ardor of the people during the Revolutionary war, supplying the place of government, commanded a degree of order sufficient at least for the temporary preservation of society. The Confederation which was early felt to be necessary was prepared from the models of the Batavian and Helvetic confederacies, the only examples which remain with any detail and precision in history, and certainly the only ones which the people at large had ever considered. But reflecting on the striking difference in so many particulars between this country and those where a courier may go from the seat of government to the frontier in a single day, it was then certainly foreseen by some who assisted in Congress at the formation of it that it could not be durable.

Negligence of its regulations, inattention to its recommendations, if not disobedience to its authority, not only in individuals but in States, soon appeared with their melancholy consequences—universal languor, jealousies and rivalries of States, decline of navigation and commerce, discouragement of necessary manufactures, universal fall in the value of lands and their produce, contempt of public and private faith, loss of consideration and credit with foreign nations, and at length in discontents, animosities, combinations, partial conventions, and insurrection, threatening some great national calamity.

71. What best summarizes the first sentence of this piece?

(A) When we first realize there was no middle ground between subservience and independence, intelligent men were less afraid of war than they were of deciding how to govern our new nation

(B) When our ancestors first realized they must be free instead of obedient, they realized that combat was far less challenging than the bureaucracy that would follow

(C) When men realized, in the past, that freedom would be hard to win, they decided to craft a new form of government to aid in this process

(D) When our new nation first achieved independence, the true struggle was not the war that followed, but the arguments between learned me who could not agree on anything

(E) When men first decided independence was necessary, they could not agree who should lead them, or how

72. **The phrase "ocean of uncertainty" is a:**

(A) Allusion

(B) Metaphor

(C) Allegory

(D) Simile

(E) Personification

73. **In the last sentence of the next to last paragraph, what does "durable" refer to?**

(A) Striking

(B) Courier

(C) Country

(D) Congress

(E) Formation

74. **What does the author identify as a problem in the second paragraph?**

(A) The similarities between his new nation and the Batavian and Helvetic confederacies

(B) The ignorance of the common people

(C) The unrestrained zeal of common citizens

(D) The vast size of this new country

(E) The brewing revolution that approaches

75. **What word does "frankly" modify in the last sentence of the first paragraph?**

(A) Cut

(B) Asunder

(C) Ties

(D) Representatives

(E) Bound

Sample Test Three

76. The author identifies all of these as problems in the third paragraph EXCEPT:

(A) Laziness

(B) Envy

(C) Poor trade

(D) Religious intolerance

(E) Increased dependence on foreign powers

77. What is "it" the first sentence of the third paragraph refers to?

(A) The new nation

(B) The Revolutionary War

(C) Congress

(D) The presidency

(E) The States

78. In the first paragraph, what does the author NOT credit with aiding the representatives?

(A) Providence

(B) Intelligence

(C) Integrity

(D) The Nation

(E) Purity

Passage 11

"You've just told me some high spots in your memories. Want to hear mine? They're all connected with the sea.

Here's one. When I was on the Squarehead square rigger, bound for Buenos Aires. Full moon in the trades. The old hooker driving 14 knots. I lay on the bowsprit, facing astern, with the water foaming into spume under me. Every mast with sail white in the moonlight - towering high above me. I became drunk with the beauty and singing rhythm of it - and for a second I lost myself, actually lost my life. I was set free! I dissolved into the sea, became white sails and flying spray - became beauty and rhythm, became moonlight and the ship and the high dim-starred sky. I belonged, without past or future, within peace and unity and a wild joy, within something greater than my own life, or the life of man, to Life itself! To God if you want to put it that way.

Then another time, on the American line, when I was lookout in the crow's nest on the dawn watch. A calm sea that time. Only a lazy ground swell and a slow drousy roll of the ship. The passengers asleep and none of the crew in sight. No sound of man. Black smoke pouring from the funnels behind and beneath me. Dreaming, not keeping lookout, feeling alone, and above, and apart, watching the dawn creep like a painted dream over the sky and sea which slept together.

Then the moment of ecstatic freedom came. The peace, the end of the quest, the last harbor, the joy of belonging to a fulfillment beyond men's lousy, greedy fears and hopes and dreams! And several other times in my life, when I was swimming far out, or lying alone on the beach, I have had the same experience. Became the sun, the hot sand, green seaweed anchored to a rock, swaying in the tide. Like a saint's vision of beatitude. Like the veil of things as they seem drawn back by an unseen hand. For a second you see - and seeing the secret, are the secret. For a second there is meaning! Then the hand lets the veil fall and you are alone, lost in the fog again, stumbling on toward no where, for no good reason!

It was a great mistake, my being born a man. I would have been much more successful as a seagull or fish. As it is, I will always be a stranger who never feels at home, who does not want and is not really wanted, who can never belong, who must always be a little in love with death."

Sample Test Three

79. What adjective best describes Edmund's tone in this piece?

(A) Disaffected

(B) Morose

(C) Longing

(D) Celebratory

(E) Inspired

80. This piece can best be described as...

(A) A poem

(B) A dramatic monologue

(C) Prose fiction

(D) An ode

(E) A dirge

Sample Test Three

Question Number	Correct Answer	Your Answer	Question Number	Correct Answer	Your Answer
1	B		31	A	
2	A		32	B	
3	D		33	B	
4	A		34	A	
5	C		35	D	
6	A		36	A	
7	B		37	D	
8	D		38	D	
9	B		39	B	
10	A		40	B	
11	A		41	A	
12	C		42	D	
13	C		43	C	
14	D		44	E	
15	B		45	A	
16	C		46	B	
17	A		47	E	
18	E		48	C	
19	A		49	A	
20	B		50	B	
21	E		51	C	
22	A		52	E	
23	B		53	D	
24	C		54	B	
25	D		55	B	
26	B		56	B	
27	A		57	C	
28	A		58	D	
29	D		59	A	
30	A		60	B	

Sample Test Three

Question Number	Correct Answer	Your Answer
61	C	
62	A	
63	B	
64	D	
65	B	
66	B	
67	E	
68	C	
69	A	
70	D	

Question Number	Correct Answer	Your Answer
71	A	
72	B	
73	C	
74	D	
75	A	
76	E	
77	C	
78	D	
79	C	
80	B	

Sample Test Three: Rationales _____

Passage 1

On the domestic front, life was not easy. England was not a wealthy country and its people endured relatively poor living standards. The landed classes – many of them enriched by the confiscated wealth of former monasteries – were determined in the interests of profile to convert their arable land into pasture for sheep, so as to produce the wool that supported the country's chief economic asset, the woolen cloth trade. But the enclosing of the land only added to the misery of the poor, many of whom, evicted and displaced, left their decaying villages and gravitated to the towns where they joined the growing army of beggars and vagabonds that would become such a feature of Elizabethan life. Once, the religious houses would have dispensed charity to the destitute, but Henry VIII had dissolved them all in the 1530s, and many former monks and nuns were now themselves beggars. Nor did the civic authorities help: they passed laws in an attempt to ban the poor from towns and cities, but to little avail. It was a common sight to see men and women lying in the dusty streets, often dying in the dirt like dogs or beasts, without human compassion being shown to them. 'Certainly,' wrote a Spanish observer in 1558, 'the state of England lay now most afflicted.' And although people looked to the new Queen Elizabeth to put matters right, there were so many who doubted if she could overcome the seemingly insurmountable problems she faced, or even remain queen long enough to begin tacking them. Some, both at home and abroad, were the opinion that her title to the throne rested on very precarious foundations. Many regarded the daughter of Henry VIII and Anne Boleyn as a bastard from the time of her birth on 7 September 1533, although, ignoring such slurs on the validity of his second marriage, Henry had declared Elizabeth his heir.

1. **Why was land confiscated from the poor?**

   (A) The town wanted to build a new monastery.

   (B) To create pastures for sheep, ultimately increasing the export of wool.

   (C) The town wanted to create housing for monks and nuns.

   (D) Queen Elizabeth wanted to expand her property.

   (E) The poor did not pay their taxes.

   The correct answer is B.
   This is stated directly in the paragraph in the opening lines.

2. **A vagabond is a _____.**

   (A) Wanderer

   (B) Prisoner

   (C) Poor person

   (D) Rich person

   (E) Fighter

   The correct answer is A.
   Using your vocabulary, should should know this; but it can also be narrowed down from the passage, where you would be able to guess between C and A.

3. **Why didn't the poor have shelter with the churches?**

   (A) They were already filled with beggars.

   (B) Religious houses have never offered shelter to the poor.

   (C) They were also being used to raise sheep.

   (D) Henry VIII had dissolved them all in the 1530s.

   (E) Queen Elizabeth dissolved them all in the 1530s.

   The correct answer is D.
   Again, this is stated directly in the paragraph. This CLEP test looks at your reading comprehension in addition to your knowledge of vocabulary and literary terms.

4. **How were civic authorities unsuccessful?**

   (A) Poor people remained within city limits

   (B) Public service funds ran out

   (C) Public housing plans extended deadlines

   (D) Churches did not open their doors to the poor

   (E) The poor overthrew them to gain their land back

   The correct answer is A.

   Using a statement in the passage, "It was a common sight to see men and women lying in the dusty streets, often dying in the dirt like dogs or beasts," it shows through analysis that they were still in the city. To eliminate the other answers, there is no indication of B or C in the passage; D is incorrect as the previous question reminded you that the churches were closed, and: E is incorrect because again, there is no indication in the passage that situation occurred.

5. **What is a synonym for precarious?**

   (A) Strong

   (B) Careful

   (C) Risky

   (D) Determined

   (E) Illegitimate

   The correct answer is C.

   This is a test of your vocabulary, but you should be able to use clues in the paragraph if you aren't sure of the answer.

6. **What is the author's view towards Queen Elizabeth?**

   (A) Doubtful

   (B) Vengeful

   (C) Resentful

   (D) Supportive

   (E) Confident

The correct answer is A.

Indications of this are found toward the end of the passage. "there were many who doubted" and the author continues to explain those doubts.

7. **How is the English culture portrayed in this passage?**

   (A) Religious

   (B) Elitist

   (C) Racist

   (D) Diverse

   (E) Spiritual

The correct answer is B.

By using contextual analysis, you can see how King Henry VII favored land-holders even early in the passage and the description of their life, "enriched by the confiscated wealth of former monasteries."

8. **What is Elizabeth's relationship to Henry?**

   (A) Wife

   (B) Cousin

   (C) Lover

   (D) Daughter

   (E) Niece

The correct answer is D.

This is explained directly in the passage, after the description of the illegitimacy of the daughter of Anne Boelyn.

Passage 2

"Mother," said little Pearl, "the sunshine does not love you. It runs away and hides itself, because it is afraid of something on your bosom. . . . It will not flee from me, for I wear nothing on my bosom yet!"

"Nor ever will, my child, I hope," said Hester.

"And why not, mother?" asked Pearl, stopping short....

"Will it not come of its own accord, when I am a woman grown?"

– *The Scarlett Letter*

9. **Who is the author of this book?**

    (A) William Faulkner

    (B) Nathaniel Hawthorne

    (C) William Blake

    (D) William Shakespeare

    (E) Frederick Douglass

    The correct answer is B.
    As this is a literature exam, you are expected to know some of the works of famous authors. Knowing the time period in which they wrote will also help, but it is not necessary to memorize lists of authors and books.

10. **What is the relationship between these two characters?**

    (A) Mother and daughter

    (B) Sisters

    (C) Aunt and niece

    (D) Cousins

    (E) Grandmother and grandchild

    The correct answer is A.
    The very first word explains this.

11. **What kind of description is the author providing of this scene?**

    (A) A symbolic, metaphorical description that provides a backstory of the main character

    (B) A characterization of what the character is like

    (C) A narrative, with the end of the selection giving thoughts in the first person

    (D) The unreliable narrative about a character

    (E) The author is using a persuasive argument

The correct answer is A.
You need to determined the meaning of passages in this CLEP to achieve the "Analyzing" component of the title.

12. **What does the "sunshine" represent?**

(A) Light

(B) Hope

(C) Purity

(D) Heaven

(E) Good luck

The correct answer is C.
This is an analogy. Being one of Hawthorne's most popular works and frequently used on tests, understanding of the phrase is important.

13. **Why doesn't Pearl have anything on her bosom?**

(A) Only one person in the village wears the symbol at a time.

(B) The symbol is used to signify divorce, and Pearl is not yet married.

(C) It represents pregnancy and she is too young to be pregnant.

(D) She will inherit the symbol to wear when her mother dies.

(E) It's a symbol of womanhood, and Pearl is still considered a child.

The correct answer is C.
Again, knowing the symbolism of one of the most important novels of that era is important. Understanding some of the plot and having read the book would have occurred in the literature classes at the early stages of college coursework, so you should understand some of the dynamics of the story.

Sample Test Three

14. The author portrays the attitude of the character Pearl as:

(A) condescending

(B) loving

(C) disrespectful

(D) innocent

(E) resentful

The correct answer is D.

There is no indication of A, C, or E being included in this passage; so even if you do not know the plot, you should be able to reason through to the correct answer between B and D.

15. "Will it not come of its own accord, when I am a woman grown?" What is the author implying that Pearl is asking for?

(A) If the scarlet letter will be handed down to her when she becomes a woman.

(B) If she will become pregnant when she becomes mature enough.

(C) Whether or not she will get divorced when she marries.

(D) If she will find true love when she grows up.

(E) If her mother will share this symbol with her when she is old enough.

The correct answer is B.

In The Scarlet Letter, there is no analysis of divorce, so C is not correct. Likewise, there are very clear parameters around the letter, so A and E are also inaccurate. If you narrow your choices down to B or D, the majority of the novel is not around components of love.

16. Which of the following best describes the author's message?

(A) Little girls are oblivious to the world around them.

(B) Daughters always question things that their mothers do.

(C) Growing up means losing your innocence.

(D) The world will know when you have sinned.

(E) None of the above.

The correct answer is C.

This is part of the novel, but if you had not read it, you may assume that B is a possible answer. You already know to eliminate E in most multiple choice answer lists. A and D are pessimistic options and not components of the plot in the book (though D does have some overtures, but are explicitly denounced as "all sin" will be discovered in the novel.

Passage 3

"Death, be not Proud"

Death, be not proud, though some have called thee
Mighty and dreadful, for thou art not so;
For those whom thou think'st thou dost overthrow
Die not, poor Death, nor yet canst thou kill me.
From rest and sleep, which but thy pictures be,
Much pleasure; then from thee much more must flow,
And soonest our best men with thee do go,
Rest of their bones, and soul's delivery.
Thou art slave to fate, chance, kings, and desperate men,
And dost with poison, war, and sickness dwell,
And poppy or charms can make us sleep as well
And better than thy stroke; why swell'st thou then?
One short sleep past, we wake eternally
And death shall be no more; Death, thou shalt die.

17. Who wrote this poem, titled "Death, be not Proud?

   (A) John Donne

   (B) William Shakespeare

   (C) Emily Dickinson

   (D) Edgar Allen Poe

   (E) William Wordsworth

The correct answer is A.

This is a famous poem, and one where you should recognize it and the author.

18. **What type of poem is this?**

(A) Ballad

(B) Epic

(C) Haiku

(D) Prose

(E) Sonnet

The correct answer is E.

These are all a literary terms that you should know. Prose is a story in the format of a novel; Haiku is a very specific short Japanese poem; An epic is a piece that tells about an adventure or a hero; Ballads typically describe events and are put to music.

19. **What is the rhyme scheme in the first stanza?**

(A) ABBAABBA

(B) AABBABBA

(C) ABCABCBC

(D) AABBCCAA

(E) ABBBAAAB

The correct answer is A.

Look at the pattern of the letters and match it to the pattern and rhymes of the poem to select the correct option.

20. **What is the author implying in the following line?**

"Die not, poor Death, nor yet canst thou kill me."

(A) He/She is invincible.

(B) His/Her soul will go to heaven; therefore, death does not end life.

(C) Death does not decide when he/she will die.

(D) Poor people do not decide when they will die.

(E) He/she will defend themselves against a murderer.

The correct answer is B.

The selection discusses not being able to kill the speaker. it doesn't talk about timing of death, so C, D and E are incorrect. A is not specific enough about living and life, so it is also not the correct answer - invincible does not mean life-everlasting, and shows that some questions will mix vocabulary and analysis in their multiple choice options.

21. **What does the following line represent?**

"One short sleep past, we wake eternally"

(A) Being buried

(B) A coma

(C) Fighting off disease

(D) A dream

(E) Resurrection

The correct answer is E.
The whole theme of the poem is that death cannot conquer the spirit that believes in God's gift of life after death. Eternal awake-ness after death is resurrection, so this is also a definition question.

22. **The last line of the poem tries to explain _____.**

(A) that heaven/the afterlife defeats death.

(B) that death dies when the human body dies.

(C) that death can be defeated with death.

(D) that death is only a threat to those that are alive.

(E) None of the above.

The correct answer is A.
Again, talking about the life after lasting (resurrection) and heaven being a gift from above, that good overcomes evil and Death (evil) cannot overcome good (heaven and resurrection).

23. Why are poison, war, and sickness mentioned?

(A) To give examples of cowardly death scenarios.

(B) To show that you can be killed by others or in a passive way.

(C) To provoke memories from the reader.

(D) To personify death as a bully.

(E) None of the above.

The correct answer is B.
This tests your analytical skills and deductive reasoning regarding the intent of an author.

24. The author speaks about death as if it's a/an _____.

(A) theory

(B) legacy

(C) person

(D) threat

(E) imaginary concept

The correct answer is C.
Many literary works portray death as "the grim reaper", and that's what Donne achieves in this piece.

Passage 4

"And if she thought anything, it was No. No. Nono. Nonono. Simple. She just flew. Collected every bit of life she had made, all the parts of her that were precious and fine and beautiful, and carried, pushed, dragged them through the veil, out, away, over there where no one could hurt them. Over there. Outside this place, where they would be safe."
—*Beloved*

25. Who wrote Beloved?

(A) Martin Luther King

(B) Frederick Douglass

(C) Maya Angelou

(D) Toni Morrison

(E) Zora Neal Hurston

The correct answer is D.
Again, one of her most famous pieces and highly used in college literary courses, you should know the answer to this. Review famous literary works and their authors so you can recognize simple questions such as this.

26. What does "No. No. Nono. Nonono." represent?

(A) Children fighting with their parents

(B) Parents defending discipline

(C) Teachers arguing with parents

(D) Children being defiant

(E) Parents defending their children

The correct answer is B.
If you are unfamiliar with the novel, this would be a harder question to answer accurately. However, you can use analysis on the answer choices to derive the correction one. A and D are the same, so eliminate them. In this context, there is no mention of teachers or situations that can be construed to have teachers represented by some other words, so C is eliminated. Of B and E, there is no indication that a parent is fighting someone/something, so it too can be eliminated.

27. What are "bits of life"?

(A) Children

(B) Belongings

(C) Crops

(D) Flowers

(E) Poems

The correct answer is A.
In context, it's "every bit of life she had made". While it could mean objects she actually made, if you had familiarity with the plot and characters in the novel, this would be an easy question. If you have to logic your way through options, crops and flowers do not make sense (as people cannot make crops or flowers) and poems is possible, but A and B are better possibilities. A is the best choice because you don't make belongings - you buy them.

28. What does the veil represent?

(A) A screen of oppression

(B) A funeral

(C) Birth

(D) Puberty

(E) None of the above

The correct answer is A.
The novel is about white oppression/white dominance and a wall (or veil) against opportunities for people of color. She thinks about breaking through the veil and coming out victorious on the other side.

29. Where is "over there"?

(A) Africa

(B) The Underground Railroad

(C) The slaves quarters

(D) The afterlife

(E) The garden

The correct answer is D.

Knowing the novel is helpful in this case, but not required. "Over there" is away from this place - so you know B, C, and E are not accurate because they are part of "this place." There is nothing to suggest Africa is the right choice. If you know the novel, it is easier to select D, but not necessary - this is another test of your analyzing skills.

30. Where would they be safe?

(A) Nowhere on this earth

(B) Off the plantation

(C) Back in Africa

(D) In school

(E) Up North

The correct answer is A.

Using the same logic as described in the previous rationale, the choices other than A are incorrect. If you know the book, these last two questions are easy points for you. If you don't know the book, you can review the top literature pieces in British and American literature, find reviews to explain the books and plots, and use that as preparation for the CLEP.

31. The author implies that the main character _____.

(A) would rather see her children die than watch them suffer.

(B) is trying to hide her children from the master.

(C) is planning on escaping on the Underground Railroad.

(D) would like to return to Africa.

(E) is hiding her belongings from fellow slaves.

The correct answer is A.

Options B through E are all relatively similar, so even if you didn't know the answer, you may be able to pick the right choice by reviewing the possible selections. But if you know this book, you can pick the right answer quickly. Even reviewing the past three questions may help you see a theme of the book's storyline.

32. What literary device is used in this passage?

(A) Alliteration

(B) Allegory

(C) Analogy

(D) Anecdote

(E) Anagram

The correct answer is B.

This is a matter of knowing your literary terms, so make sure you review the terms for poetry and for literary devices.

Passage 5

"Then you must tell 'em dat love ain't somethin' lak uh grindstone dat's de same thing everywhere and do de same thing tuh everything it touch. Love is lak de sea. It's uh movin' thing, but still and all, it takes its shape from de shore it meets, and it's different with every shore."

– *Their Eyes Were Watching God*

33. Who wrote this novel?

(A) Toni Morrison

(B) Zora Neal Hurston

(C) W.E.B. Dubois

(D) Maya Angelou

(E) Richard Wright

The correct answer is B.

There are many questions like this in past CLEP tests; reviewing the literature lists as previously suggested helps you score more points easily and quickly!

34. What literary device is used to show the similarity between love and the sea?

(A) Simile

(B) Metaphor

(C) Euphemism

(D) Flashback

(E) Foreshadowing

The correct answer is A.

Remember to review your literary terms!

35. In what form is this written?

(A) Phonetic

(B) Informal

(C) With an accent

(D) Vernacular

(E) Stream of consciousness

The correct answer is D.

Some of the words listed are literary devices, but this option is a word you should be able to recognize - both its use and meaning.

36. _____ is used to describe the sea.

(A) Imagery

(B) Alliteration

(C) Action

(D) Personification

(E) All of the above

The correct answer is A.

Remember, "all of the above" and "none of the above" are rarely right when given as options by The College Board. Action is not a literary term applicable in this instance. Of the three remaining, you need to know your literary terms.

37. How does the author portray love?

(A) It's different for each relationship.

(B) It's unobtainable.

(C) It causes waves in your life.

(D) It comes and goes like the tide.

(E) None of the above.

The correct answer is D.
The selection describes lobe being like the sea, and the next phrase is nearly identical to this correct option.

38. What is a grindstone?

(A) A stone made of sand

(B) A workday

(C) A square stone used to grind sediment

(D) A round stone used to sharpen tools

(E) A plantation

The correct answer is D.
Sometimes, The College Board will ask questions to make sure you know definitions of literary terms, but other times - like this - they ask for definitions of routine/regular words. This allows them to determine if you know the actual words and can then extrapolate to determine the meaning of a passage in the literary sense.

39. What best describes love in this passage?

(A) Grindstone

(B) Uh movin' thing

(C) Still

(D) Same thing

(E) Everyone

The correct answer is B.
Option C and even D are the opposite of the phrasing used to describe

Sample Test Three

love. Choice E gives an answer as to who can experience love but it doesn't answer the question - always make sure you are answering the question they ask, not just selecting something that is accurate from the passage; it's a favorite trick to give a statement that is true in the passage but not applicable to the question asked! Of A and B, the correct choice should be clear to you given the emotional description of love from the passage.

Passage 6

"Oh, Jake," Brett said, "we could have had such a damned good time together."
Ahead was a mounted policeman in khaki directing traffic. He raised his baton. The car slowed suddenly pressing Brett against me.
"Yes," I said. "Isn't it pretty to think so?"
– *The Sun Also Rises*

40. Who wrote this novel?

    (A) Henry David Thoreau

    (B) Ernest Hemmingway

    (C) F. Scott Fitzgerald

    (D) Harper Lee

    (E) J.R.R. Tolkien

The correct answer is B.
Refer to a top or most popular literature works and famous authors list and you'll see this listed and this author's most famous works.

41. What is the significance of the policeman waiting his baton?

    (A) It symbolizes that it's time to move along

    (B) Their love will never be legal

    (C) If they get caught they will go to jail

    (D) It shows their love stuck, as if in traffic

    (E) All of the above

The correct answer is A.

There is no indication that B is correct or D. You should recall by now that E – all of the above – is rarely a correct statement in The College Board tests. Of the remaining A or C, when considering that the cop has already seen them together, the portion of the answer "if they get caught" has already happened – and they didn't go to jail.

42. Which is true about Brett?

(A) She has always been in love with Jake.

(B) She refuses to go anywhere without Jake.

(C) She sees Jake in her future.

(D) She regrets the past.

(E) All of the above.

The correct answer is D.

The first phrase of the passage is delivered in a wistful way, as if she were longing for a different past. This takes some skill to analyze the author's intention, and is a classic way that The College Board will test your abilities.

43. Which is true about Jake?

(A) He sees Brett in his future.

(B) He wants to marry Brett.

(C) He doesn't think their relationship would ever work out.

(D) He loves Brett as a friend.

(E) He thinks Brett is pretty.

The correct answer is C.

By using the word "pretty" when answering the first statement of the passage, it is the author's meaning that needs to be calculated. By not immediately agreeing, and in fact answering in a seemingly non-committal way, Jake is being agreeable in conversation by not directly saying it wouldn't work out, but the author's word choice for the speaker indicates there is more meaning than agreement.

Sample Test Three

44. Which literary device would be most appropriate before this dialogue?

(A) Flashforward

(B) Foreshadowing

(C) Backflash

(D) Metaphor

(E) Flashback

The correct answer is E.
This is a time when knowing the meanings of various literary devices is critical to answering correctly. You could see C is not even a real literary term. D is a device but a type of phrasing, not a device used as a whole precursor passage. Of the three remaining, A doesn't make sense that something was said years ahead and then this passage is a flashback to that future event. Narrowing down to B or E, and how the first phrase discusses what could have been - it implies that a certain event changed the course that brought them to that point in the conversation, so E is the best choice.

45. Which literary device would be most appropriate after this dialogue?

(A) Flashforward

(B) Foreshadowing

(C) Backflash

(D) Metaphor

(E) Flashback

The correct answer is A.
Similar to the previous rationale, in this case C is still not a real literary term and D still isn't appropriate. Using the remaining options, there is a strong possibility that the "pretty" thought continues into what could be lost if they would be married on the part of Jake's ideas, so A is the best option.

46. Which is the best description of this dialogue and its placement in the story?

(A) Introduction

(B) Cliffhanger

(C) Frame story

(D) Backstory

(E) Setting

The correct answer is B.

Knowing literary devices terms, the choices of A, C, and E aren't possible. While this could be backstory, if you know the meaning of the terms, then you realize that isn't correct as it doesn't fit what a backstory means. The preceding passage that is not included in this test is likely is the backstory. The correct choice is cliffhanger.

47. Why did the car slow down?

(A) There was traffic.

(B) The policeman waved his baton.

(C) The driver needed directions.

(D) The driver was picking up another passenger.

(E) It was time to get out.

The correct answer is E.

There is no indication of C or D being accurate, and when reading passages it is not a good idea to "make up" pieces when answering. That's not how the items are constructed. There also is no indication of traffic. Of the two remaining options, the baton being waved isn't directly correlated with their actions, so the best answer is E.

Passage 7

O for a Muse of fire, that would ascend
The brightest heaven of invention,
A kingdom for a stage, princes to act
And monarchs to behold the swelling scene!
Then should the warlike Harry, like himself,

Sample Test Three

Assume the port of Mars; and at his heels,
Leash'd in like hounds, should famine, sword and fire
Crouch for employment. But pardon, and gentles all,
The flat unraised spirits that have dared
On this unworthy scaffold to bring forth
So great an object: can this cockpit hold
The vasty fields of France? or may we cram
Within this wooden O the very casques
That did affright the air at Agincourt?
O, pardon! since a crooked figure may
Attest in little place a million;
And let us, ciphers to this great account,
On your imaginary forces work.
Suppose within the girdle of these walls
Are now confined two mighty monarchies,
Whose high upreared and abutting fronts
The perilous narrow ocean parts asunder:
Piece out our imperfections with your thoughts;
Into a thousand parts divide one man,
And make imaginary puissance;
Think when we talk of horses, that you see them
Printing their proud hoofs i' the receiving earth;
For 'tis your thoughts that now must deck our kings,
Carry them here and there; jumping o'er times,
Turning the accomplishment of many years
Into an hour-glass: for the which supply,
Admit me Chorus to this history;
Who prologue-like your humble patience pray,
Gently to hear, kindly to judge, our play.

48. The first four lines could best be described as...

(A) A warning of violence to come.

(B) A celebration of military victory.

(C) An exultation of creative vision.

(D) A lamentation of the inadequacy of mortals.

(E) A plea for patience from the audience.

The correct answer is C.

The lines (O for a Muse of fire, that would ascend/ The brightest heaven of invention,/ A kingdom for a stage, princes to act/ And monarchs to behold the swelling scene!) are very descriptive of a scene. It has nothing to do with things mentioned in A, D or E. Between B and C, the poem's additional contents do not describe any sort of military action, so the correct answer is C.

49. What can the reader infer from lines 5-8?

(A) Harry was a man who inspired awe and fear.

(B) Harry was a god.

(C) Harry will soon rule over all people.

(D) Harry is the villain of the play.

(E) Harry was a sailor.

The correct answer is A.

There are no clues in the selection to lead to other answers being the best choice.

50. What is meant by the line "since a crooked figure may attest in little place a million"?

(A) Small men can enact great change if they fulfill their potential.

(B) One actor can play many parts.

(C) Trials can be overcome through perseverance.

(D) Some tests are insurmountable to any man.

(E) There are mysteries we cannot solve.

Sample Test Three

The correct answer is B.
This is the introduction of Shakespeare's Henry V, and the prologue of explaining one actor will take the place of millions in battle while representing the drama on stage.

51. **What does the narrator wish for the audience to do in lines 20-28?**

   (A) Draw upon their own experiences at the theater.

   (B) Imagine the horror and glory of war.

   (C) Pretend the physical aspects of the theater reflect things far greater than can be shown onstage.

   (D) Appreciate history, both the good and bad aspects.

   (E) Understand their own smallness in the face of this epic tale.

The correct answer is C.
Again, this is like the preceding answer, where it is relaying the constraints of theater.

52. **What is the narrator's attitude towards the audience?**

   (A) Egocentric disdain

   (B) Haughty dismissal

   (C) Meek terror

   (D) Wide-eyed fascination

   (E) Humble entreating

The correct answer is E.
The speaker is apologetic for not being able to adequately do justice to the tale being presented. If you recognize this as one of Shakespeare's most famous plays, that would help these questions be answered quickly.

Sample Test Three

53. What is the "unworthy scaffold"?

(A) A run-down building

(B) A poorhouse

(C) The barracks

(D) The stage itself

(E) A church

The correct answer is D.

Again, the orientation of the prologue of the play represents a major key into getting these questions correct. Context and inferring context plays a big role in The College Board questions.

54. The narrator wishes to

(A) Deceive the audience with propaganda.

(B) Relay a tale too great for the stage to contain.

(C) Repent for the sins committed by his people.

(D) Slander the memory of a great leader.

(E) Absolve himself of any guilt he may be feeling.

The correct answer is B.

The play itself describes the great drama while injecting commentary about it not being nearly adequate of a venue to relay such events. These first questions on this passage are all related to the context of Shakespeare's play.

55. Who are the "ciphers to this great account"?

(A) Soldiers

(B) Actors

(C) Women

(D) Scholars

(E) Royalty

The correct answer is B.

If you didn't recognize the play, you may have had difficulty with all of

Sample Test Three

these related questions. In this case, a cipher is something that relays meaning; in a play, that would be the actors. Even if the story is about royalty or soldiers in battle, nothing has meaning without the efforts of the actors.

Passage 8

In a village of La Mancha, the name of which I have no desire to call to mind, there lived not long since one of those gentlemen that keep a lance in the lance-rack, an old buckler, a lean hack, and a greyhound for coursing. An olla of rather more beef than mutton, a salad on most nights, scraps on Saturdays, lentils on Fridays, and a pigeon or so extra on Sundays, made away with three-quarters of his income. The rest of it went in a doublet of fine cloth and velvet breeches and shoes to match for holidays, while on week-days he made a brave figure in his best homespun. He had in his house a housekeeper past forty, a niece under twenty, and a lad for the field and market-place, who used to saddle the hack as well as handle the bill-hook. The age of this gentleman of ours was bordering on fifty; he was of a hardy habit, spare, gaunt-featured, a very early riser and a great sportsman. They will have it his surname was Quixada or Quesada (for here there is some difference of opinion among the authors who write on the subject), although from reasonable conjectures it seems plain that he was called Quexana. This, however, is of but little importance to our tale; it will be enough not to stray a hair's breadth from the truth in the telling of it.

You must know, then, that the above-named gentleman whenever he was at leisure (which was mostly all the year round) gave himself up to reading books of chivalry with such ardour and avidity that he almost entirely neglected the pursuit of his field-sports, and even the management of his property; and to such a pitch did his eagerness and infatuation go that he sold many an acre of tillageland to buy books of chivalry to read, and brought home as many of them as he could get. But of all there were none he liked so well as those of the famous Feliciano de Silva's composition, for their lucidity of style and complicated conceits were as pearls in his sight, particularly when in his reading he came upon courtships and cartels, where he often found passages like "the reason of the unreason with which my reason is afflicted so weakens my reason that with reason I murmur at your beauty;" or again, "the high heavens, that of your divinity divinely fortify you with the stars, render you deserving of the desert your greatness deserves." Over conceits of this sort the poor gentleman lost his wits, and used to lie awake striving to understand them and worm the meaning out of them; what Aristotle himself could not have made out or extracted had he come to life again for that special purpose. He was not at all easy about the wounds which Don Belianis gave and took, because it seemed to him that, great as were the surgeons who had cured him, he must have had his face and body covered all over with seams and scars. He commended, however, the author's way of ending his book with the promise of that interminable adventure, and many a time was he tempted to take up his pen and finish it properly as is there proposed, which no doubt he would have done, and made a successful piece of work of it too, had not greater and more absorbing thoughts prevented him.

56. The author's tone in this piece can best be described as...

(A) Heroic

(B) Comedic

(C) Florid

(D) Epic

(E) Mysterious

The correct answer is B.

This is the story of Don Quixote. The author writes about the enthusiasm of the lead character, eliminating options C, D and E. Between the first and second choice, if you know the play, it is easy to select the correct answer. If you need to infer the meaning, you need to select key words that lead to B. There are not many depictions of a hero, but there are allusions to entertaining situations, so that is the answer even if you have not read the book.

57. **The line "were as pearls to his site" is an example of a...**

(A) Metaphor

(B) Analogy

(C) Simile

(D) Allegory

(E) Conceit

The correct answer is C.

Remember to know your literary device terms, and this answer would be apparent.

58. **Our main character's attitude towards reading can best be described as...**

(A) Lackadaisical

(B) Unusual

(C) Illiterate

(D) Obsessive

(E) Joyous

The correct answer is D.

The phrase "buy books of chivalry to read, and brought home as many of them as he could get" gives some insight as well as other clues to the nature of the lead character. While B may also be true, D is the best answer.

59. **The passage "the high heavens, that of your divinity divinely fortify you with the stars, render you deserving of the desert your greatness deserves" contains several examples what poetic device?**

(A) Alliteration

(B) Onomatopoeia

(C) Diction

(D) Resonance

(E) Enjambment

The correct answer is A.

If you review the meaning of any of these terms you didn't know, the right choice will be readily apparent. Make sure you learn them before you take the CLEP.

60. **According to the text, who is Count Belianis?**

(A) A historical champion

(B) A fictional character

(C) A competing nobleman

(D) A romantic rival

(E) A dead family member

The correct answer is B.

The many scars and wounds are described as well as his grand thoughts in the last sentence. Thus, in context of the passage, B is false as well as D and E. While C may be true to some degree (or rather, appear true), you need to select the best answer and that is A.

61. **The passage "it will be enough not to stray a hair's breadth from the truth in the telling of it" characterizes the previous passage as...**

(A) Essential

(B) Metaphorical

(C) Unimportant

(D) Esoteric

(E) Bland

The correct answer is C.

The prior sentence is about the spelling of the main character's name. In perspective and context, that is unimportant as when compared to the events. When given a snippet of the passage, read around the phrase for context to help you - especially when they direct you to a particular area of the passage (such as the "previous passage" in the selection.

62. What are the two defining traits of the main character described above?

(A) Laziness and obsessiveness

(B) Ignorance and piousness

(C) Diligence and valor

(D) Prideful and vain

(E) Curious and kindhearted

The correct answer is A.
This selection refers in part to his compulsiveness on reading (explained earlier). Before selecting A and the other half could be blatantly wrong, look at the other options. Perhaps valor in C is accurately portrayed in the selection, but none of the others are true. Between A and C, use the context of the passage to determine if laziness or diligence is more appropriate, and you'll note that A is the better answer.

63. The final sentence of this excerpt is an example of…

(A) Satire

(B) Foreshadowing

(C) Interstitial

(D) Subtext

(E) Premonition

The correct answer is B.
The ending of the introduction (which this is) sets the stage for the book and what is to follow. Knowing your literary terms is helpful, as you can narrow the possible answers to B and E, but the actual definitions show B is more correct. Promotion is a character's particular feeling or description whereas foreshadowing is the casting of mood prior to arriving to a scene.

Passage 9

O wild West Wind, thou breath of Autumn's being,

Thou, from whose unseen presence the leaves dead
Are driven, like ghosts from an enchanter fleeing,

Yellow, and black, and pale, and hectic red,
Pestilence-stricken multitudes: O thou,
Who chariotest to their dark wintry bed

The winged seeds, where they lie cold and low,
Each like a corpse within its grave, until
Thine azure sister of the Spring shall blow

Her clarion o'er the dreaming earth, and fill
(Driving sweet buds like flocks to feed in air)
With living hues and odors plain and hill:

Wild Spirit, which art moving everywhere;
Destroyer and preserver; hear, oh, hear!

Thou on whose stream, 'mid the steep sky's commotion,
Loose clouds like earth's decaying leaves are shed,
Shook from the tangled boughs of Heaven and Ocean,

Angels of rain and lightning: there are spread
On the blue surface of thine aery surge,
Like the bright hair uplifted from the head

Of some fierce Maenad, even from the dim verge
Of the horizon to the zenith's height,
The locks of the approaching storm. Thou dirge

Of the dying year, to which this closing night
Will be the dome of a vast sepulchre,
Vaulted with all thy congregated might

Of vapors, from whose solid atmosphere
Black rain, and fire, and hail will burst: oh, hear!

Sample Test Three

64. The first line of this poem exhibits what poetic devices?

I. Alliteration

II. Personification

III. Onomatopoeia

(A) Only I

(B) Only II

(C) Only III

(D) I and II

(E) I, II, and III

The correct answer is D.

This is a favorite style of question for The College Board. There is no "typical" way these types of options go; while usual for all options to be accurate, it can happen. Don't discount an answer in these styles as "all or nothing" - use the passage to help determine the correct answer (and, of course, the definitions of words).

65. What best describes the final stanza of this selection?

(A) Slant rhyme

(B) Heroic couplet

(C) Hyperbole

(D) Irony

(E) Blank verse

The correct answer is B.

Review the last stanza and apply what you know about the options. Choices C and D describe content, not the format - so they are not correct. Of the three remaining, you should be able to eliminate blank verse. That leaves a 50/50 chance if you don't know the definitions of A or B.

66. "Wild Spirit, which art moving everywhere;

Destroyer and preserver; hear, oh, hear!"
This passage displays a...

(A) Enjambment

(B) Slant rhyme

(C) Simile

(D) Iamb

(E) Allegory

The correct answer is B.
Similar to the preceding option, apply what you know. Definitions are important. You should readily see that choice C is not correct, neither is D or E. If you get to the two remaining choices, you again have a 50/50 shot... but should recognize "displays" wants you to talk about the style not the content - B is style. You can see why knowing the main words you are seeing in definition questions is so important. There aren't that many - create flashcards to reinforce the definitions leading up to exam day.

67. This poem is written in what style?

(A) Vers libre

(B) Heroic couplet

(C) Epic saga

(D) Imagist soliloquy

(E) Iambic pentameter

The correct answer is E.
Not to belabor the importance of definitions, but iambic pentameter is one of the most important poetic devices and you should know what it means. It is very likely you will see this included in at least one question's list of possible options.

68. What in the poem is compared to "Angels of rain and lightning"?

(A) The wind

(B) Maenads

(C) Clouds

(D) Human souls

(E) Autumn

The correct answer is C.
It is in the poem.

69. "Of the dying year, to which this closing night/ Will be the dome of a vast sepulchre, / Vaulted with all thy congregated might"

This passage exhibits…

(A) A metaphor

(B) An allegory

(C) A comparison

(D) A consonance

(E) An allusion

The correct answer is A.
Know your definitions!

70. How many stanzas does this poem contain?

(A) Four

(B) Five

(C) Eight

(D) Ten

(E) Twelve

The correct answer is D.
Just count them (as long as you know what a stanza means).

71. What best summarizes the first sentence of this piece?

(A) When we first realize there was no middle ground between subservience and independence, intelligent men were less afraid of war than they were of deciding how to govern our new nation

(B) When our ancestors first realized they must be free instead of obedient, they realized that combat was far less challenging than the bureaucracy that would follow

(C) When men realized, in the past, that freedom would be hard to win, they decided to craft a new form of government to aid in this process

(D) When our new nation first achieved independence, the true struggle was not the war that followed, but the arguments between learned me who could not agree on anything

(E) When men first decided independence was necessary, they could not agree who should lead them, or how

The correct answer is A.
This type of question - ensuring your reading comprehension skills and rephrasing are at the collegiate level - is important on The College Board tests. You can improve this by reading more, and then checking what passages mean.

72. The phrase "ocean of uncertainty" is a

(A) Allusion

(B) Metaphor

(C) Allegory

(D) Simile

(E) Personification

The correct answer is B.
It's a definition question, again.

73. In the last sentence of the next to last paragraph, what does "durable" refer to?

(A) Striking

(B) Courier

(C) Country

(D) Congress

(E) Formation

The correct answer is C.

This is checking intent and comprehension. The sentence discusses the creation of Congress and the nature of it. Durable describes the nature of what they hoped to achieve by creating the Congress. While it is not typical that non-fiction passages are used (just like World Literature is not always incorporated), it is possible - that is why we included in your sample tests these options, so you would be familiar with their style and how questions could be asked about comprehension and context.

74. What does the author identify as a problem in the second paragraph?

(A) The similarities between his new nation and the Batavian and Helvetic confederacies

(B) The ignorance of the common people

(C) The unrestrained zeal of common citizens

(D) The vast size of this new country

(E) The brewing revolution that approaches

The correct answer is D.

So even if you aren't certain what this non-fiction passage was originally discussing, by the end and the mention of the creation of Congress, you should have an idea it's about America and the challenges of a new country. That reduces best possible answer options down to D.

75. **What word does "frankly" modify in the last sentence of the first paragraph?**

(A) Cut

(B) Asunder

(C) Ties

(D) Representatives

(E) Bound

The correct answer is A.

Modifiers are typically proximal - close - to the word they describe, even when English several hundred years old.

76. **The author identifies all of these as problems in the third paragraph EXCEPT:**

(A) Laziness

(B) Envy

(C) Poor trade

(D) Religious intolerance

(E) Increased dependence on foreign powers

The correct answer is E.

Go through the options listed and simply see what's there and what's not. Caution about the wording of the question, though - make sure it's the answer they want. Sometimes they look for an exception whereas sometimes they look for the exact answer (and options are close but aren't exact). Always read questions carefully.

77. **What is "it" the first sentence of the third paragraph refers to?**

(A) The new nation

(B) The Revolutionary War

(C) Congress

(D) The presidency

(E) The States

The correct answer is C.

Similar to question 73, you must read and understand the passage and apply the question to the context of the selection.

78. **In the first paragraph, what does the author NOT credit with aiding the representatives?**

(A) Providence

(B) Intelligence

(C) Integrity

(D) The Nation

(E) Purity

The correct answer is D.

Like question, 76, review the options listed, cross-check them to the actual passage, and simply see what's there and what's not.

79. **What adjective best describes Edmund's tone in this piece?**

(A) Disaffected

(B) Morose

(C) Longing

(D) Celebratory

(E) Inspired

The correct answer is C.

You likely know all of these words that are possible answers, so The College Board will just try to make sure you didn't skim and make assumptions on what the answer will be based on one or two words. Read carefully the passages, questions, and answer options.

80. This piece can best be described as...

(A) A poem

(B) A dramatic monologue

(C) Prose fiction

(D) An ode

(E) A dirge

The correct answer is B.

The piece is an excerpt from fiction, so C is not correct. An ode is a style, and this selection isn't an ode (know your vocabulary). It's also not a dirge or poem, so you should have selected B rather easily.

Sample Test Three

XAMonline

The CLEP Specialist

Individual Sample Tests in ebook format with full explanations

eBooks

All 33 CLEP sample tests are available as ebook downloads from retail websites such as **Amazon.com** and **Barnesandnoble.com**

American Government	9781607875130
American Literature	9781607875079
Analyzing and Interpreting Literature	9781607875086
Biology	9781607875222
Calculus	9781607875376
Chemistry	9781607875239
College Algebra	9781607875215
College Composition	9781607875109
College Composition Modular	9781607875437
College Mathematics	9781607875246
English Literature	9781607875093
Financial Accounting	9781607875383
French	9781607875123
German	9781607875369
History of the United States I	9781607875178
History of the United States II	9781607875185
Human Growth and Development	9781607875444
Humanities	9781607875147
Information Systems	9781607875390
Introduction to Educational Psychology	9781607875451
Introductory Business Law	9781607875420
Introductory Psychology	9781607875154
Introductory Sociology	9781607875352
Natural Sciences	9781607875253
Precalculus	9781607875345
Principles of Macroeconomics	9781607875406
Principles of Microeconomics	9781607875468
Principles of Marketing	9781607875475
Principles of Management	9781607875468
Social Sciences and History	9781607875161
Spanish	9781607875116
Western Civilization I	9781607875192
Western Civilization II	9781607875208

TO ORDER: Individual full length sample test are available online **amazon** BARNES&NOBLE
BOOKSELLERS

XAMonline

CLEP

Full Guides

TO ORDER: Complete study guides are available from **amazon** or **BARNES&NOBLE** BOOKSELLERS

CLEP College Algebra
ISBN: 9781607875307
Price: $34.99

CLEP Biology
ISBN: 9781607875314
Price: $34.99

CLEP Analyzing and
Interpreting Literature
ISBN: 9781607875260
Price: $34.99

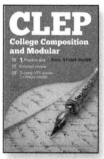

CLEP College Composition
and Modular
ISBN: 9781607875277
Price: $14.99

CLEP College Mathematics
ISBN: 9781607875321
Price: $34.99

CLEP Psychology
ISBN: 9781607875291
Price: $34.99

CLEP Spanish
ISBN: 9781607875284
Price: $34.99

XAMonline
CLEP Subject Samplers

Collection by Topic

Sample Test Approach

CLEP Literature
ISBN: 9781607875833
Price: $34.99

CLEP Foreign Language
ISBN: 9781607875772
Price: $34.99

CLEP History
ISBN: 9781607875789
Price: $34.99

CLEP Sociology
ISBN: 9781607875796
Price: $14.99

CLEP Science
ISBN: 9781607875802
Price: $34.99

CLEP Mathematics
ISBN: 9781607875819
Price: $34.99

CLEP Business
ISBN: 9781607875826
Price: $34.99

TO ORDER: Complete sample tests are available from **amazon** or **BARNES&NOBLE** BOOKSELLERS

XAMonline

CLEP Favorites

Collection by Topic
Sample Test Approach

CLEP 5
ISBN: 9781607875765
Price: $24.95

TITLE
ISBN: 9781607875512
Price: $24.95

TO ORDER: Complete sample tests are available from **amazon** or **BARNES&NOBL**
BOOKSELLERS

CPSIA information can be obtained at www.ICGtesting.com
Printed in the USA
BVOW06s0110030816

457664BV00026B/134/P

9 781607 875260